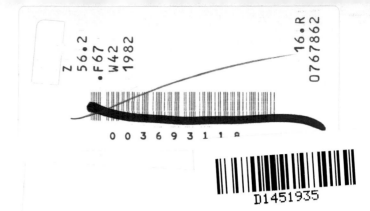

forkner SHORTHAND

FOR COLLEGES

GLORIA H. WEBER

EDWIN J. WEBER
The University of New Mexico

HAMDEN L. FORKNER, JR.

Shorthand outlines by Mary S. Lore

Forkner Publishing Corporation

A SUBSIDIARY OF CANADA PUBLISHING CORPORATION

ISBN 0-912036-44-3
Library of Congress Catalog Card No. 81-67853
4 5 6 7 8 9 10 11 12 13 14 K 4 3 2 1 0 9 8 7
Printed and Bound in the United States of America

TO THE INSTRUCTOR

Forkner Shorthand was introduced in 1952 after ten years of research. Today, it is taught in thousands of high school and college classrooms throughout the world.

Forkner Shorthand students succeed in business because they can write at high speeds and transcribe accurately. They consistently win awards for writing speeds and transcription accuracy in contests sponsored by national organizations.

Forkner programs succeed in secondary schools and colleges because the system is easy to learn to write. It combines 19 letters of the alphabet with a few symbols. Because Forkner Shorthand is based on what students already know—how to read and write longhand—they need not learn a whole new language to become competent in shorthand. Consequently, many high school and college students acquire a marketable shorthand skill in one year.

Motivation is high in Forkner programs because shorthand writing begins the first class period. Students make speedy progress toward their goals. Shorthand enrollments go up. These new materials are designed to equip the student to meet the current challenge of the administrative assistant in business and government.

This Edition

Those who have taught post-secondary Forkner Shorthand classes over the years will feel at home with this new college text. All of the writing rules are concisely presented and thoroughly illustrated. The materials are self-keyed to provide immediate reinforcement for the learner. Every fourth chapter provides a review and applies previously learned theory through the medium of business correspondence. The *Skill Builder* includes a series of self-tests for each text chapter so that both student and instructor can monitor progress.

Features of the College Edition

The textbook. This new first-semester text contains the following features:

1. A new sequence of theory presentation gives students a more gradual introduction to shorthand theory.

2. The number of theory principles has been reduced. This reduction cuts even further the time required to learn Forkner theory. More class time is available for building speed and for teaching essential transcription skills.

3. The number of abbreviated words has been reduced by some 40 percent, thus lessening the memory burden.

4. Heavy emphasis is placed on transcription and on English skills. Every fourth chapter provides a special section, "Building Transcription Skills."

5. Ample dictation material is included within chapters, in Appendix A, and in the Instructor's Manual.

The Skill Builder. Correlated chapter-by-chapter with the textbook, the *Skill Builder* gives students additional practice in applying writing principles. It consists of 32 units of self-tests, and is completely self-keyed. Designed for out-of-class work, each unit requires about 30 minutes to complete.

The examinations. After each four chapters, a preview examination is provided at the back of the *Skill Builder* for students to test their ability to write, transcribe, and to deal with English skills. A key to each examination is also provided at the back of the *Skill Builder* so that students may evaluate their progress before taking a more formal examination.

Dictation tapes. *Theory and Speed-Building Tapes for Colleges* are correlated with the text and *Skill Builder*. Sixteen cassettes give students additional practice on all material presented in the 32 text chapters and *Skill Builder* units. A variety of speed-forcing dictation plans is used. Two additional cassettes provide compact reviews for use periodically during the course. Together the 18 cassettes provide almost 18 hours of dictation practice for classroom use, for make-up work for students absent from class, or for homework.

Other teaching aids for beginning classes. A complete range of materials is available for teaching beginning shorthand. Contact the publisher for specific details.

Second Semester—Dictation and Transcription

Forkner Shorthand for Colleges is designed to be completed in one semester of classroom study. Most students, however, should take a second-semester course in Forkner Shorthand to increase dictation and transcription skills and to improve language arts skills.

Forkner Dictation and Transcription for Colleges has been prepared for second-semester college courses in Forkner Shorthand. This program, consisting of textbook and tape library, provides ample dictation and transcription material to assist the student in the refinement of grammar, punctuation, spelling, and word usage skills, and to develop faster writing and transcription speeds.

Correlated Dictation and Transcription, Third Edition, may also be used for second-semester courses in Forkner Shorthand. Consisting of textbook, study guide, and tape library, this program will be beneficial in classes containing students who have previously studied either Forkner or Gregg Series 90 Shorthand.

Advanced Study

Advanced Dictation and Transcription for Colleges has been prepared for college students requiring or desiring additional instruction in Forkner Shorthand. Like other college materials, this text is supplemented with a tape library.

ACKNOWLEDGEMENTS

The authors and publisher of Forkner Shorthand for Colleges are indebted to the late Dr. Hamden L. Forkner, Sr., who invented the system and who was an author of the four previous editions. His inventiveness and outstanding achievements have laid the foundation for this first college edition.

We are grateful to schools, colleges, universities, and educators everywhere who have used the four previous editions of Forkner Shorthand and who continue to hold workshops and conferences to acquaint teachers with the benefits of the Forkner Shorthand system.

We are indebted to Robert McElman, consultant, who gave invaluable direction to us as we developed the manuscript, and who contributed a great deal to the final draft. We are most grateful also to Margaret Turner, editor of the program.

CONTENTS

TO THE STUDENT

Learning Forkner Shorthand in the shortest possible time (so that you will be able to use it effectively on the job) will depend primarily on these two factors: how much time you allocate to your study of shorthand and how effectively you manage that time.

Here are some suggestions for effective study:

1. *Plan a work schedule*. Try to work on your shorthand regularly—at least some time *each* day. Frequent, short, purposeful sessions on a regular schedule are far more efficient than long sessions scheduled irregularly. This is true when learning any skill—learning to typewrite, learning shorthand, or learning to play a musical instrument.

2. *Work in a quiet place*. Intense mental concentration is one key to learning shorthand efficiently and in completing assignments quickly and on time. Time spent studying while listening to music or watching television is largely wasted.

3. Follow the instructions for learning given in your textbook and *Skill Builder*. You will find this shorthand program unique in that it gives you both *content* to be learned and a variety of proven *methods* for learning and doing the various exercises. As a special aid to study, the entire textbook and *Skill Builder* are self-keyed so that you get immediate feedback about the quality of your work.

Developing writing speed

In order to write shorthand rapidly, you must be able to move your hand quickly. How fast can you write longhand?

To find out, write the following speed sentence in longhand as many times as you can in ten seconds (one-sixth of a minute). Your instructor will time you. Then multiply the total number of words you write by 6 to get your longhand writing rate. Try writing this sentence a number of times to see whether you can double your longhand writing rate.

Speed sentence: **They will make sure each page will look very good.**

Forkner Shorthand is easy to learn because it blends letters of the alphabet with a few symbols. If you follow your instructor's directions, you will soon have a skill that will give you an excellent start in your business career.

Materials required

You should have the following materials: *Forkner Shorthand for Colleges*, and *Forkner Shorthand Skill Builder for Colleges*. Although not required for the successful completion of this course, you will find either the *Forkner Shorthand Dictionary for Beginners* or the *Comprehensive Forkner Shorthand Dictionary* a valuable reference. Both include, with Forkner outlines, the words presented in your text and *Skill Builder*.

To assist you in learning the writing principles and to build speed, you should have available the *Theory and Speed-Building Tapes for Colleges*. These tapes enable you to work at your own speed and, when necessary, to review material that is difficult for you. This 18-cassette audio program is normally purchased by colleges offering the course.

You will also need a ball-point pen with a fairly fine point. Pencils or felt-tip pens are not suitable. You will need one or more shorthand notebooks. The best notebook for taking shorthand has a spiral binding at the top and a center vertical rule. You will likely use several of these during the course, and the instructor may designate that a separate notebook be used for homework, special exercises, or transcription from tapes.

WRITING IN YOUR SHORTHAND NOTEBOOK

As a student of Forkner Shorthand, you will need a shorthand notebook in which to practice and to take shorthand dictation for transcription. Note that each page in your shorthand notebook has a line down the center. When writing shorthand, begin at the top left edge of the page and write to the center line. When you have completed the left column, begin at the top of the right column and write until all lines are filled. (See illustration below).

As you complete the right column, use your left hand to flip the left corner, ready to turn quickly to the next sheet. Turn the page and write on the next sheet (not on the back of the page just completed). Thus, you will write through an entire notebook in one direction and then turn the notebook over and write in the other direction. Write the current date at the bottom of each notebook page.

For efficiency, attach an elastic band to the cover of your notebook so that as shorthand is transcribed, pages are slipped under the band.

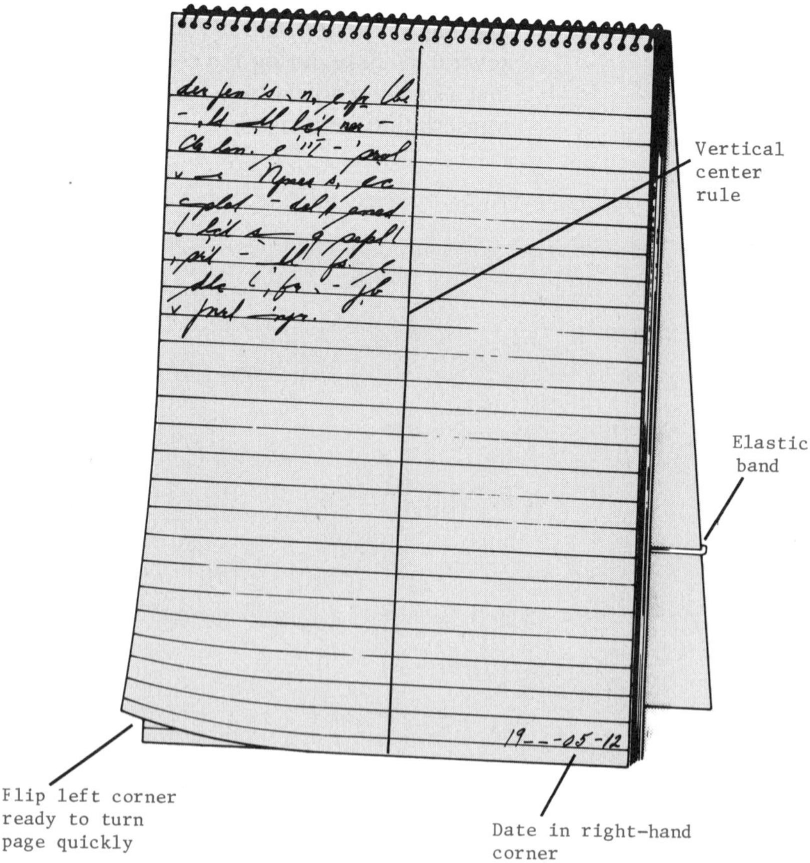

Chapter 1

WRITING SOUNDS OF LONG AND SHORT E AND LONG I

Saving writing strokes

Extra strokes at the beginning and ending of words are eliminated when writing Forkner Shorthand. The samples below show how to eliminate unneeded strokes on letters that *begin a word*. Write each letter without hesitating, several times, in your shorthand notebook. Try to write your letters *exactly* like those shown.

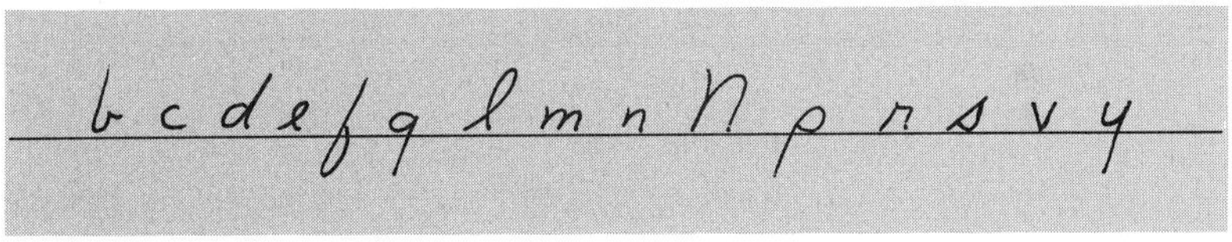

Learning tips:

1. When *b* or *f* begins a word or stands alone, start writing at the top of the letter.
2. When *p* begins a word or stands alone, start below the line and make an upward stroke with the loop on the line.

When writing the *last letter in a word*, omit any extra ending strokes. Write each letter several times in your notebook, remembering to omit ending strokes.

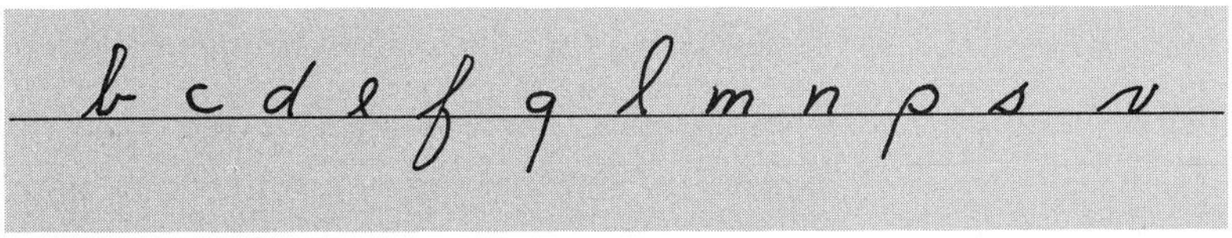

Writing by sound

When you write shorthand, you write only the sounds you hear. You save writing strokes because you omit silent letters. Study the examples below to see how to write by sound.

people	p-e-p-l	(You hear only *p*, *e*, *p*, and *l*. The *o* and final *e* are silent.)
judge	j-u-j	(The *d* and *e* are silent. The *g* sounds like *j*.)
scene	s-e-n	(The *c* and final *e* are silent.)
light	l-i-t	(The *g* and *h* are silent.)

Application—**Writing by sound**. Identify the sounds you hear in each of the following words. Write these sounds in your notebook. Check your answers with the key located in Appendix G at the back of the text.

field	leave	dry	free	straight	might	slow	day
edge	treaty	goal	sign	own	pay	bright	

WRITING PRINCIPLES

Sound of long e

Write *e* for the *long e* sound.

fel	feld	les	pepl	ner	ev
feel	field	lease	people	near	Eve

se	del	delr	den	ledr	red
see-sea	deal	dealer	dean	leader	read

fe	dep	fre	lev	ned	evn	nede
fee	deep	free	leave	need	even	needy

Cover the print of the first line of words with an index card and read the shorthand outlines until you can read each outline fluently. Read each line of outlines until you can read all outlines easily.

Cover the shorthand outlines of the preceding words and write each word in shorthand in your notebook until you can do so without hesitation. Say each word to yourself as you write it.

Learning tips:

1. Do not use capital letters when writing proper names in shorthand. Place a check mark under the outline to indicate that it is to be capitalized (see *Eve* above).
2. When an outline stands for more than one word, as in *see-sea*, the meaning of the sentence (context) tells you the correct word to use.
3. In some words the final *y* has a *long e* sound (See *needy* above).

Sound of short e

Omit *e* when the short sound of *e* occurs in the *body* of a word.

nvr	rde	srv	svrl	fdrl	sd
never	ready	serve	several	federal	said

vre	ern	eg	ys	ld	ls	lvl
very	earn	egg	yes	led-lead (n)	less	level
fl	brd					
fell	bread					

Cover the print of the first line of words and read the outlines until you can read them easily. Then quickly write the outline for each word three times in your shorthand notebook. Follow the same procedure with each line of words. Do not move ahead until you can read and write quickly and accurately all the words illustrating the sound of *short e*.

Learning tips:

1. The *short e* in *earn* and *egg* does not occur in the body of the word. Therefore, it is written.
2. The *(n)* after *lead* indicates that the word is a noun.

Sound of long *i*

Write an *i* without the dot for the sound of *long i*.

i	fin	lif	fir	dri	sin
I-eye	fine	life	fire	dry	sign
idel	driv	bi	di	sirn	rid
ideal	drive	buy	die-dye	siren	ride
lin	fil	drivr	din	idl	dil
line	file	driver	dine	idle	dial

Cover the print of each line of words and read each outline. Then, write the outline several times in your notebook.

Learning tip:

The undotted *i* is written with a short downward stroke when it stands alone or when it comes first in a word.

Abbreviated words

Some words that occur frequently have special shorthand outlines that are called *abbreviations*. These abbreviations must be memorized so that you can read and write each one automatically. To learn the six abbreviated words that follow, write each outline several times in your shorthand notebook. Say each word to yourself as you write the shorthand. Write the outlines quickly. Remember to leave out all extra beginning and ending strokes.

can · for · go-good · he · his-is-us · the

In subsequent chapters *abbreviated words* will appear first in New Vocabulary sections. The longhand for each will appear in italics and be underlined with a solid color line.

Learning tip:

The outline for *the* is the cross of the letter *t*. Make it short, and write it above the line when it stands alone.

Phrases

Joining two or more words together when writing shorthand is called *phrasing*. Read the outlines for the following phrases with the print covered until you can read them easily. Then cover the outlines and write each outline several times in your notebook. Say each phrase to yourself each time you write it.

for the · he is · I can · he can

In subsequent chapters, phrases will appear at the end of the New Vocabulary sections.

APPLYING NEW PRINCIPLES

Throughout this shorthand program you will find sentences, letters, and other passages that will help you apply the writing principles you have learned. To develop writing speed, it is essential that you read and write this type of material until you can do so quickly and without hesitation.

Read the shorthand sentences that follow until you can read them as fast as you can read the same sentences from print. If you cannot read an outline after sounding it out, look at the Transcript of Shorthand Sentences which follows. After you can read the outlines fluently, write each sentence in shorthand as you read it from the transcript. Say each sentence to yourself as you write it. Write each sentence in shorthand until you can do so without hesitation.

1. -fdrl ledr c srv svrl pepl.
2. ic se s sin.
3. -sin sd nvr g ner -dep se.
4. -drivr sd es rde f rid.
5. ec br -di f eg.
6. -fe f del s vre fin.
7. -fir sirn ner -feld s idel.
8. ec lev -brd f nede.
9. svrl pepl cse -fir.
10. -den sd ev s -idel ledr.
11. -idel les s rde f s.
12. ev c sin -les f pepl.

Learning tips:

1. When writing shorthand, do not use the capitalization symbol to indicate that the first word in a sentence is capitalized. Of course, you will capitalize the first word of a sentence when you transcribe.

2. Sentences that end with a period are punctuated with a period in shorthand.

TRANSCRIPT OF SHORTHAND SENTENCES

1. The federal leader can serve several people.
2. I can see his sign.
3. The sign said never go near the deep sea. (20)
4. The driver said he is ready for the ride.
5. He can buy the dye for the egg.
6. The fee for the deal is very fine. (40)
7. The fire siren near the field is ideal.
8. He can leave the bread for the needy.
9. Several people can see the fire. (60)
10. The dean said Eve is the ideal leader.
11. The ideal lease is ready for us.
12. Eve can sign the lease for the people. (80)

DICTATION AND TRANSCRIPTION

Write from dictation the Transcript of Shorthand Sentences. Your instructor will dictate each group of 20 words to you at various speeds. In order to build speed, your instructor will often dictate at a rate faster than you can write comfortably. Taking dictation at speeds that "force" you to write faster is the best way to build your writing speed.

Note that certain sentences contain numbers in parentheses. These numbers indicate that number of *standard words* up to that point. A standard word contains 1.4 syllables. For example, the first three sentences contain 20 standard words or a total of 28 syllables (20 × 1.4).

This indication of standard words enables a dictator to dictate at a given rate of speed. For example, to dictate this passage at 60 words per minute the dictator should complete the first three sentences in 20 seconds; the first six sentences in 40 seconds; and the entire passage in 80 seconds.

The following chart shows the precise amount of time to allow for dictating 20-word groups at various speeds.

	Speed of Dictation									
	50	60	70	80	90	100	110	120	130	140
	Seconds Elapsed									
First	24	20	17	15	13	12	11	10	09	08
Minute	48	40	34	30	26	24	22	20	18	17
Second	12	60	51	45	40	36	33	30	27	25
Minute	36	20	08	60	53	48	44	40	37	34
	60	40	25	15	06	60	55	50	46	42
		60	42	30	20	12	06	60	55	51
			60	45	33	24	17	10	04	60
				60	47	36	28	20	14	08
					60	48	39	30	23	17
						60	50	40	32	25
							60	50	41	34
								60	51	42
									60	51
										60

To dictate for more than two minutes, simply repeat the cycle.

50 wpm--20 words every 24 seconds	100 wpm--20 words every 12 seconds
60 wpm--20 words every 20 seconds	110 wpm--20 words every 11 seconds
70 wpm--20 words every 17 seconds	120 wpm--20 words every 10 seconds
80 wpm--20 words every 15 seconds	130 wpm--20 words every 9 seconds
90 wpm--20 words every 13 seconds	140 wpm--20 words every 8 seconds

BUILDING WRITING AND TRANSCRIPTION SPEEDS

New vocabulary

Read and write the following words and phrases until you can do so without hesitation.

Fred	press	for us-for his	I feel

Passage 1

You should be able to read and write the following passage. Read each sentence until you can read it easily. Then write each sentence twice in your notebook. If you cannot read a word, refer to the transcript which follows.

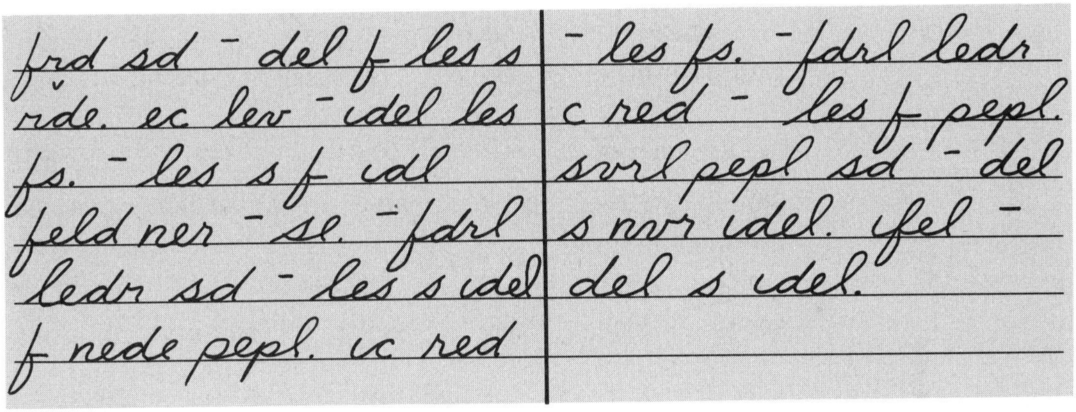

Passage 1 transcript

Fred said the deal for the lease is ready. He can leave the ideal lease for us. The lease is for the idle field near (20) the sea. The federal leader said the lease is ideal for the needy people. I can read the lease for us. The (40) federal leader can read the lease for the people. Several people said the deal is never ideal. I feel (60) the deal is ideal. (64)

SKILL-BUILDING ASSIGNMENTS

1. Complete Unit 1 in *Forkner Shorthand Skill Builder for Colleges*.
2. Select Cassette 1 Side A of the *Theory and Speed-Building Tapes for Colleges* and follow the directions on the tape.
3. If instructed to do so, read, write, and transcribe the supplementary passage for this chapter found in Appendix A, Supplementary Dictation and Transcription.
4. Take additional live dictation as provided by your instructor.

Chapter 2

WRITING SOUNDS OF A, T, AND SHORT I

WRITING PRINCIPLES

Sounds of *a*

Write an apostrophe ' for all sounds of *a*.

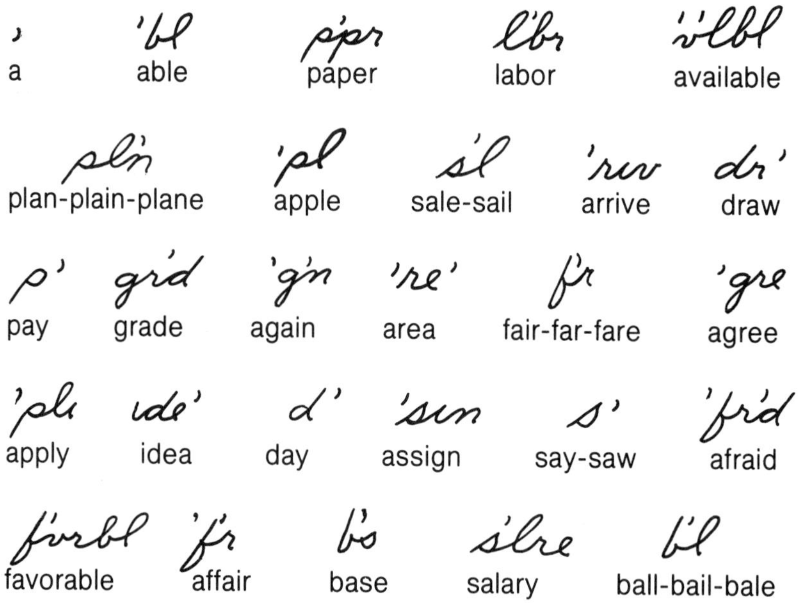

With the print covered, read the outlines for words illustrating the sounds of *a*. When you can read the outlines fluently, cover them and write the outlines from the print. When finished, check your outlines with those in the text. Are you remembering to omit extra beginning and ending strokes? Did you write the initial *p* correctly in *paper* and *pay*? Write correctly any words you may have written incorrectly. Then write all outlines again from the print to build your writing speed.

Learning tips:

1. Write an apostrophe for all *a* sounds—the *a* sound in *able*, the *a* sound in *bad*, the *a* sound in *agree*, and the *a* sound in *ball*.
2. Write the *a* first if the *a* sound occurs first in a word. Write it last at all other times.
3. The *o* in *labor* has an indistinct neutral sound. For discussion on such sounds, see page 10, Learning tip No. 2.

Sound of *t*

Write the *t* without the cross.

try fight date title table better

trade rate-rat settle tell get left

data late night treaty set type

later-latter Ted

Cover the print of each line of words and read the outlines until you can read them as fast as you can read the print. Then cover the outlines and write them from print until you can write each outline rapidly and accurately.

Learning tip:
When the *t* begins a word or when it stands alone, write the *t* with a single downward stroke (see *try* and *type* above).

Sound of short *i*

Write a dot above the line to show where the sound of *short i* occurs in a word.

if did bill trip little fill

give till fit built

As you read each word, write its outline several times in your notebook. After you have read and written the outlines for all the words, you should be able to read and write them fluently.

Learning tip:
If the short sound of *i* occurs first in a word, write the dot first. Write it last at all other times.

New vocabulary

Study the print and the outlines below until you can read the outlines as fast as you can read the print. Then cover the outlines and write them in shorthand from print as fast as you can several times. Remember, the abbreviated words must be memorized.

l	t	v	y	b	fnl
<u>*all*</u>	<u>*at-it-to*</u>	<u>*of*</u>	<u>*your*</u>	<u>*be-by-bye-but*</u>	final
v	tg	tse	ttp	esd	cb
of the	to go	to see	to type	he said	can be
ttri	tgv				
to try	to give				

Learning tips:

1. Note that the word *to* can be joined to most words that follow it.
2. The *a* in *final* does not have an *a* sound. It has an indistinct neutral sound. Several longhand letters sometimes express this same indistinct sound. For example, the *i* in *possible*, the *o* in *method*, and the *u* in *butter* all have the same indistinct sound. To save writing time, we do not use a symbol or letter to express the neutral sounds in the body of a word. However, neutral vowel sounds must be expressed at the beginning and ending of a word.

Examples: above 'bv; data dt'

APPLYING NEW PRINCIPLES

Follow these procedures in learning to read and write the sentences on page 11.

1. Read the first three sentences until you can do so easily.
2. Dictate the first three sentences to yourself as you write them in shorthand. This process is called *self-dictation*. Read a group of words. Then say the group of words to yourself as you write the corresponding outlines in your shorthand notebook. Repeat this process until you have written all the outlines in the three sentences.
3. Check your outlines and write correct outlines for any words you may have written incorrectly.
4. Repeat this procedure for each three-sentence group until you can read and write all the sentences without hesitation.

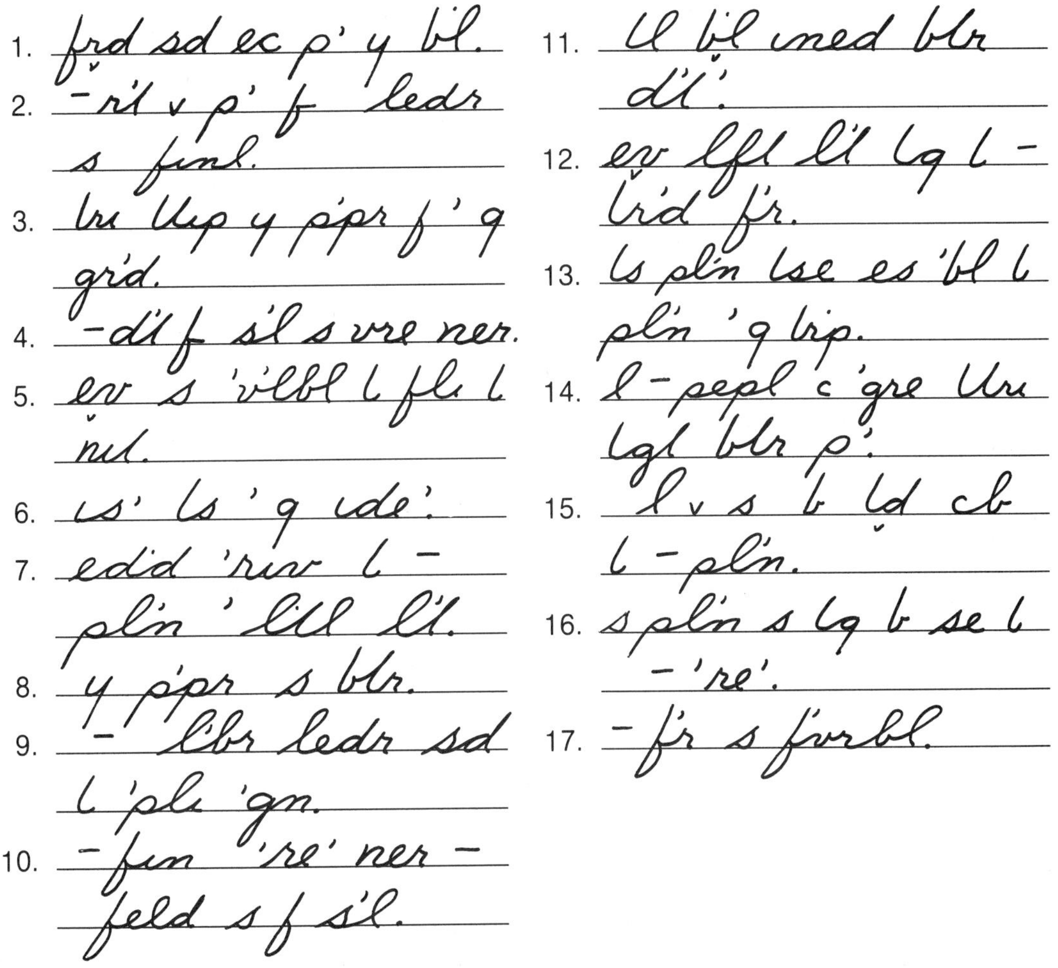

TRANSCRIPT OF SHORTHAND SENTENCES

1. Fred said he can pay your bill.
2. The rate of pay for the leader is final.
3. Try to type your paper for a good grade. (20)
4. The date for the sale is very near.
5. Eve is available to fly at night.
6. I say it is a good idea. (40)
7. He did arrive at the plane a little late.
8. Your paper is better.
9. The labor leader said to apply again. (60)
10. The fine area near the field is for sale.
11. Tell Bill I need better data.

12. Eve left late to go to the trade fair. (80)
13. It is plain to see he is able to plan a good trip.
14. All the people can agree to try to get better pay. (100)
15. All of us but Ted can be at the plane.
16. His plan is to go by sea to the area.
17. The fare is favorable. (120)

DICTATION AND TRANSCRIPTION

Write from dictation the Transcript of Shorthand Sentences. Your instructor will dictate each group of 20 words to you at various speeds. In order to build speed, your instructor will often dictate at a rate faster than you can write comfortably. Taking dictation at speeds that "force" you to write faster is the best way to build your writing speed.

BUILDING WRITING AND TRANSCRIPTION SPEEDS

New vocabulary

Read and write the following words until you can do so without hesitation.

fall-fail	freight	editor	written	slight	dear	Betty

Letter 1

Read the letter until you can do so fluently. Check the transcript if you cannot read an outline. Write the letter until you can write each outline accurately and rapidly. Then, from the transcript, write one good set of notes. Transcribe your notes at your best typing rate. Check your transcript.

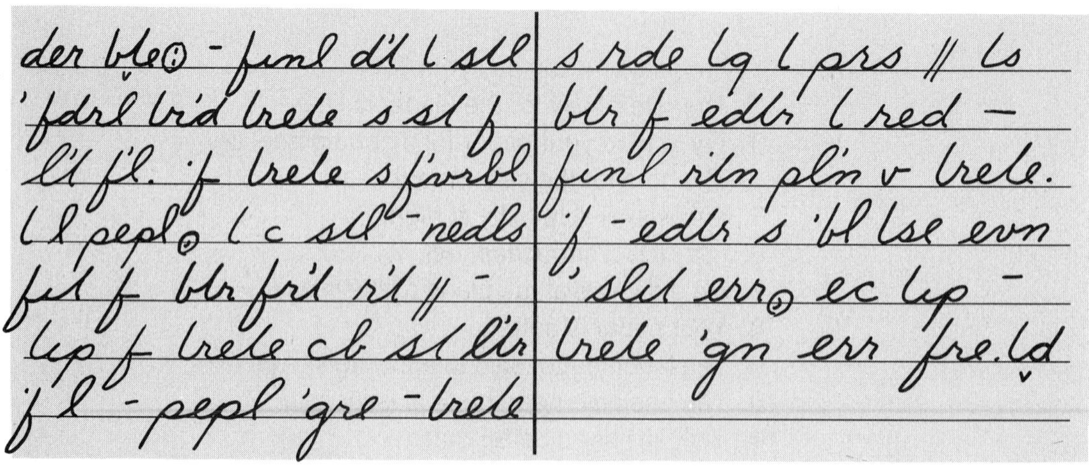

Learning tips:

1. Use a double diagonal (//) to indicate the beginning of a new paragraph.
2. Punctuation marks within a sentence are circled to distinguish them from shorthand symbols.

Letter 1 transcript

Dear Betty: The final date to settle a federal trade treaty is set for late fall. If the treaty is (20) favorable to all people, it can settle the needless fight for the better freight rate.

The type for the treaty can (40) be set later if all the people agree the treaty is ready to go to press.

It is better for the (60) editor to read the final written plan of the treaty. If the editor is able to see even a slight (80) error, he can type the treaty again error free. Ted (90)

LETTER STYLES

Do not take the time to set up letters in business-letter form unless instructed to do so. When transcribing letters, set your typewriter margins for a 60-space line and type the letters in the form shown under the heading, "Letter 1 transcript."

You will have an opportunity to transcribe letters in business-letter form later in the program. A model of a letter is shown on page 23.

SKILL-BUILDING ASSIGNMENTS

1. Complete Unit 2 in *Forkner Shorthand Skill Builder for Colleges*.
2. Select Cassette 2 Side A of the *Theory and Speed-Building Tapes for Colleges* and follow the directions on the tape.
3. If instructed to do so, read, write, and transcribe the supplementary letter for this chapter found in Appendix A, Supplementary Dictation and Transcription.
4. Take additional live dictation as provided by your instructor.

Chapter 3

WRITING SOUNDS OF HARD C AND K, O, AND SOFT C

WRITING PRINCIPLES

Sound of hard *c* and *k*

For the hard *c* and *k* sound, write the longhand *c*.

keep   ask   desk   take-talk-tack   car-care

capitol-capital   key   kept   ticket   taken   carry

class   call   clear   back-bake   case   risk

Cover the printed words and read the outlines until you can read them without hesitating. Then cover the outlines and write each word in shorthand as you read it from print. Check your outlines and correct any errors you may have made. Write all the outlines until you can read and write them rapidly and accurately.

Sounds of *o*

Write a comma , on or below the line for all sounds of *o*.

copy   operate   catalog/ue   telephone   told   goal

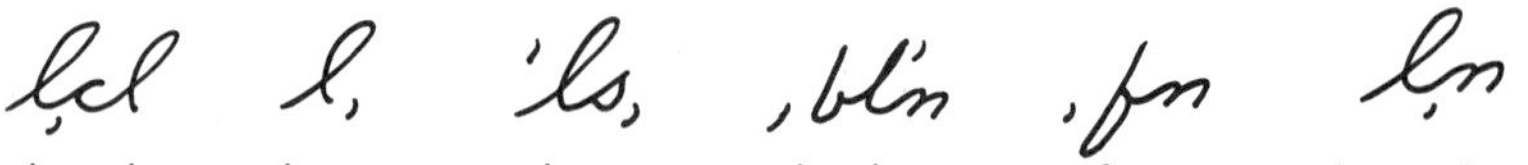

local   low   also   obtain   often   loan-lone

offer   open   total   box   lower   owner

sailboat   possible   alone   course-coarse   own-on

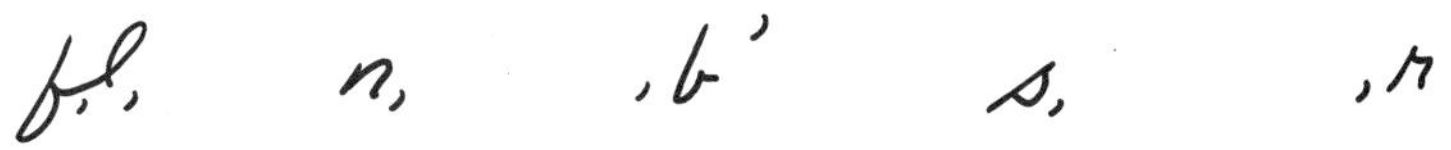

follow   no-know   obey   so-sew-sow   or-ore-oar

As you read each outline, write it three times in your notebook. When you have written all the words, you should be able to read and write them rapidly and accurately. Now cover the outlines and write them in shorthand from print. Read back your notes and correct any errors you may have made.

Learning tips:

1. Note that the *o*-comma is written for all sounds of *o* — the *o* in *total*, the *o* in *off* and *bought*, and the *o* in *copy*.
2. Note how the final *x* is written in *box* to save writing time.
3. Some English words have variant spellings. *Catalog/catalogue* is an example. Your instructor will indicate the spelling preferred in your community.

Sound of soft c

When *c* has an *s* sound, write a longhand *s*. Remember, you always write what you hear.

place   notice   policy   office   price   service

face   race   nice   cell-sell   officer   peace-piece

circle   civil   civic   practice   slice   source

As you read each word, write the shorthand outline several times in your notebook. When finished, cover the shorthand and write each word once in shorthand from the print. Try to read your own notes. If any of the outlines are difficult to read, write them until you can read and write them easily.

New vocabulary

Read and write the following outlines until you can do so fluently. Note that many phrases can be written using the word *not*.

not   *do*   *and*   *next*   cannot   tonight

today	before	I cannot	he cannot	is not	he is not

it is not	did not	I did not	he did not	on the	do not

Learning tip:

Note that the word *cannot* is made up of two abbreviated words — *can* and *not*. Words that are made up of two abbreviated words or of an abbreviated word and another word or syllable are known as *derivatives*. The word *tonight* is a derivative because it is made up of the abbreviated word *to* and the word *night*. Similarly, *today* and *before* are derivatives. Derivatives are underlined with a dotted black line.

APPLYING NEW PRINCIPLES

Follow these procedures in learning to read and write the sentences below.

1. Read the shorthand outlines for each of the sentences until you can read all the sentences without hesitation.
2. Using the Transcript of Shorthand Sentences, write the shorthand outlines for each sentence in your notebook.
3. Check your outlines.
4. Write correctly, three times, each outline that you may have written incorrectly.
5. Rewrite the shorthand outlines as you read the sentences once again from the Transcript of Shorthand Sentences.
6. Transcribe the sentences from your own notes. Compare your transcript with the text transcript and circle any errors you may have made, including spelling errors.

1. 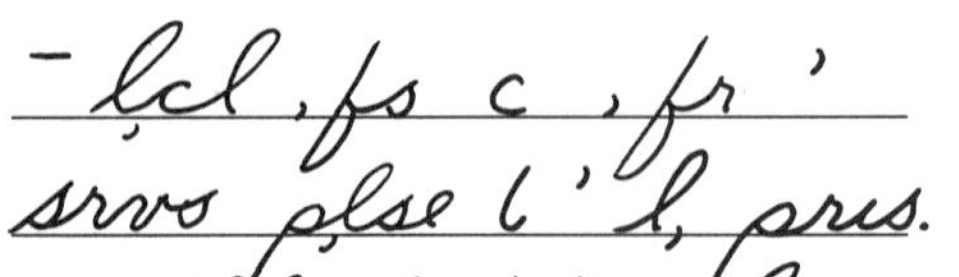

2. 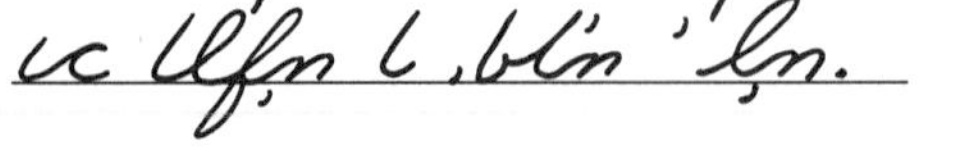

3. 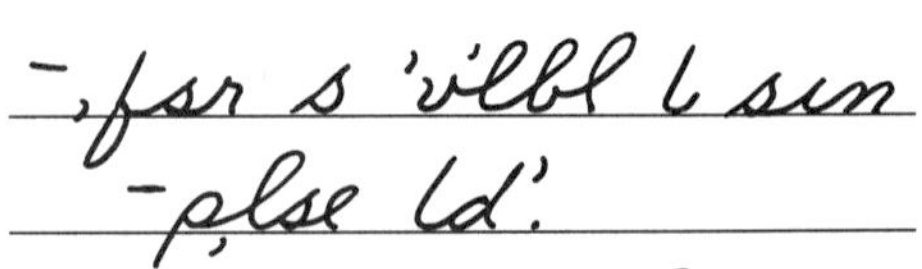

4. 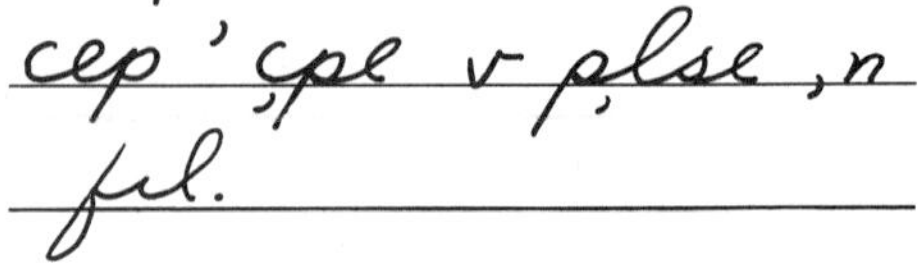

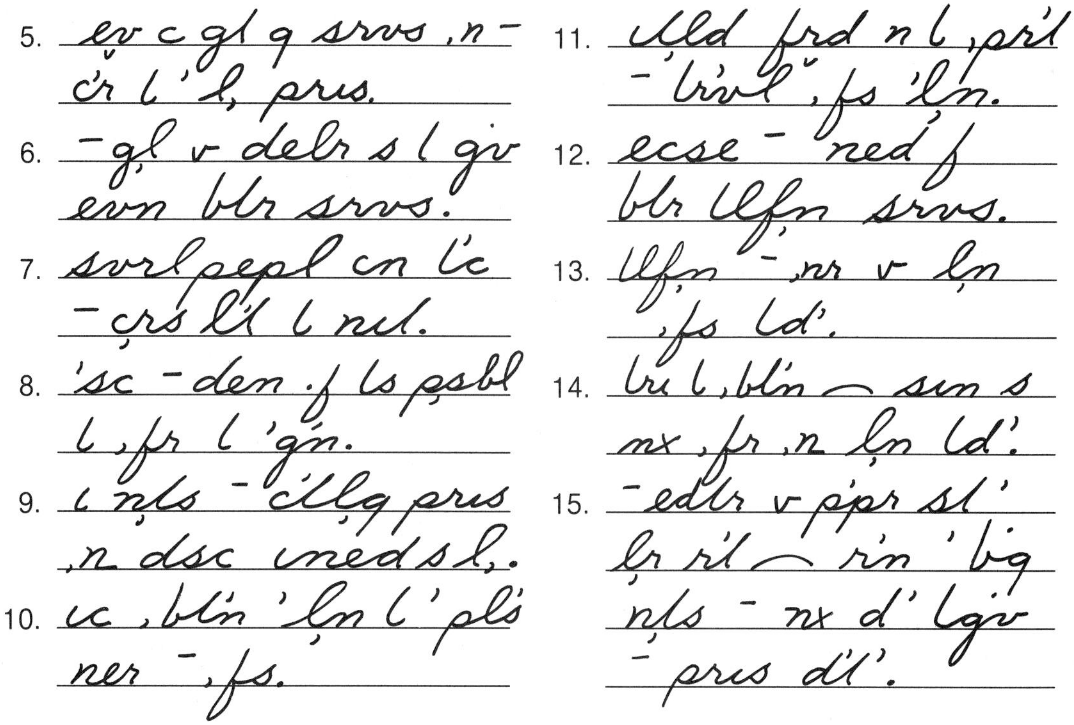

TRANSCRIPT OF SHORTHAND SENTENCES

1. The local office can offer a service policy at a low price.
2. I can telephone to obtain a loan. (20)
3. The officer is available to sign the policy today.
4. Keep a copy of the policy on file. (40)
5. Eve can get good service on the car at a low price.
6. The goal of the dealer is to give even better service. (60)
7. Several people cannot take the course late at night.
8. Ask the dean if it is possible to offer it again. (80)
9. I notice the catalog price on the desk I need is low.
10. I can obtain a loan at a place near the office. (100)
11. I told Fred not to operate the travel office alone.
12. He can see the need for better telephone service. (120)
13. Telephone the owner of the loan office today.
14. Try to obtain and sign his next offer on the loan today. (140)
15. The editor of the paper set a lower rate and ran a big notice the next day to give the price data. (160)

DICTATION AND TRANSCRIPTION

Write from dictation the Transcript of Shorthand Sentences. Your instructor will dictate each group of 20 words to you at various speeds. In order to build speed, your instructor will often dictate at a rate faster than you can write comfortably. Taking dictation at speeds that "force" you to write faster is the best way to build your writing speed.

VOWEL SYMBOLS

Some writers find they can omit many vowel symbols in words that appear in context and still transcribe their notes accurately. Others find that they must insert most vowels. In the shorthand passages in this and succeeding chapters, some vowel symbols have been omitted because the writer felt the passage could be accurately transcribed without them. In some cases, the writer has inserted a vowel in a word and later in the same passage may have omitted the vowel in that same word. This was done because it was felt that the vowel was necessary for clarification in some sentences and not in others.

The flexibility in the use of vowel symbols is one of the important features of Forkner Shorthand. The more vowel symbols you can omit and still read your writing, the faster you will be able to take and transcribe your dictation.

All vowel symbols should be inserted when writing isolated words.

BUILDING WRITING AND TRANSCRIPTION SPEEDS

Letter 1

Write the following letter in shorthand in your notebook. Say each word as you write it. Check your outlines with the outlines in the text. To build shorthand speed, have someone dictate the letter to you two or three times while you take notes. Then make one good set of notes and transcribe it at the typewriter. If you have time, or if your instructor prefers, transcribe your notes more than once, trying to increase your transcription rate each time.

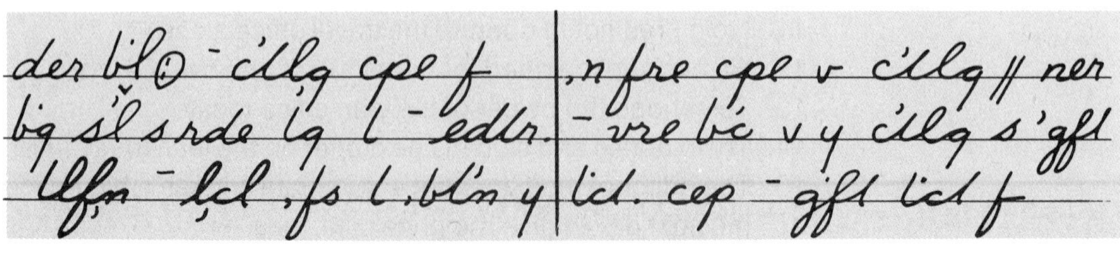

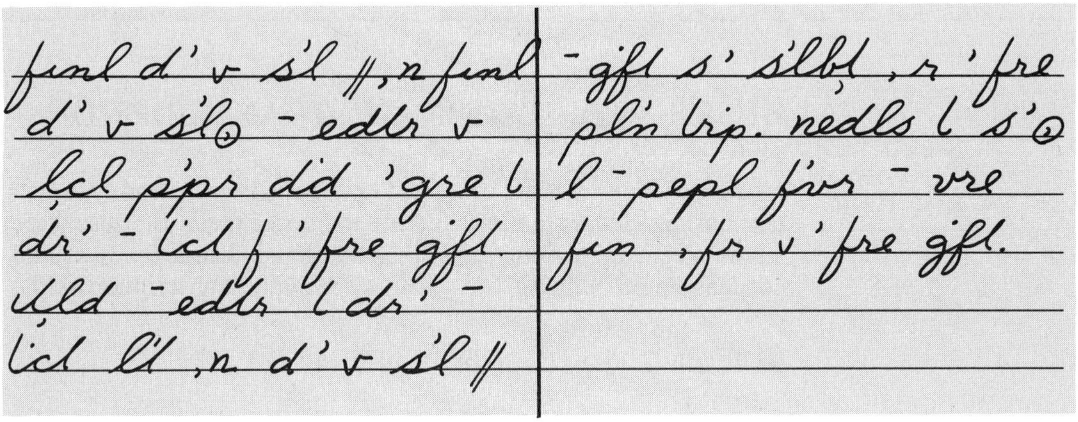

Letter 1 transcript

Dear Bill: The catalog copy for the big sale is ready to go to the editor. Telephone the local (20) office to obtain your own free copy of the catalog.

Near the very back of your catalog is a gift (40) ticket. Keep the gift ticket for the final day of the sale.

On the final day of the sale, the editor of (60) the local paper did agree to draw the ticket for a free gift. I told the editor to draw the ticket (80) late on the day of the sale.

The gift is a sailboat or a free plane trip. Needless to say, all the people favor (100) the very fine offer of a free gift. (107)

SKILL-BUILDING ASSIGNMENTS

1. Complete Unit 3 in *Forkner Shorthand Skill Builder for Colleges*.
2. Select Cassette 3 Side A of the *Theory and Speed-Building Tapes for Colleges* and follow the directions on the tape.
3. If instructed to do so, read, write, and transcribe the supplementary letter for this chapter found in Appendix A, Supplementary Dictation and Transcription.
4. Take additional live dictation as provided by your instructor.

Chapter 4

BUSINESS DICTATION AND TRANSCRIPTION

No new writing rules are presented in this chapter. Instead, you will take business letters in shorthand and transcribe them. Because these letters *review* the writing rules you have already learned, you should concentrate on building your writing speed and transcription skills.

BUILDING TRANSCRIPTION SKILLS

Various chapters in this text *preview* the specific transcription skills needed in order to transcribe effectively the material in that chapter. For example, in this chapter you will transcribe business letters that include a salutation, a complimentary close, the names of days of the week and months, and introductory expressions.

Salutations

The *salutation* is the greeting that comes before the body of a letter. When writing to an individual, the salutation usually begins with *Dear*, includes the title of the person addressed (*Mr.*, *Mrs.*, *Miss*, *Ms.*, *Dr.*, etc.), and usually ends with a colon. Examples include:

Dear Mrs. Smith:	Dear Miss Lombardi:	Dear Ms. Gomez:
Dear Mr. Rogers:	Dear Dr. Green:	Dear Madam:

When writing to an organization, the following salutations are frequently used:

Gentlemen:	Ladies and Gentlemen:
Ladies:	Mesdames:

Note that all salutations begin with a capital letter.

Complimentary closes

The *complimentary close* follows the body of the letter and begins with a capital. A comma follows the complimentary close if the salutation ends with a colon. Common complimentary closes include:

Yours very truly,	Sincerely yours,	Sincerely,
Cordially yours,	Yours sincerely,	Yours truly,

Capitalization

When transcribing, always capitalize names of places, days of the week, months, and names of holidays. Do not abbreviate days of the week or months when transcribing.

1. Our annual meeting is the first Monday in October.

2. It happens that New Year's Day falls on Saturday this year.

3. Jean will report for work on Tuesday.

Punctuating introductory expressions

Introductory words, phrases, and clauses introduce the reader to the rest of the sentence. Place a comma after all such expressions.

The most common introductory words and expressions include: *therefore*, *however*, *nevertheless*, *even so*, *furthermore*, and *for example*. Introductory phrases and clauses usually begin with one of the following words: *if*, *since*, *when*, *after*, *although*, *as*, *because*, *in*, *unless*, *upon*, *whenever*, and *while*.

The business letters in this chapter include introductory expressions. Study the examples that follow and note how they are punctuated so that you will be able to punctuate the letters properly.

1. As I predicted, we received a rush order today.
2. To ship the order on time, our entire crew worked late.
3. Having completed the job, we took the next morning off.
4. Consequently, the office was closed until after lunch.
5. When she flies to San Juan, she should go through Miami.
6. If the weather is bad, she can go later.
7. Of course, she will save money if she flies at night.
8. Furthermore, she would arrive early in the day.

Application — **Punctuating introductory expressions; capitalization**. In your notebook, number from 1 – 10. If the sentences below require a comma, place the preceding word and the comma opposite the appropriate sentence number. If a word requires capitalization, write the capitalized word after the appropriate sentence number. Some sentences may require both punctuation and capitalization corrections. If a sentence is correct, write OK after the number. Check your work with the key located in Appendix G at the back of this text.

1. As you know he received an award for his work.
2. Their home was in buenos aires.
3. Consequently it is the only action we can take.
4. If you wish to go with us, you are welcome.
5. As a result jean spent her vacation in mexico.

6. She did not, however, visit Mexico City.
7. To do the job right we will need more workers.
8. christmas will be on a tuesday this year.
9. The fultons live at 134 west fourth street Los Angeles, California.
10. Furthermore the game will be replayed tomorrow.

Letter styles

There are many acceptable business letter styles. One of the more common styles is the *block style* which is illustrated on page 23. Unless otherwise instructed, use this style when transcribing the remaining letters in this text.

The following points will assist you in attractively positioning your transcript on letterhead.

1. Side margins should not exceed $1^1/_2$ inches (35–40 mm).
2. Position the date 2 inches (50 mm) from the top of the page.
3. Depending on letter length, leave 4–8 blank lines between the date and the inside address. The shorter the letter, the greater the space.
4. Leave 1 blank line between paragraphs, between the salutation and the body, between the body and complimentary close, and between the typed signature or title of the dictator and reference initials.
5. Leave sufficient space (usually 3–4 blank lines) between the complimentary close and the typed signature for the signature.

Standard abbreviations

Words that are commonly abbreviated in longhand are called *standard abbreviations*. To increase your writing speed, you should learn and use these abbreviations. As you can see from the following outlines, the shorthand writing principles are applied in writing these shortened forms. All standard abbreviations are underlined with a dotted color line. Read and write the following standard abbreviations until you can do so rapidly and accurately.

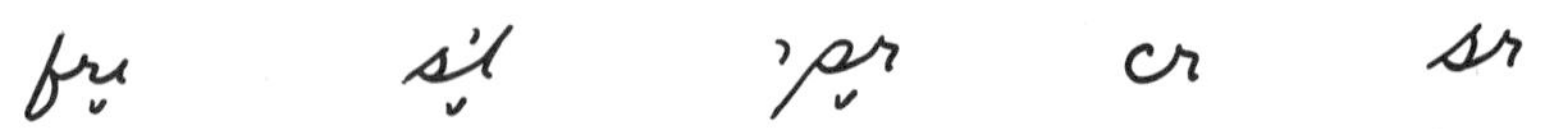

Friday   Saturday   April   credit   senior

Fast Fast Floor Merchandisers Incorporated
27 Avenue A, Newark, NJ 07114 (201) 733-3200

October 20, 19--

Mr. William French
375 Banks Street
Lansing, MI 48924-1140

Dear Mr. French

There are many acceptable styles for business letters. This is an example of the block style.

Punctuation styles also vary in business letters. This letter has open punctuation. With this style, you omit punctuation at the ends of lines in the address, after the salutation, and after the complimentary close.

You begin the date at the left margin two spaces below the last line of the printed letterhead. Then type the name and address at least four spaces below the date. With short letters, add more space between the date and the name and address so that the letter is well placed.

Now type the salutation at the left margin two spaces below the address. The first paragraph begins at the left margin two spaces below the salutation. Double space between paragraphs.

Begin the complimentary close at the left margin two spaces below the last paragraph. Then place the typed signature of the dictator four spaces below the complimentary close. Add the title of the dictator on the next line if required.

The secretary's identifying initials are typed two spaces below the typed signature or title of the dictator. Some employers prefer to have the dictator's initials typed before those of the secretary. In this case, the two sets of initials are separated by a colon.

Yours truly

Kenneth R. Nelson

Kenneth R. Nelson

js

BUILDING WRITING AND TRANSCRIPTION SPEEDS

Follow these steps in learning to read and write the business letters in this chapter. Complete all steps for Letter 1 first; then repeat the procedures for Letter 2.

1. Read and write the "new vocabulary" words and phrases until you can do so rapidly and accurately.

2. Read the letter until you can read the shorthand outlines without hesitation.

3. As you read the letter a final time, *scribble-write* the letter so that you become familiar with the writing of each outline. Scribble-writing is a technique used to learn to write shorthand rapidly and accurately. To scribble-write, keep your eyes on the outlines in the text as you write them in your shorthand notebook. Because you are not looking at your paper, you simply write one outline over the previous one. You do not move your hand across the page as you write. Say the words as you write them. Your notes will look something like this:

4. Write the shorthand outlines for the letter as you dictate it to yourself from the transcript.

5. Read your shorthand notes. If you are unable to read your notes, check them against the outlines in the text.

6. Write correctly any outlines you may have written incorrectly.

7. Rewrite from the print the shorthand outlines for each letter.

Letter 1 new vocabulary

basket   craft   got   pottery   snack   Debby

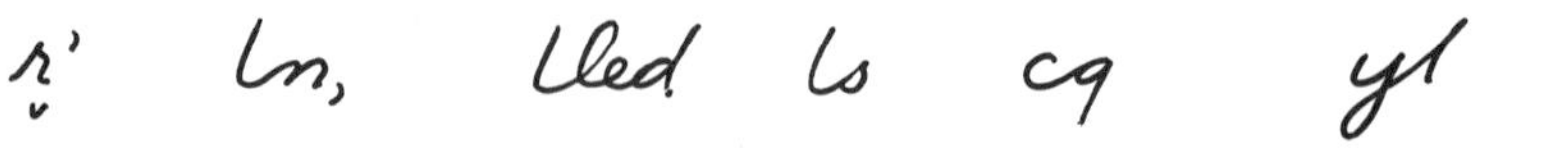

Ray   to know   to lead   it is   can go   Yours truly

Learning tips:

1. The outline for the phrase, *it is*, can also stand for *to us*, *to his*, *at his*, and *at us*.

2. *Yours truly* is an example of an abbreviated *correspondence form*. Additional correspondence forms will be introduced as they are used.

Letter 1

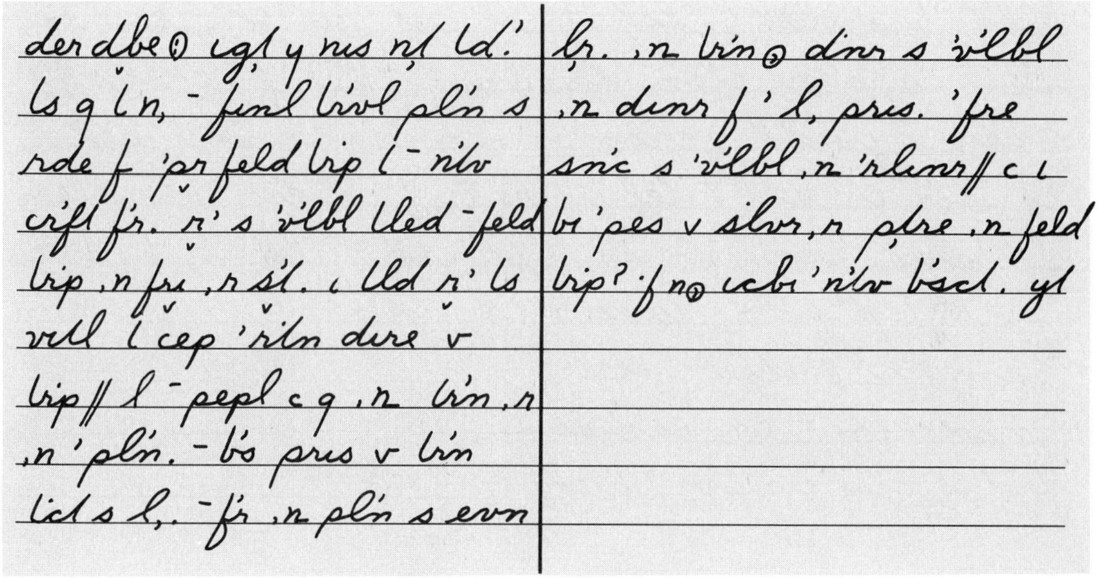

Learning tip:
Punctuate questions with a question mark without the period.

Letter 1 transcript

Dear Debby: I got your nice note today. It is good to know the final travel plan is ready for the April (20) field trip to the native craft fair. Ray is available to lead the field trip on Friday or Saturday. I told (40) Ray it is vital to keep a written diary of the trip.

All the people can go on the train or on a plane. (60) The base price of the train ticket is low. The fare on the plane is even lower. On the train, dinner is (80) available on the diner for a low price. A free snack is available on the airliner.

Can I buy a piece (100) of silver or pottery on the field trip? If not, I can buy a native basket. Yours truly, (117)

Letter 2 new vocabulary

brief cancel fix cover I plan to sign he said

Letter 2

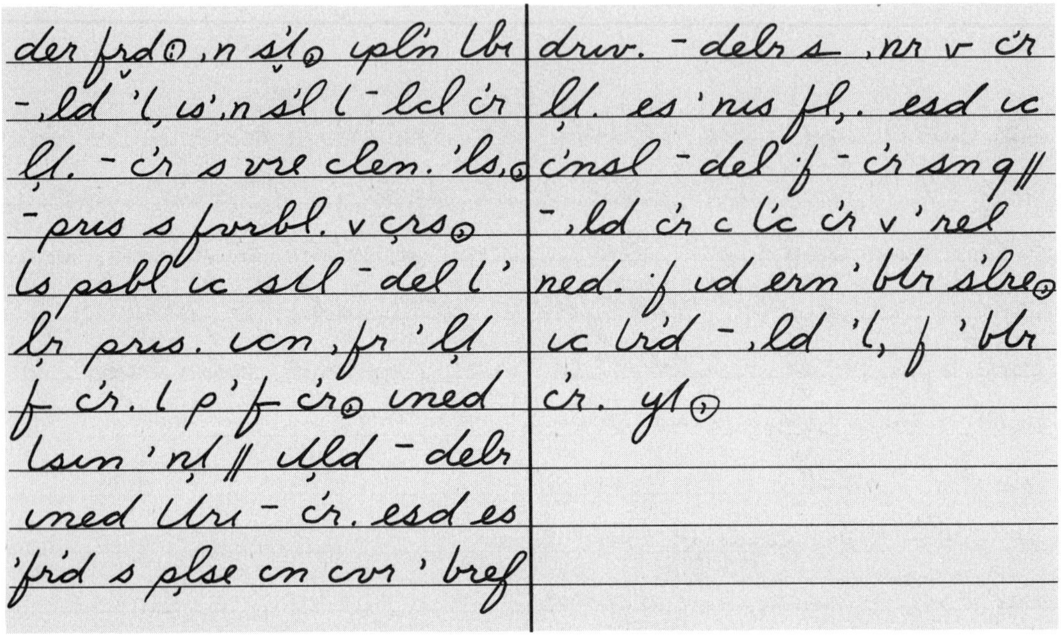

Letter 2 transcript

Dear Fred: On Saturday, I plan to buy the old auto I saw on sale at the local car lot. The car is very (20) clean. Also, the price is favorable. Of course, it is possible I can settle the deal at a lower (40) price. I cannot offer a lot for the car. To pay for the car, I need to sign a note.

I told the dealer I (60) need to try the car. He said he is afraid his policy cannot cover a brief drive. The dealer is the (80) owner of the car lot. He is a nice fellow. He said I can cancel the deal if the car is not good.

The old car (100) can take care of a real need. If I do earn a better salary, I can trade the old auto for a better (120) car. Yours truly, (123)

DICTATION AND TRANSCRIPTION

Write from dictation the transcripts of letters 1 and 2. Your instructor will dictate each letter to you at various speeds.

Using your own notes, transcribe both letters using the block style illustrated in this chapter. Use a fictitious inside address. Use your own name for the typed signature line.

SKILL-BUILDING ASSIGNMENTS

1. Complete Unit 4 in *Forkner Shorthand Skill Builder for Colleges*.

2. Select Cassette 4 Side A of the *Theory and Speed-Building Tapes for Colleges* and follow the directions on the tape.

3. If instructed to do so, read, write, and transcribe the supplementary letter for this chapter found in Appendix A, Supplementary Dictation and Transcription.

4. Take additional live dictation as provided by your instructor.

PREVIEW EXAMINATION 1

Remove Preview Examination 1 from your *Forkner Shorthand Skill Builder for Colleges*. It follows Unit 32. This informal preview examination will help you in assessing your understanding of the Forkner principles presented in Chapters 1–4. It is similar to Examination 1 which may be administered at a later date by your instructor.

Complete Preview Examination 1 and then check your answers carefully with the key in your *Forkner Shorthand Skill Builder for Colleges*. Correct any errors you may have made.

Chapter 5

WRITING SOUNDS OF U-OO, M, AND MENT

WRITING PRINCIPLES

Sounds of *u-oo*

Write a short, slanted, downward stroke on or below the line of writing to express all sounds of *u* and *oo*.

new-knew   school   value   soon   full-fool-fuel

look   too   few   up   upon   due-dew   approve

booklet   approval   book   food   useful   revenue

noon   regular   bulletin   secure   opinion

Cover the print of the first line of words and read the outlines until you can read them easily. Then quickly write the outline for each word three times in your shorthand notebook. Follow the same procedure for each line of words. When you can write all the outlines fluently, cover them and write the outlines from the print. When finished, check your outlines carefully. Write correctly any words you may have written incorrectly.

Learning tip:

The letter *u* has several sounds, all of which require the *u* stroke. The following sounds illustrate various words in which the *u* stroke is written: *value*, *up*, *full*, *few*. The *u* stroke is also used for all *oo* sounds. Examples include school, book, and stood. In some words a lightly sounded *y* comes before a *u* or other vowel sound. Examples include: *value*, *secure*, *familiar*, and *ammonia*. In such words, omit the lightly sounded *y* and write the *u* stroke.

Sound of *m*

Write a long, straight line on or above the line of writing to express *m*.

me   same   complete   material   make   many

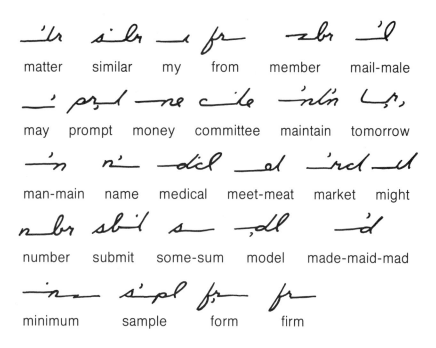

matter similar my from member mail-male

may prompt money committee maintain tomorrow

man-main name medical meet-meat market might

number submit some-sum model made-maid-mad

minimum sample form firm

As you read each outline, write it several times. Do this for all the words. When you can read all the outlines fluently, cover the print and write each outline once. Then read your own notes. If you have difficulty reading your outlines, compare them with those in the text. Then, rewrite them and read them again.

Learning tips:

1. Make the *m* stroke long. It is the letter *m* stretched out into a straight line.

2. Note that there is a slight jog between the *m*'s in *member* and *minimum* so that the two *m*'s can be easily recognized. Make the jog very small so it will not be mistaken for an *i*.

Syllable *ment*

Write the longhand *m* for the syllable *ment*.

payment agreement mental commitment improvement

assignment settlement

Cover the printed words and read the outlines until you can read them without hesitating. Then, cover the outlines and write each word as you read it from print. Check your notes and correct any errors you may have made. Write all the outlines until you can read and write them rapidly and accurately.

New vocabulary

Study the print and the outlines below until you can read the outlines as fast as you can read the print. Then cover the outlines and write them from print several times as fast as you can.

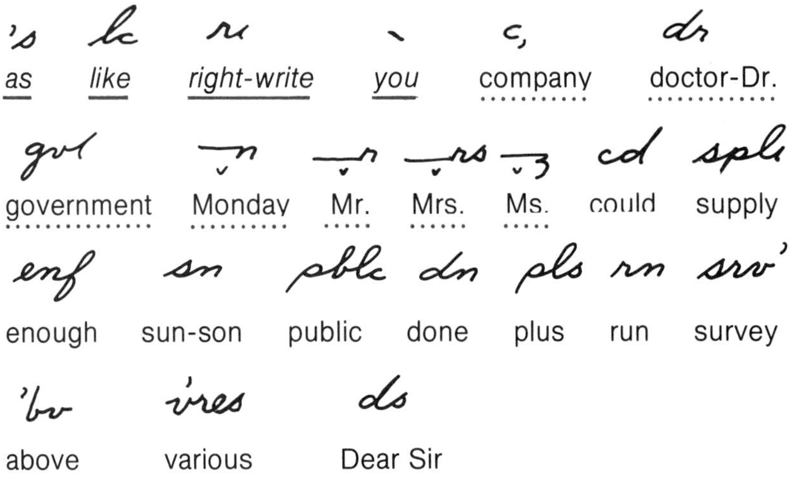

Learning tip:

Dear Sir is another example of an abbreviated correspondence form.

APPLYING NEW PRINCIPLES

Follow these procedures in learning to read and write the sentences on page 31.

1. Read the shorthand outlines for each of the sentences until you can read all the sentences without hesitation.
2. Using the Transcript of Shorthand Sentences, write the shorthand outlines for each sentence in your notebook.
3. Check your outlines.
4. Write correctly three times each outline that you may have written incorrectly.
5. Rewrite the shorthand outlines as you read the sentences once again from the Transcript of Shorthand Sentences.

6. Transcribe the sentences from your own notes. Compare your transcript with the text transcript and circle any errors you may have made, including spelling and punctuation errors.

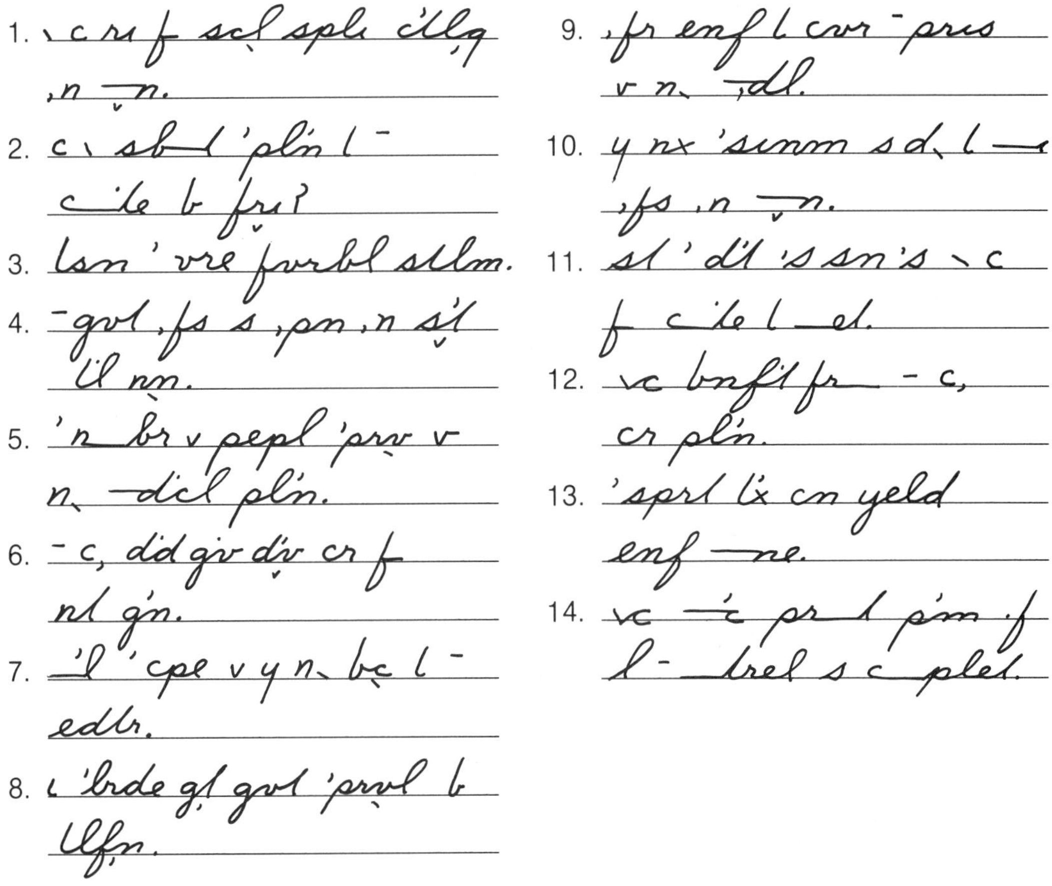

TRANSCRIPT OF SHORTHAND SENTENCES

1. You can write for the school supply catalog on Monday.
2. Can you submit a plan to the committee by Friday? (20)
3. It is not a very favorable settlement.
4. The government office is open on Saturday till noon. (40)
5. A number of people approve of the new medical plan.
6. The company did give Dave credit for the net gain. (60)
7. Mail a copy of your new book to the editor.
8. I already got government approval by telephone. (80)

9. Offer enough to cover the price of the new model.
10. Your next assignment is due at my office on Monday. (100)
11. Set a date as soon as you can for the committee to meet.
12. You can benefit from the company credit plan. (120)
13. A separate tax cannot yield enough money.
14. You can make prompt payment if all the material is complete. (140)

DICTATION AND TRANSCRIPTION

Write from dictation the Transcript of Shorthand Sentences. Your instructor will dictate each group of 20 words to you at various speeds. Select one set of notes, and transcribe it quickly and accurately.

BUILDING WRITING AND TRANSCRIPTION SPEEDS

Letter 1

Using the self-dictation method, write the shorthand outlines for the following letter in your shorthand notebook. As you read your notes, compare them with the outlines in the text. Circle any words you may have written incorrectly and write them correctly several times. Then write the letter again from print, using the self-dictation technique. Transcribe your notes as an attractively arranged block-style letter. Use a fictitious inside address. Use your own name for the typed signature line.

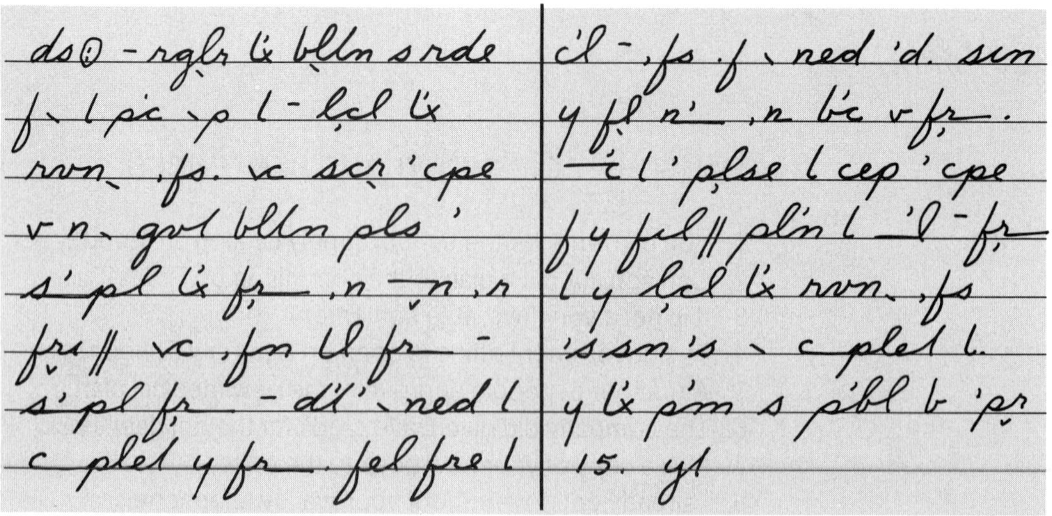

Letter 1 transcript

Dear Sir: The regular tax bulletin is ready for you to pick up at the local tax revenue office. (20) You can secure a copy of the new government bulletin plus a sample tax form on Monday or Friday. (40)

You can often tell from the sample form the data you need to complete your form. Feel free to call the office if (60) you need aid. Sign your full name on the back of the form. Make it a policy to keep a copy for your file.

Plan (80) to mail the form to your local tax revenue office as soon as you complete it. Your tax payment is payable (100) by April 15. Yours truly, (105)

Learning tip:

When writing and transcribing dates, use figures. For example: April 15; November 5.

SKILL-BUILDING ASSIGNMENTS

1. Complete Unit 5 in *Forkner Shorthand Skill Builder for Colleges*.
2. Select Cassette 5 Side A of the *Theory and Speed-Building Tapes for Colleges* and follow the directions on the tape.
3. If instructed to do so, read, write, and transcribe the supplementary letter for this chapter found in Appendix A, Supplementary Dictation and Transcription.
4. Take additional live dictation as provided by your instructor.

Chapter 6

WRITING SOUNDS OF SOFT G AND J, EN-IN-UN, AND D OR ED ADDED TO A ROOT WORD

WRITING PRINCIPLES

Sound of soft *g* and *j*

Write an undotted *j* for all sounds of soft *g* and *j*.

job college large budget major average

manage manager management age page cage

general coverage knowledge original June John

judge package

As you read each outline, write it three times in your notebook. When you have learned all the words, you should be able to read and write them rapidly and accurately. Cover the outlines and write them from the print. Read back your notes and correct any errors you may have made.

Learning tip:

To save time, omit the final upward stroke in words ending with *g* or *j*. (See *college* and *judge* above).

Prefixes *in-en-un*

Write a longhand capital N to express the prefixes *in-en-un*.

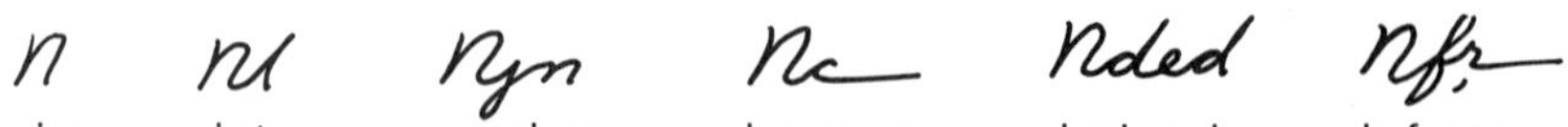

in into engine income indeed inform

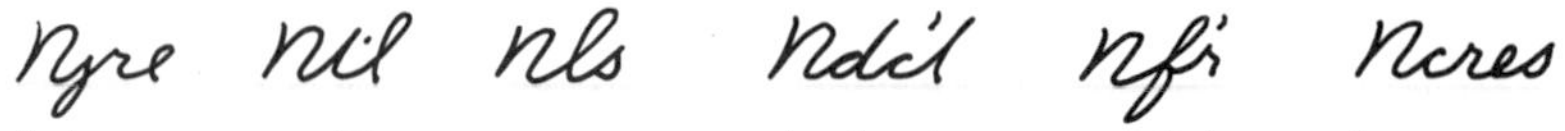

injury until unless indicate unfair increase

envelope — enroll/enrol — unpaid — energy — engage

Cover the printed words and read the outlines until you can read them without hesitating. Then cover the outlines and write each word in shorthand as you read it from the print. Check your notes and correct any errors you may have made. Write all the outlines until you can read and write them rapidly and accurately.

Expressing past tense

Make a short dash under the last letter or symbol in an outline to show that *d* or *ed* is added to a root word to form the past tense. This method of indicating past tense will help you transcribe accurately words that sound alike.

For example: *build*  *billed* .

placed — needed — offered — submitted — mailed — signed

obtained — played — approved — involved — indicated

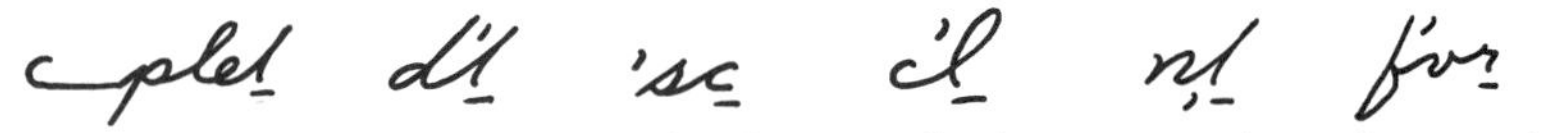

completed — dated — asked — called — noted — favored

Cover the printed words and read the outlines until you can read them without hesitating. Then build your writing speed by scribble-writing the outlines in your notebook.

New vocabulary

Study the print and the outlines below until you can read the outlines as fast as you can read the print. Then cover the outlines and write them from print as fast as you can several times.

accept — *am-more* — *great* — *opportunity* — *glad*

satisfy-satisfactory   I am   to be

BUILDING TRANSCRIPTION SKILLS

Parenthetical expressions

Parenthetical expressions are words or groups of words that may be omitted from a sentence without changing its meaning. Place a comma before and after all parenthetical words or phrases. Study the examples that follow and note how each is punctuated.

1. We will, however, spend the winter in our cabin.
2. The United States and Canada, which have been settled by many immigrants, have developed multicultural societies.
3. The company will, of course, refund your money.
4. The old inn, in regular use for over a century, was in excellent condition.
5. Our instructor, who is confined to a wheelchair, gives excellent lectures.
6. I must say, frankly, I do not understand the question.
7. It is necessary, nevertheless, to time the examination.
8. Everyone, regardless of age, has formed habits and attitudes.

Application – **Punctuating parenthetical expressions**. In your notebook number from 1 – 10. If the sentences below require a comma, place the preceding word followed by the comma after the appropriate number. If the sentence is correct, write OK after the number. Check your work with the key located in Appendix G at the back of this text.

1. We shall of course work on the problem.
2. Mr. Fields who is an expert computer programmer walked into the office.
3. Our new computer although smaller than its predecessor has a large capacity.
4. I was not, as you know, aware of your illness.
5. You should try nevertheless to attend the meeting.

6. We do not as a rule buy our food at that store.
7. The factory is operating according to my information at full capacity.
8. Mr. Davis, who contributed much to the community, was honored at a banquet.
9. It is difficult unfortunately to assess the extent of the damage.
10. Please accept the package regardless of its condition when it arrives.

Spelling review

Each of the following sentences contains an outline for a word that is often misspelled. Transcribe the shorthand outline in your notebook. You may use a dictionary, a standard word reference list, or the *Forkner Shorthand Dictionary for Beginners* to verify the spelling. Compare your answers with the key located at the end of the chapter. Review any words you may have misspelled. Then write all the outlines until you can write them fluently.

1. The motel will 'c-d'l two hundred people each night.
2. The old bridge 'crs the river needs to be repaired.
3. Please do not e-brs me in front of the other students.
4. Studies of the Nvrnm are becoming very popular.
5. Are you f'-lr with the tax laws?
6. Solar heating made a nlsbl difference in our house.
7. Has it ,cr to you that daily practice is necessary?
8. You really fsn'l me.
9. The performance was held for the bnfil of the Student Council.
10. The two books about birds are very si-lr.

APPLYING NEW PRINCIPLES

Follow these procedures in learning to read and write the sentences on page 38.

1. Read the shorthand outlines for each of the sentences until you can read all the sentences without hesitation.

2. Using the Transcript of Shorthand Sentences, write the shorthand outlines for each sentence in your notebook.

3. Check your outlines.

4. Write correctly three times each outline that you may have written incorrectly.

5. Rewrite the shorthand outlines as you read the sentences once again from the Transcript of Shorthand Sentences.

6. Transcribe the sentences from your own notes. Compare your transcript with the text transcript and circle any errors you may have made, including spelling and punctuation errors.

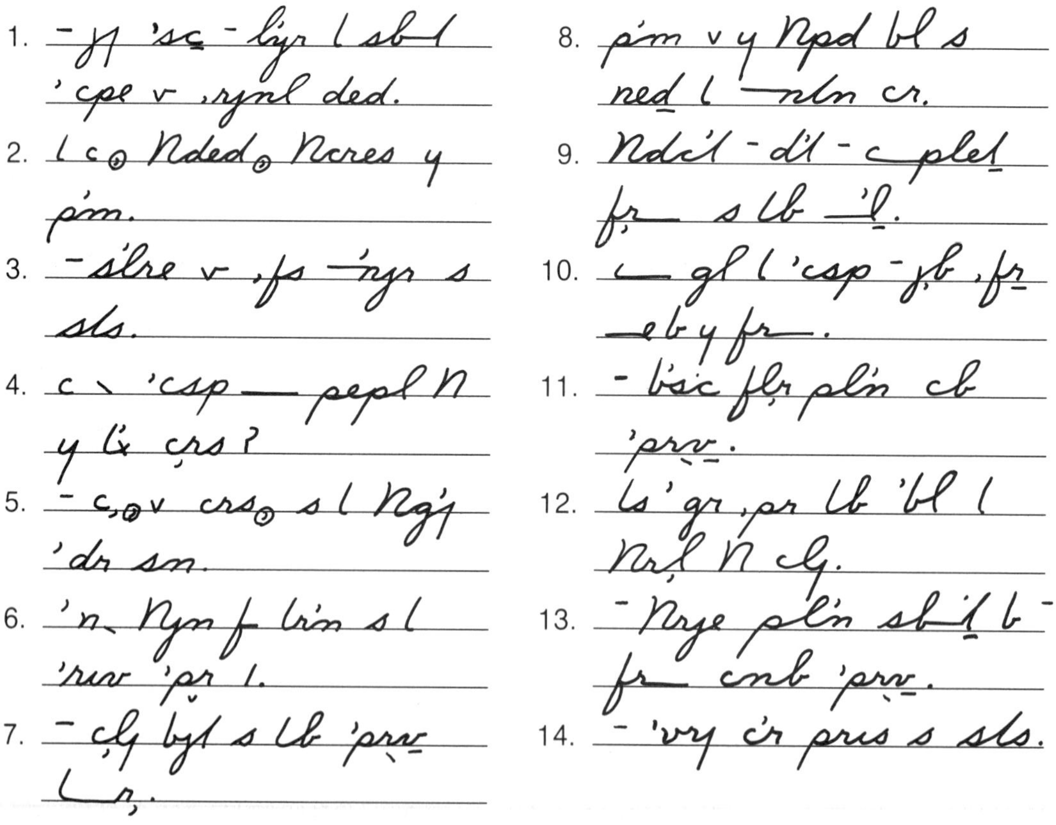

TRANSCRIPT OF SHORTHAND SENTENCES

1. The judge asked the lawyer to submit a copy of the original deed.
2. It can, indeed, increase your payment. (20)
3. The salary of the office manager is satisfactory.
4. Can you accept more people in your tax course? (40)
5. The company, of course, is to engage a doctor soon.
6. A new engine for the train is to arrive April 1. (60)
7. The college budget is to be approved tomorrow.
8. Payment of your unpaid bill is needed to maintain credit. (80)
9. Indicate the date the completed form is to be mailed.
10. I am glad to accept the job offered me by your firm. (100)
11. The basic floor plan can be approved.
12. It is a great opportunity to be able to enroll in college. (120)
13. The energy plan submitted by the firm cannot be approved.
14. The average car price is satisfactory. (140)

Learning tip:
For ease in transcribing, some shorthand writers prefer to circle all numbers in shorthand notes.

DICTATION AND TRANSCRIPTION

Write from dictation the Transcript of Shorthand Sentences. Your instructor will dictate each group of 20 words to you at various speeds. Select one set of notes, and transcribe it quickly and accurately.

BUILDING WRITING AND TRANSCRIPTION SPEEDS

New vocabulary

Read and write the following shorthand outlines until you can do so without hesitation.

February January opened use (n) facility tour

panel capable impossible located scheduled

individual agreed

Letter 1

Read the following letter until you can do so fluently. Then, using the self-dictation method, write the shorthand outlines for the letter in your shorthand notebook. As you read your notes, compare them with the outlines in the text. Circle any words you may have written incorrectly and write them correctly several times. Then write the letter again from print, using the self-dictation technique. Transcribe your notes as an attractively arranged block-style letter. Use a fictitious inside address. Use your own name for the typed signature line.

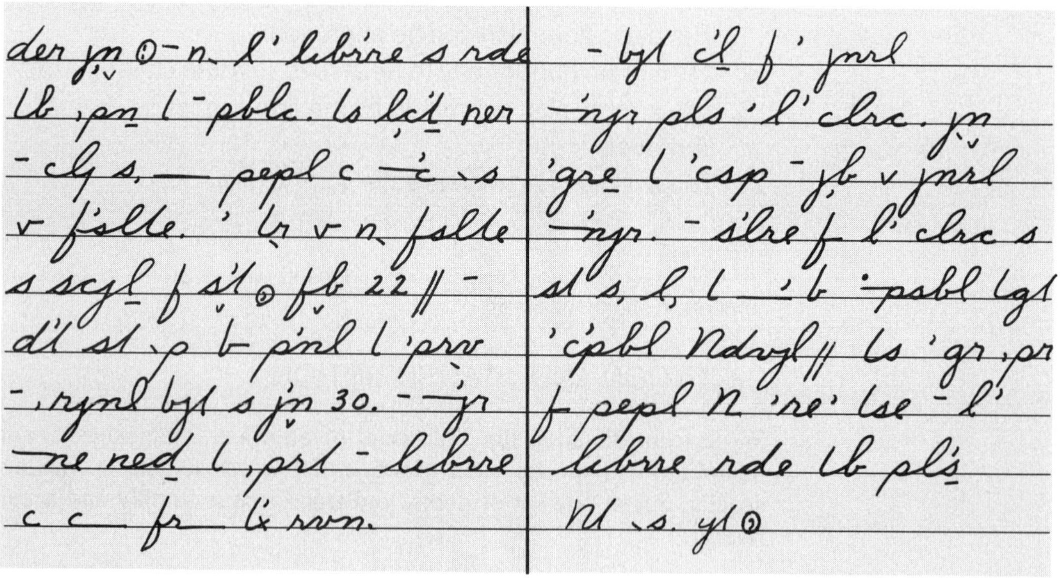

Letter 1 transcript

Dear John: The new law library is ready to be opened to the public. It is located near the college (20) so more people can make use of the facility. A tour of the new facility is scheduled for Saturday, (40) February 22.

The date set up by the panel to approve the original budget is (60) January 30. The major money needed to operate the library can come from tax revenue. (80) The budget called for a general manager plus a law clerk. June agreed to accept the job of general (100) manager. The salary for the law clerk is set so low it may be impossible to get a capable (120) individual.

It is a great opportunity for the people in the area to see the law (140) library ready to be placed into use. Yours truly, (149)

SKILL-BUILDING ASSIGNMENTS

1. Complete Unit 6 in *Forkner Shorthand Skill Builder for Colleges*.
2. Select Cassette 6 Side A of the *Theory and Speed-Building Tapes for Colleges* and follow the directions on the tape.
3. If instructed to do so, read, write, and transcribe the supplementary letter for this chapter found in Appendix A, Supplementary Dictation and Transcription.
4. Take additional live dictation as provided by your instructor.

Spelling review key

1. accommodate 2. across 3. embarrass 4. environment
5. familiar 6. noticeable 7. occurred 8. fascinate
9. benefit 10. similar

Chapter 7

WRITING SOUNDS OF W-WH, AWA-AWAY, AND CON-COUN-COUNT

WRITING PRINCIPLES

Sounds of *w-wh*

Write a long upward, slanted, straight line for the sounds of *w* and *wh*. When the *w-wh* stroke comes first in a word, begin the stroke below the line so the next downstroke rests on the line.

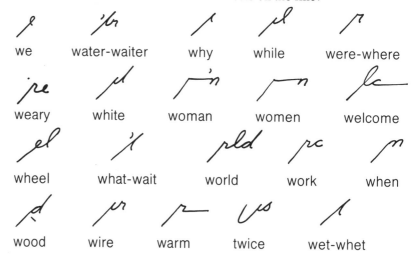

we | water-waiter | why | while | were-where

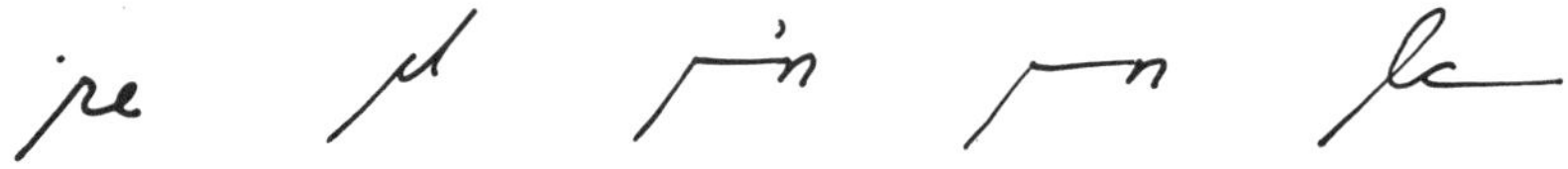

weary | white | woman | women | welcome

wheel | what-wait | world | work | when

wood | wire | warm | twice | wet-whet

As you read each outline, write it several times. Do this for all the words. When you can read all the words fluently, cover the print and write each outline once. Then read your own notes. If you have difficulty reading your notes, rewrite the outlines and read them again.

Combination *awa*

Write two *a* symbols ›› to express the combination *awa* and *away*.

away | aware | awake | await | awaited | unaware

As you read each outline, write it three times in your notebook. When you have written all the words, you should be able to read and write each one rapidly and accurately.

Prefixes *con-coun-count*

Write a capital C to express the prefixes *con*, *coun*, and *count*.

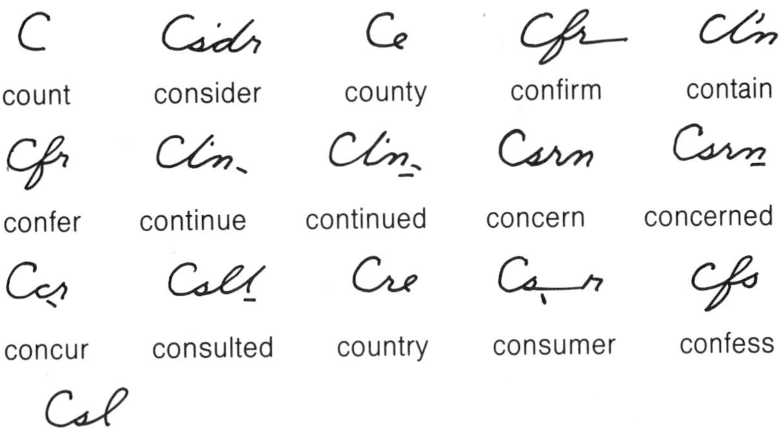

count consider county confirm contain

confer continue continued concern concerned

concur consulted country consumer confess

council-counsel

Cover the print of the first line of words and read the outlines until you can read them easily. Then quickly write the outline for each word several times in your notebook. Follow the same procedure for each line of words. When you can read the outlines fluently, cover them and write them from the print. Check your outlines. Rewrite correctly any words you may have written incorrectly.

New vocabulary

Read and write the following words and phrases until you can read and write them without hesitation. Always memorize the abbreviated words.

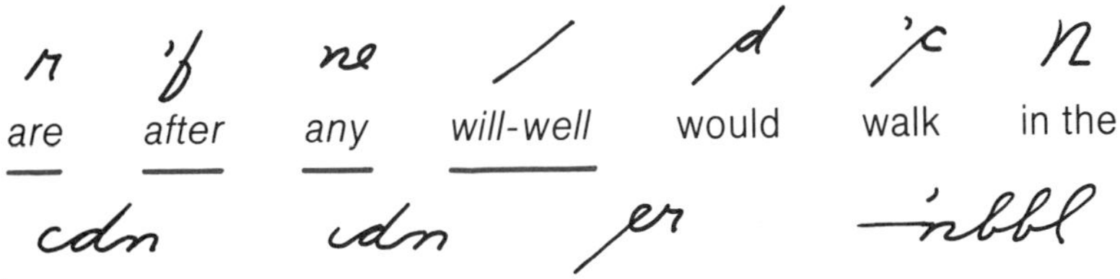

<u>are</u> <u>after</u> <u>any</u> <u>will-well</u> would walk in the

could not I do not we are may not be able

BUILDING TRANSCRIPTION SKILLS

Spelling review

The shorthand outlines which follow are for commonly misspelled words. Transcribe the outlines in your notebook. You may use a dictionary, a standard word reference list, or the *Forkner Shorthand Dictionary for Beginners* to verify the spelling. Compare your answers with the key located at the end of the chapter. Review any words you may have misspelled. Then write each outline three times.

1. bnfl
2. gr'r
3. lrjde
4. Csev
5. jjm
6. sfle
7. dfnl
8. librre
9. dvid
10.

Word usage

Study the following groups of words. Notice that within the groups the words sound similar or alike, but have different meanings. Learn the meaning of each word.

Words Commonly Misused	Definition
adapt	to adjust
adopt	to choose
affect	to influence
effect	(n) result (v) to bring about
cite	to quote
sight	a view
site	a place
counsel	(n) an attorney (v) to give advice
council	an assembly
grate	(n) a frame of bars (v) to scrape
great	large, famous
its	possessive form of *it*
it's	contraction of *it is*

later	after a time
latter	second in a series of two
stationary	immovable, fixed
stationery	writing paper
their	belonging to them
there	in that place
they're	contraction of *they are*
to	toward
too	also, to an excessive degree
two	a number: 2

Application — **Word usage.** In your notebook number from 1 – 10. Complete each of the following sentences by writing the correct word opposite the appropriate sentence number. Check your work with the key located in Appendix G at the back of this text.

1. (It's, Its) time to go to the game.
2. Please (cite, sight, site) the source of your information.
3. What will be the (affect, effect) of your decision?
4. May I make an appointment (later, latter) in the week?
5. The new tax forms caused the citizens a (grate, great) deal of trouble.
6. Most of the employees have received (their, there, they're) raises.
7. Send the package (to, too, two) my attention.
8. The storm front remained (stationary, stationery) all day.
9. Why not (adapt, adopt) a child?
10. Her legal (counsel, council) advised her not to answer the question.

APPLYING NEW PRINCIPLES

Follow these procedures in learning to read and write the sentences below.

1. Read the shorthand outlines for each of the sentences until you can read all the sentences without hesitation.
2. Using the Transcript of Shorthand Sentences, write the shorthand outlines for each sentence in your notebook.
3. Check your outlines.
4. Write correctly three times each outline that you may have written incorrectly.
5. Rewrite the shorthand outlines as you read the sentences once again from the Transcript of Shorthand Sentences.
6. Transcribe the sentences from your own notes. Compare your transcript with the text transcript and circle any errors you may have made, including spelling and punctuation errors.

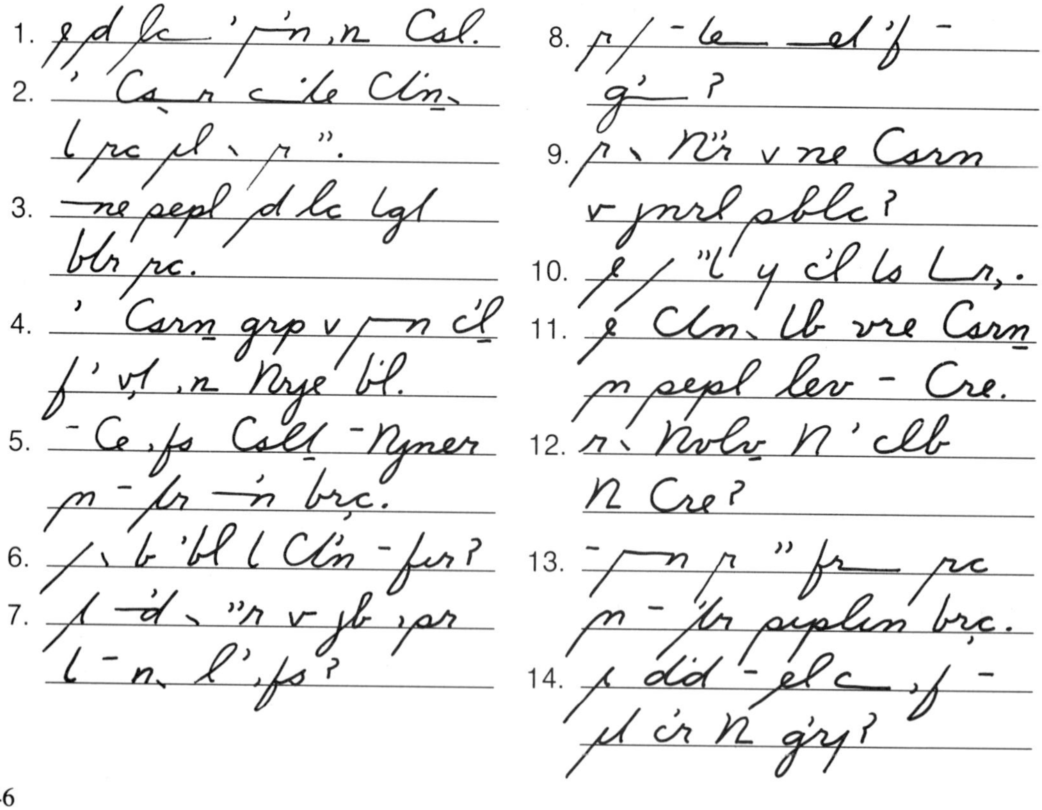

TRANSCRIPT OF SHORTHAND SENTENCES

1. We would welcome a woman on the council.
2. A consumer committee continued to work while you were away. (20)
3. Many people would like to get better work.
4. A concerned group of women called for a vote on the energy bill. (40)
5. The county office consulted the engineer when the water main broke.
6. Will you be able to contain the fire? (60)
7. What made you aware of the job opportunity at the new law office?
8. Where will the team meet after the game? (80)
9. Were you unaware of any concern of the general public?
10. We will await your call to us tomorrow. (100)
11. We continue to be very concerned when people leave the country.
12. Are you involved in a club in the country? (120)
13. The women were away from work when the water pipeline broke.
14. Why did the wheel come off the white car in the garage? (140)

DICTATION AND TRANSCRIPTION

Write from dictation the Transcript of Shorthand Sentences. Your instructor will dictate each group of 20 words to you at various speeds. Select one set of notes, and transcribe it quickly and accurately.

BUILDING WRITING AND TRANSCRIPTION SPEEDS

Letter 1

You can read the following letter because you have learned all of the theory principles used in the words. Read the letter repeatedly until you can read it fluently. Then transcribe it. Check your transcript with the text transcript and correct any errors you may have made.

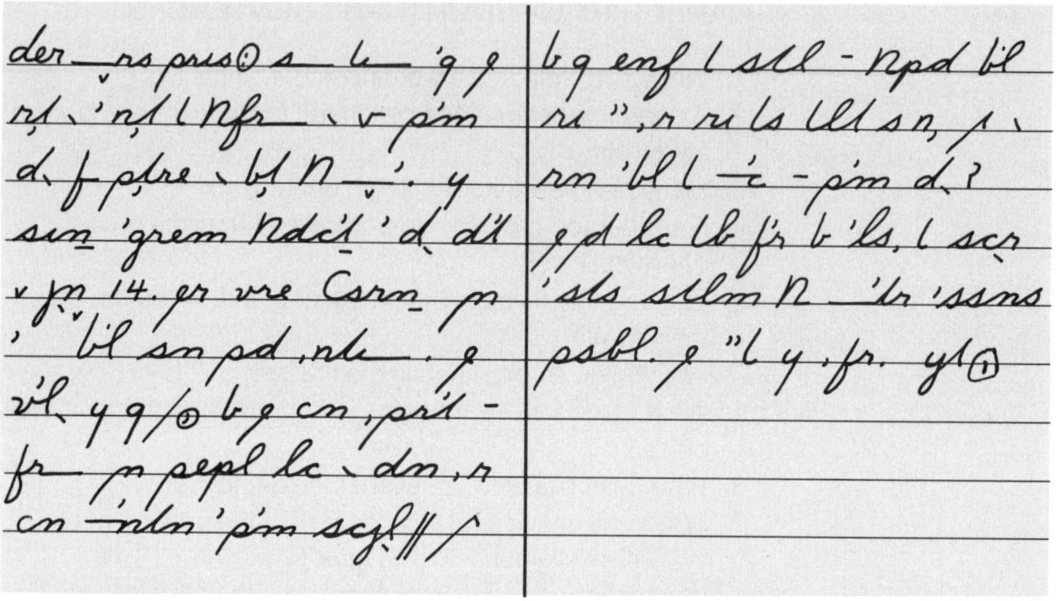

Letter 1 transcript

Dear Mrs. Price: Some time ago we wrote you a note to inform you of the payment due for the pottery you (20) bought in May. Your signed agreement indicated a due date of June 14. We are very concerned when a bill (40) is not paid on time. We value your good will, but we cannot operate the firm when people like you do not or (60) cannot maintain a payment schedule.

Will you be good enough to settle the unpaid bill right away or write to (80) us to let us know why you are not able to make the payment due? We would like to be fair but also to (100) secure a satisfactory settlement in the matter as soon as possible. We await your offer. Yours truly, (120)

Responding to a business letter

In addition to taking letters in shorthand, many secretaries are responsible for composing business letters. How creative are you? In your notebook write your own response to the letter you just read and transcribed. Write as much of your reply in shorthand as you can; however, you may use longhand for words you cannot yet write in shorthand. One possible reply appears as the supplementary letter for this chapter. A second possible reply is in Unit 7 of *Forkner Shorthand Skill Builder for Colleges*.

SKILL-BUILDING ASSIGNMENTS

1. Complete Unit 7 in *Forkner Shorthand Skill Builder for Colleges*.

2. Select Cassette 7 Side A of the *Theory and Speed-Building Tapes for Colleges* and follow the directions on the tape.

3. If instructed to do so, read, write, and transcribe the supplementary letter for this chapter found in Appendix A, Supplementary Dictation and Transcription.

4. Take additional live dictation as provided by your instructor.

Spelling review key

1. benefited* 2. grammar 3. tragedy 4. conceive
5. judgment* 6. safety 7. definite 8. library
9. divide 10. omit

Learning tip:
* Variant spellings: benefited/benefitted; judgment/judgement. Your instructor will indicate the spellings preferred in your community.

Chapter 8

BUSINESS DICTATION AND TRANSCRIPTION

BUILDING TRANSCRIPTION SKILLS

Punctuating items in a series

Use a comma to separate more than two words, phrases, or clauses in a series. A comma should be used before *and*, *nor*, and *or* when they connect the last two elements in a series. Study the examples which follow.

1. The children were named Shawn, Amy, and Renee.
2. Find the material for your report in a current magazine, in a newspaper, or from a TV or radio news broadcast.
3. The fire was started by a careless camper, then spread to nearby brush, and soon became a raging forest fire.
4. Do you want a job as a typist, as a secretary, or as an administrative assistant?
5. You may set your goals higher and become an office manager, a member of the board, or an officer of the corporation.
6. An examination of charts, graphs, diagrams, or illustrations may help you understand the materials you are studying.
7. Tennis, soccer, and racquet ball are popular sports today.
8. She speaks English, French, and Spanish fluently.
9. New computer systems can accept information from many sources, including magnetic tape, optical scanners, and terminals.

Application — **Punctuating items in a series.** In your notebook number from 1 – 10. If a sentence requires one or more commas, write the preceding word followed by a comma opposite the appropriate number. Check your work with the key located in Appendix G at the back of this text.

1. The softball player hit a single a double and a home run.
2. We looked for the lost toy in the house in the garage and in the barn.

3. She did her homework watched television and had breakfast before going to school.
4. Books, stationery, and other supplies are available at the bookstore.
5. Maria toured in Canada in the United States and in Mexico last year.
6. The doctor who is well educated who keeps up to date and who cares about his patients keeps very busy.
7. Our committee included a teacher one of the counselors and an administrator.
8. Be sure to take courses in typewriting, shorthand, and accounting.
9. Clouds gathered overhead the wind came up and soon we found ourselves trapped in a rainstorm.
10. He always won, whether it was a game of soccer a tennis match or a cross-country run.

Spelling review

Here is another list of commonly misspelled words. Write each word in your notebook, filling in the missing letters. The number of blanks indicate the number of letters missing. Then write the shorthand outline for each word. Check your answers and outlines with the key located at the end of the chapter. Write the outlines several times for speed development.

1. _ntil	6. com_it_ee	11. u_efu_
2. a_ready	7. conc__vable	12. n__ghbor
3. carefu_	8. de_lt	13. med__ine
4. colum_	9. el_g_ble	14. pr_ve
5. co__itted	10. en_my	15. jew_lr_

Writing salutations and complimentary closes in shorthand

Most business letter salutations and closings can be expressed quickly in shorthand by writing the first letter of each word as a unit. Here are some examples you can already write. As you say the salutation or closing, write the shorthand outline in your notebook.

Dear Sir Dear Mrs. Dear Mr. Dear Ms. Yours very truly

Yours truly Sincerely yours Very truly yours

BUILDING WRITING AND TRANSCRIPTION SPEEDS

Except for the new vocabulary words that follow, no new words are included in the three letters in this chapter. Therefore, each letter should be easy for you to write in shorthand and to transcribe. Your instructor may dictate these letters to you at various speeds. For each letter, follow the procedures suggested to build your speed in taking and transcribing shorthand.

New vocabulary

Read and write each word until you can do so quickly and accurately.

typewriter anytime Morris arrived Jackson suited

worker treat dream

Letter 1

Read the following letter until you can read it without hesitation. Then write the shorthand for the letter in your notebook, making certain your outlines are readable. Read them back to be sure. Insert paper into your typewriter and transcribe the letter twice: first, from the shorthand in the text, and then from your own notes. Were you able to transcribe your own notes as easily as those in the text? If so, you have written excellent shorthand.

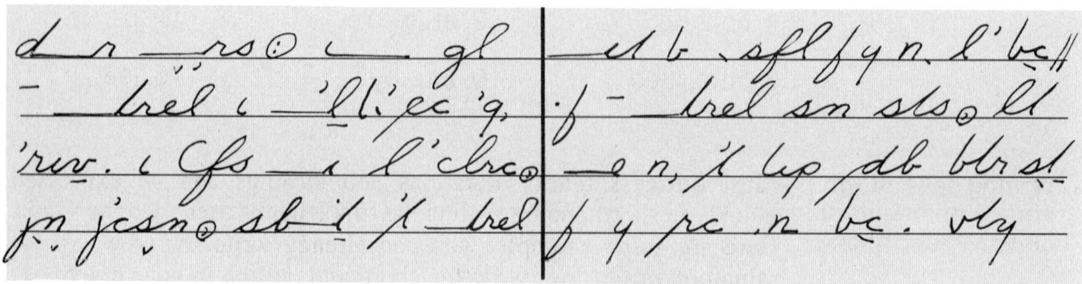

Letter 1 transcript

Dear Mr. Morris: I am glad the material I mailed to you a week ago arrived. I confess my law clerk, (20) June Jackson, submitted what material might be useful for your new law book.

If the material is not (40) satisfactory, let me know what type would be better suited for your work on the book. Very truly yours, (60)

Letter 2 As you read the following letter, scribble-write it in your notebook until you can read and write the letter easily.

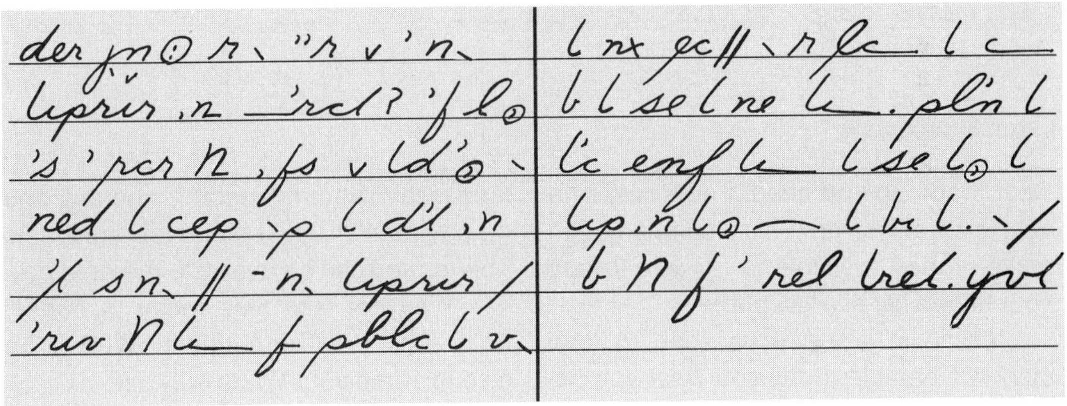

Letter 2 transcript

Dear June: Are you aware of a new typewriter on the market? After all, as a worker in the office of (20) today, you need to keep up to date on what is new.

The new typewriter will arrive in time for the public to (40) view it next week.

You are welcome to come by to see it any time. Plan to take enough time to see it, to type on (60) it, and to buy it. You will be in for a real treat. Yours very truly, (73)

Letter 3 Read Letter 3 following this procedure: Read sentence one. Then go back and read sentences one and two. Then go back to the beginning and read sentences one, two, and three. Follow this plan for reading the entire letter. Each time add a new sentence. By the time you have completed reading the letter, you should be able to transcribe the outlines easily. Transcribe the letter from the outlines in the text. Then, using the self-dictation method, write the letter from the text transcript.

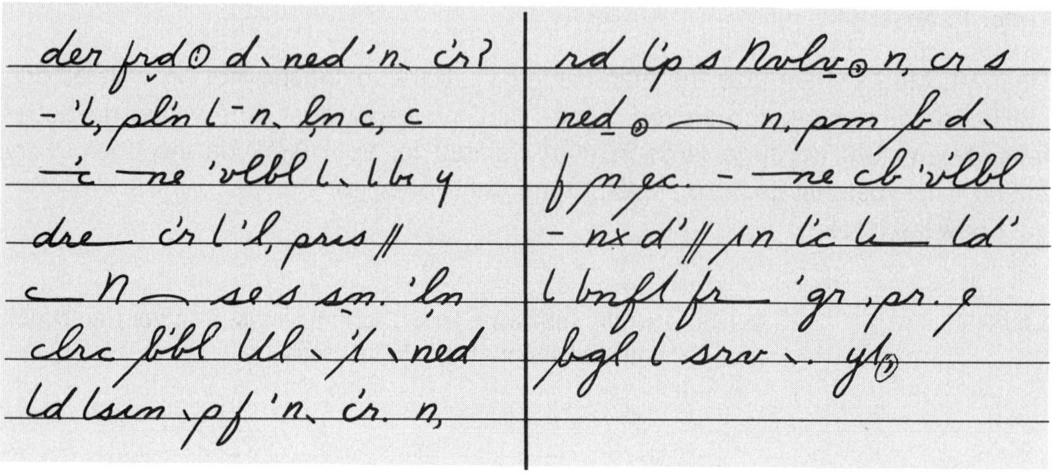

Letter 3 transcript

Dear Fred: Do you need a new car? The auto plan at the new loan company can make money available to (20) you to buy your dream car at a low price.

Come in and see us soon. A loan clerk will be able to tell you what you (40) need to do to sign up for a new car. No red tape is involved, no credit is needed, and no payment will be (60) due for one week. The money can be available the next day.

Why not take time today to benefit from a (80) great opportunity. We will be glad to serve you. Yours truly, (91)

DICTATION AND TRANSCRIPTION

Write from dictation the transcripts of Letters 1, 2, and 3. Your instructor will dictate each letter to you at various speeds.

Using your own notes, transcribe all letters using the block style illustrated in Chapter 4. Use a fictitious inside address. Use your name for the typed signature line.

SKILL-BUILDING ASSIGNMENTS

1. Complete Unit 8 in *Forkner Shorthand Skill Builder for Colleges*.
2. Select Cassette 8 Side A of the *Theory and Speed-Building Tapes for Colleges* and follow the directions on the tape.
3. If instructed to do so, read, write, and transcribe the supplementary letter for this chapter found in Appendix A, Supplementary Dictation and Transcription.

4. Take additional live dictation as provided by your instructor.

REVIEWING THE WRITING PRINCIPLES

All the writing rules, abbreviated words, and standard abbreviations you have learned in Chapters 1 through 8 are reviewed on Cassette 17 Side A of the *Theory and Speed-Building Tapes for Colleges*. Take dictation from this tape before completing Preview Examination 2.

PREVIEW EXAMINATION 2

Remove Preview Examination 2 from your *Forkner Shorthand Skill Builder for Colleges*. It follows Unit 32. This informal preview examination will help you in assessing your understanding of the Forkner principles presented in Chapters 4–8. It is similar to Examination 2 which may be administered at a later date by your instructor.

Complete Preview Examination 2 and then check your answers carefully with the key in your *Forkner Shorthand Skill Builder for Colleges*. Correct any errors you may have made.

Spelling review key

1. until
2. already
3. careful
4. column
5. committed
6. committee
7. conceivable
8. dealt

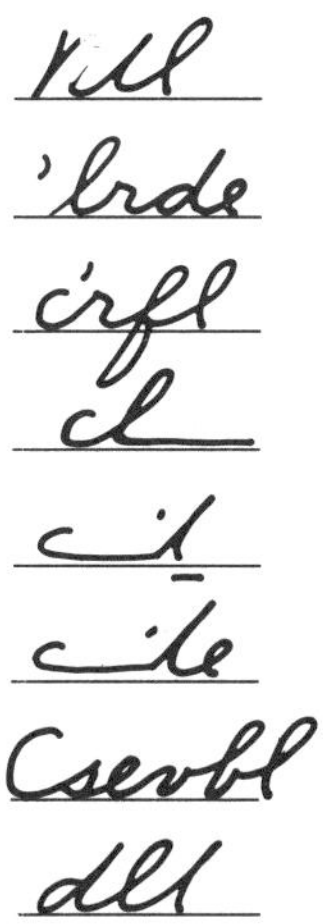

9. eligible
10. enemy
11. useful
12. neighbor
13. medicine
14. prove
15. jewelry*

Learning tip:

Variant spelling jewelry/jewellery. Your instructor will indicate the spelling preferred in your community.

Chapter 9

WRITING SOUNDS OF H, SH, AND BE-DE-RE

WRITING PRINCIPLES

Sound of *h*

Write a short dash – to express the sound of *h*.

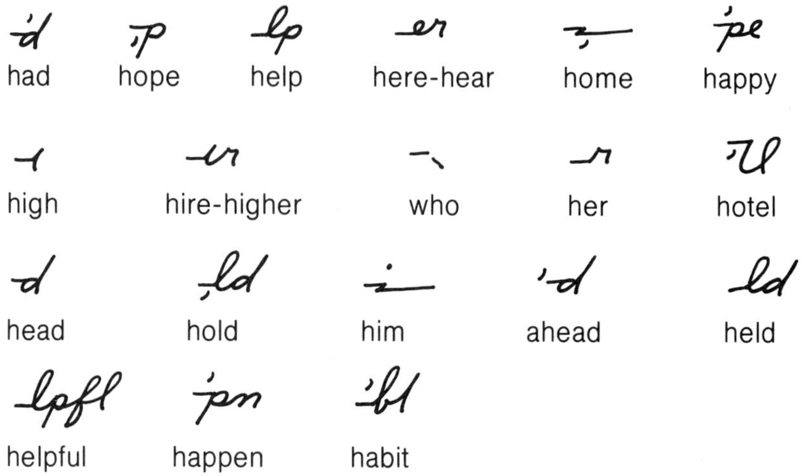

Cover the print, and read the outlines until you can read from them as fast as you can read from the print. Then cover the shorthand, and write the outlines from the print until you can write all of them rapidly and accurately.

Learning tips:

1. Make the *h* dash short so you will not confuse it with the long line for *m*.
2. Make a slight jog when joining *h* – to *m* —— in words such as *him* and *home*.
3. Note how the *h* is joined to the long *i* in *high*, the *t* in *hotel*, and the *p* in *hope*.

Sound of *sh*

Write an *h* dash through *s* to express *sh* sounds.

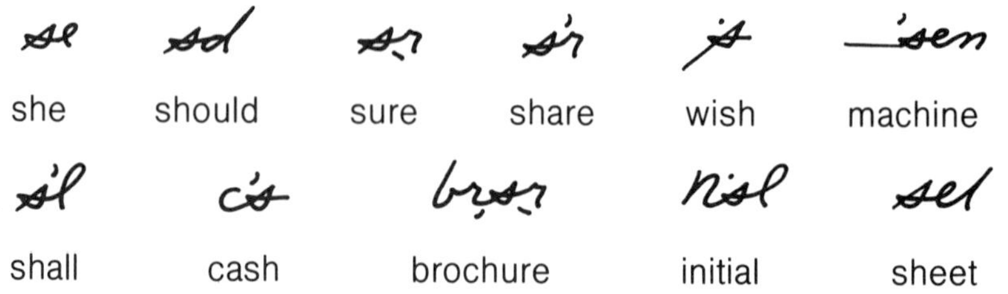

issue insure financial publish finish

pleasure show

Write each outline several times as you read each word illustrating the writing of the sound of *sh*. When you have completed this exercise, you should be able to read and write the shorthand rapidly and accurately.

Prefixes *be-de-re*

Omit the *e* in the prefixes *be*, *de*, and *re*.

believe become below-blow deliver determine

return develop development receipt delay

begin belief refer remain retirement

Read the first line of words until you can read each word fluently. Then cover the outlines and write each outline as you read from the print. Write each word in shorthand until you can do so rapidly and accurately. Follow the same procedure for each line.

New vocabulary

A technique known as the Longhand/Shorthand (L/S) Recognition Drill can be used to learn and remember new words. Using lined paper, draw vertical lines similar to the example shown on page 58. Notice that the first column contains the print of the new vocabulary words in this chapter. In the next column, the new vocabulary words have been written in shorthand. Your job will be to fill in all the columns on your lined paper, alternating between longhand and shorthand. When completed, all columns will be filled as is illustrated for *have* and *side*. Remember to say each word as you write the shorthand.

have	v	have	v	have	v
side	si	side	si	side	si
appreciate	'prs				
receive	rs				
put-please	p				
ship-short	s				
decide	dsi				
Wednesday	d				
appreciated	'prs				
pleased	p				
received	rs				
decided	dsi				
shipment	sm				
shipped	s				
membership	brs				

BUILDING TRANSCRIPTION SKILLS

Application—**Spelling**. In your notebook number from 1–15. Scan the following words. Place a check mark (√) opposite the appropriate number if the corresponding word is spelled correctly. If the word is misspelled, spell it correctly. Check your answers with a dictionary, a standard word reference list, or the *Forkner Shorthand Dictionary for Beginners*. The key showing the correct spelling of the words is located in Appendix G at the back of this text.

1. hopeing
2. scene
3. suprize
4. arrangment
5. nickel
6. several
7. heigt
8. sense
9. neice
10. shining

11. loneleness	13. seperate	15. refered
12. criticise	14. skedule	

APPLYING NEW PRINCIPLES

Follow these procedures in learning to read and write the sentences below.

1. Read the shorthand outlines for each of the sentences until you can read all the sentences without hesitation.
2. Using the Transcript of Shorthand Sentences, write the shorthand outlines for each sentence in your notebook.
3. Check your outlines.
4. Write correctly three times each outline that you may have written incorrectly.
5. Rewrite the shorthand outlines as you read the sentences once again from the Transcript of Shorthand Sentences.
6. Transcribe the sentences from your own notes. Compare your transcript with the text transcript, and circle any errors you may have made, including spelling and punctuation errors.

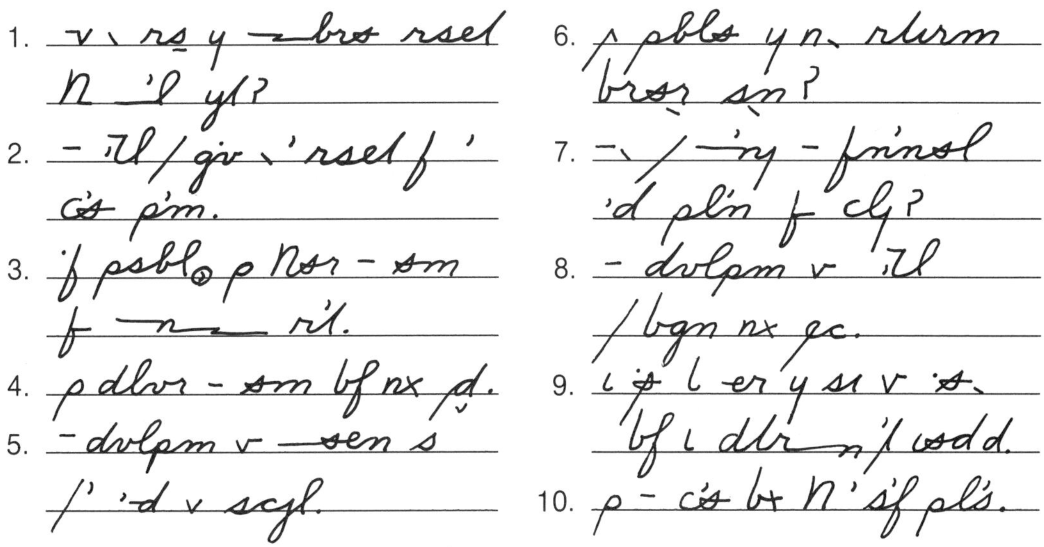

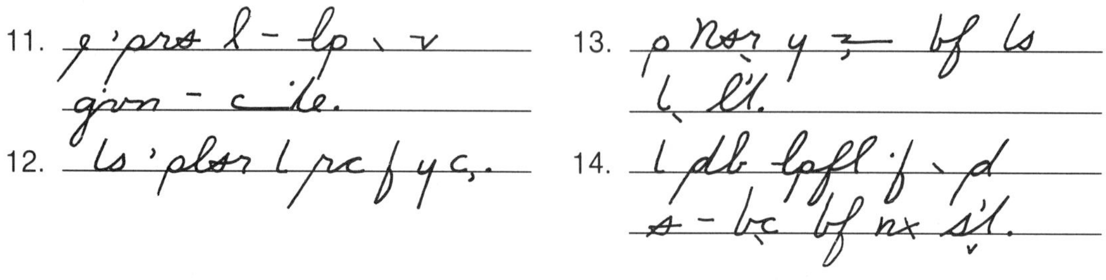

TRANSCRIPT OF SHORTHAND SENTENCES

1. Have you received your membership receipt in the mail yet?
2. The hotel will give you a receipt for a cash payment. (20)
3. If possible, please insure the shipment for the minimum rate.
4. Please deliver the shipment before next Wednesday. (40)
5. The development of the machine is way ahead of schedule.
6. Will you publish your new retirement brochure soon? (60)
7. Who will manage the financial aid plan for the college?
8. The development of the hotel will begin next week. (80)
9. I wish to hear your side of the issue before I determine what I should do.
10. Put the cash box in a safe place. (100)
11. We appreciate all the help you have given the committee.
12. It is a pleasure to work for your company. (120)
13. Please insure your home before it is too late.
14. It would be helpful if you would ship the book before next Saturday. (140)

DICTATION AND TRANSCRIPTION

Write from dictation the Transcript of Shorthand Sentences. Your instructor will dictate each group of 20 words to you at various speeds. Select one set of notes, and transcribe it quickly and accurately.

BUILDING WRITING AND TRANSCRIPTION SPEEDS

New vocabulary

Read and write each word or phrase until you can do so without hesitation.

maybe hot referred half recover repair

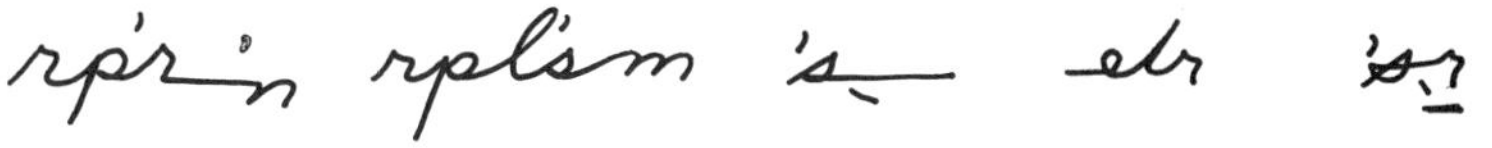

repairman replacement assume heater assured

trouble will not I do not would be he could

Letter 1

The following letter begins a sequence of correspondence related to a single matter. The sequence will continue in the *Forkner Shorthand Skill Builder For Colleges* and in Chapter 10. Read the letter until you can do so fluently. Using the self-dictation method, write the letter as you read from the transcript. Check your outlines. Write a second set of notes and transcribe it at your best typing rate.

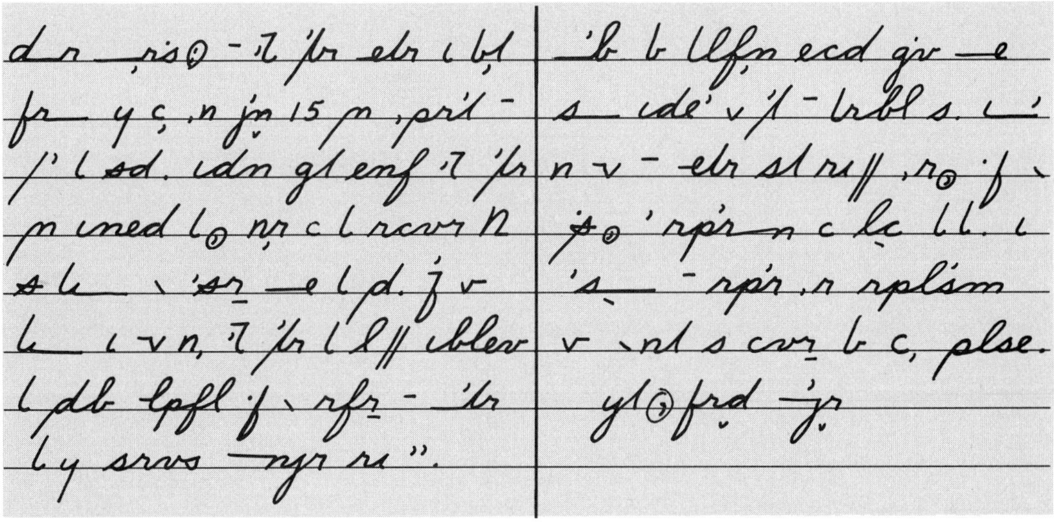

Letter 1 transcript

Dear Mr. Morris: The hot water heater I bought from your company on January 15 will not (20) operate the way it should. I do not get enough hot water when I need it, nor can it recover in the short (40) time you assured me it would. Half of the time I have no hot water at all.

I believe it would be helpful if (60) you referred the matter to your service manager right away. Maybe by telephone he could give me some (80) idea of what the trouble is. I may not have the heater set right.

Or, if you wish, a repairman can look at (100) it. I assume the repair or replacement of the unit is covered by company policy. Yours truly, (120) Fred Major (122)

SKILL-BUILDING ASSIGNMENTS

1. Complete Unit 9 in *Forkner Shorthand Skill Builder for Colleges*.
2. Select Cassette 9 Side A of the *Theory and Speed-Building Tapes for Colleges* and follow the directions on the tape.
3. If instructed to do so, read, write, and transcribe the supplementary letter for this chapter found in Appendix A, Supplementary Dictation and Transcription.
4. Take additional live dictation as provided by your instructor.

Chapter 10

WRITING SOUNDS OF CH, TH, AND HARD S AND Z

WRITING PRINCIPLES

Sound of *ch*

Write an *h* dash through *c* ∈ to express *ch* sounds.

charge child chapter children such branch

research teacher future church much which

check/cheque* picture approach chairman

As you read each outline, write it three times in your notebook. When you have written all the words, you should be able to read and write them rapidly and accurately. Now cover the outlines and write them in shorthand from print. Read your notes and correct any errors you may have made.

Learning tips:

1. When *ch* is the first sound in a word, as in *charge*, write the *c* first and then write the *h* dash through the *c*.

2. When *ch* occurs in the body of a word or at the end of a word, as in *church*, write the *h* dash as an extension of the preceding letter and write the *c* through the extended *h* dash.

3. Some words such as *feature* have the *ch* sound, but do not have the letters *ch* in them. Remember to write what you hear.

* 4. Variant spelling check/cheque. Your instructor will indicate the spelling acceptable in your community.

Sound of *th*

Join the *h* dash to the *t* ⊢ to express *th* sounds.

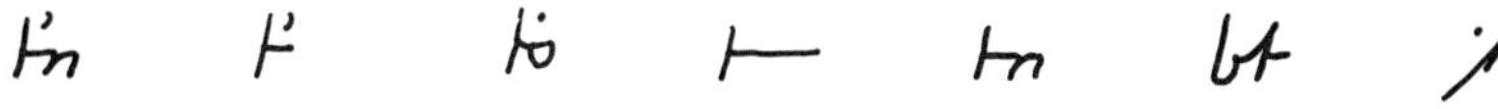

than they this them then both with

there-their together either month method

thought within although therefore rather

Cover the print of the first line of words and read the outlines until you can read them easily. Then quickly write the outline for each word several times in your notebook. Follow the same procedure for each line of words. When you can read the outlines fluently, cover them and write the outlines from the print. When finished, check your outlines with those in the text. Write correctly any words you may have written incorrectly.

Learning tip:

Most writers find it is easier to join the *h* to *t* part way up and then writing the *h* dash. Some writers prefer to cross the *t* to make the *th* combination.

Sound of hard s and z

Write a small longhand z to express the hard sound of *s* and *z*.

size ease easy season does these those

use (v) magazine hesitate cause reason was

design desire result revise deposit busy

zoo used series casualty

Cover the print, and read the outlines until you can read from them as fast as you can read from the print. Then cover the shorthand, and write the outlines from the print until you can write all of them rapidly and accurately.

New vocabulary

Memorize the following abbreviated words so that when you hear them, you can write them automatically. Then write the words in shorthand until you can do so rapidly and accurately.

each   merchandise   that-thank   manufacture

BUILDING TRANSCRIPTION SKILLS

Punctuating compound sentences

Two or more sentences that are combined into a single sentence are known as a *compound sentence*. There are three ways to form a compound sentence.

1. The most common way to form a compound sentence is to join two complete sentences with a **comma and** one of these **connecting words**: *and*, *but*, *for*, *or*, *either*, *neither*, and *nor*.

2. Two complete sentences may be joined with a **semicolon** followed by a **transitional word or phrase**. Common transitional words or phrases include: *accordingly*, *however*, *then*, *so*, *therefore*, *still*, *finally*, *consequently*, *hence*, *in fact*, *as a matter of fact*.

3. Two or more complete sentences may be joined with a **semicolon** *without* a **connecting word** or a **transitional word or phrase**.

The example which follows shows similar sentences joined in each of the three ways. Compare the various ways of forming compound sentences.

The instructions were well written. They were easy to follow. (two complete sentences)

1. The instructions were well written, and they were easy to follow. (comma plus connecting word)

2. The instructions were well written; therefore, they were easy to follow. (semicolon plus transitional word and comma)

3. The instructions were well written; they were easy to follow. (semicolon only)

Application— **Punctuating compound sentences**. Below are two sets of simple sentences.

Set 1. Our financial kit has been updated and expanded. It will help you to determine actual costs.

Set 2. The fire was burning brightly. It kept the room warm and cozy.

In your notebook, rewrite each set of sentences three times to illustrate the following ways of forming compound sentences:

1. comma plus connecting word
2. semicolon plus transitional word and comma
3. semicolon only

Check your sentences with the suggested sentences in the key located in Appendix G at the back of this text.

Application— **Word Usage**. Below are pairs of words that sound very much alike. Write the shorthand outlines for each word several times as you say the word to yourself. Then in your notebook, use each of the words correctly in a sentence. You may use a dictionary to verify your definitions. Try to use words in your sentences that you have learned to write in shorthand. Sample sentences are provided in the key located in Appendix G at the back of this text.

Word group	Shorthand outline
choose	
chose	
than	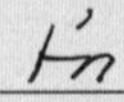
then	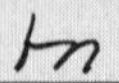

their
there
loose
lose
thorough
through

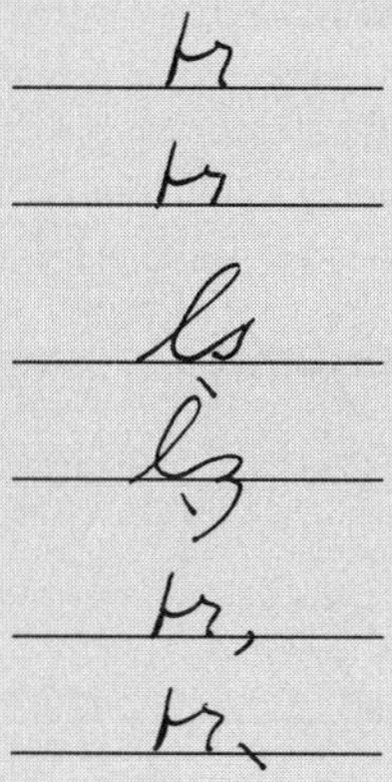

APPLYING NEW PRINCIPLES

Follow these procedures in learning to read and write the sentences below.

1. Read the shorthand outlines for each of the sentences until you can read all the sentences without hesitation.
2. Using the Transcript of Shorthand Sentences, write the shorthand outlines for each sentence in your notebook.
3. Check your outlines.
4. Write correctly three times each outline that you may have written incorrectly.
5. Rewrite the shorthand outlines as you read the sentences once again from the Transcript of Shorthand Sentences.
6. Transcribe the sentences from your own notes. Compare your transcript with the text transcript and circle any errors you may have made, including spelling and punctuation errors.

1. 

2. 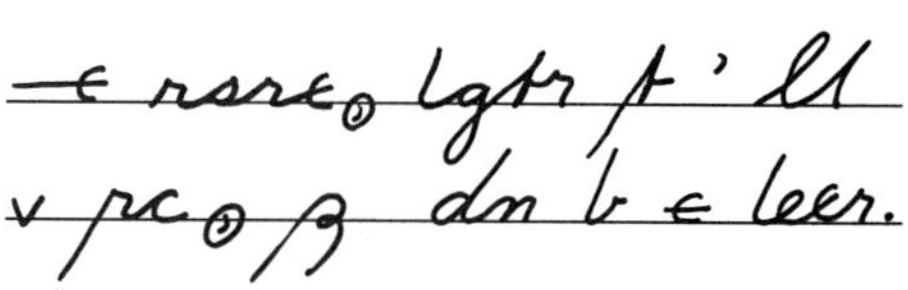

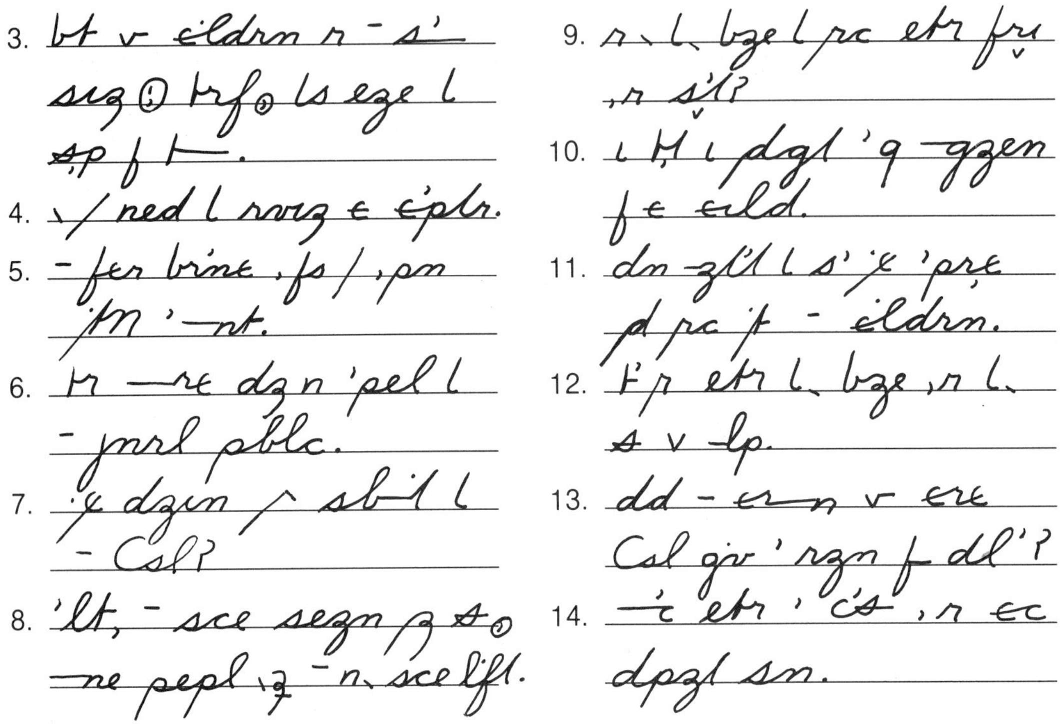

TRANSCRIPT OF SHORTHAND SENTENCES

1. Thank you for the picture of the local zoo.
2. Much research, together with a lot of work, was done by each teacher. (20)
3. Both of the children are the same size; therefore, it is easy to shop for them.
4. You will need to revise each chapter. (40)
5. The future branch office will open within a month.
6. Their merchandise does not appeal to the general public. (60)
7. Which design will you submit to the council?
8. Although the ski season was short, many people used the new ski lift. (80)
9. Are you too busy to work either Friday or Saturday?
10. I thought I would get a good magazine for each child. (100)
11. Do not hesitate to say which approach would work with the children.
12. They were either too busy or too short of help. (120)

13. Did the chairman of the church council give a reason for the delay?
14. Make either a cash or check deposit soon. (140)

DICTATION AND TRANSCRIPTION

Write from dictation the Transcript of Shorthand Sentences. Your instructor will dictate each group of 20 words to you at various speeds. Select one set of notes, and transcribe it quickly and accurately.

BUILDING WRITING AND TRANSCRIPTION SPEEDS

Carbon copies

Copies of correspondence are required in most businesses for permanent records. Sometimes it is important for a second person to receive a carbon in order to be informed about a matter. When a carbon is to go to another person, the typist uses a *carbon copy notation*. The notation, which is typed at the left margin one or two spaces below the reference initials, is usually a *cc* followed by the name of the person to whom the copy is being sent.

New vocabulary

Read and write the following words until you can do so easily.

anyone attached hotter reach

Letter 1

The following letter is the third in the defective water heater series. The letter, with a carbon copy to Mr. Morris, is to Ms. White, Chairwoman, Consumer Aid Committee. Read the letter until you can do so fluently. Then, using the transcript of the letter, write it in shorthand in your notebook. Read your notes. If there are any words you cannot read, circle them and after you have completed reading your notes, check those outlines with the text shorthand and rewrite them several times. Write a second set of notes and transcribe it at your best typing rate.

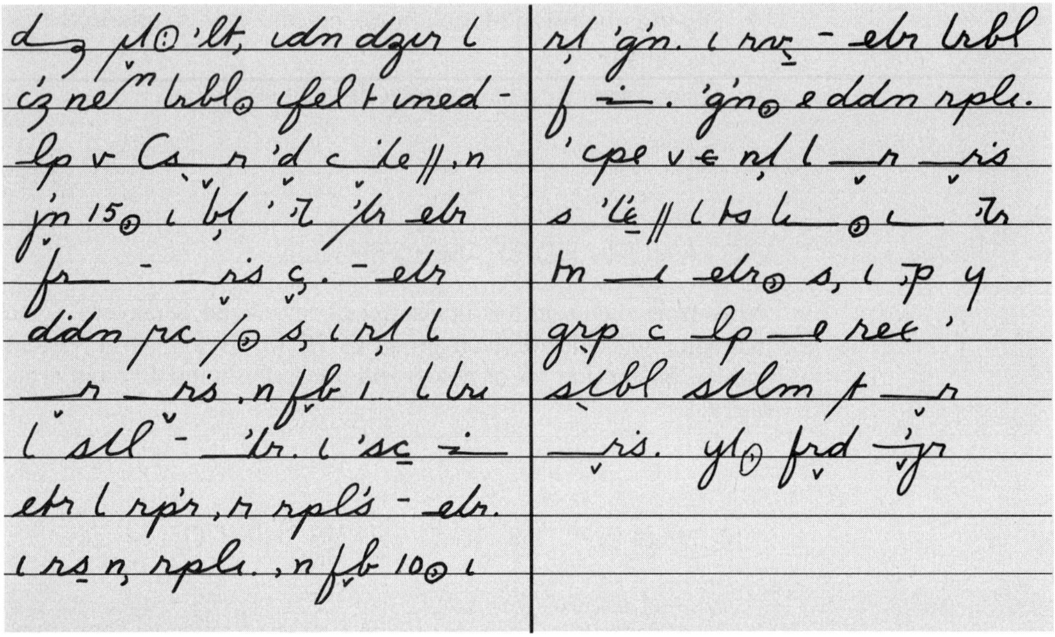

Letter 1 transcript

Dear Ms. White: Although I do not desire to cause anyone trouble, I feel that I need the help of the Consumer (20) Aid Committee.

On January 15, I bought a hot water heater from the Morris Company. The heater (40) did not work well, so I wrote to Mr. Morris on February 1 to try to settle the matter. I asked him (60) either to repair or replace the heater. I received no reply. On February 10, I wrote again. I reviewed (80) the heater trouble for him. Again, he did not reply. A copy of each note to Mr. Morris is (100) attached.

At this time, I am hotter than my heater, so I hope your group can help me reach a suitable settlement (120) with Mr. Morris. Yours truly, Fred Major (128)

SKILL-BUILDING ASSIGNMENTS

1. Complete Unit 10 in *Forkner Shorthand Skill Builder for Colleges*.
2. Select Cassette 10 Side A of the *Theory and Speed-Building Tapes for Colleges* and follow the directions on the tape.
3. If instructed to do so, read, write, and transcribe the supplementary letter for this chapter found in Appendix A, Supplementary Dictation and Transcription.
4. Take additional live dictation as provided by your instructor.

Chapter 11

WRITING SOUNDS OF NG-ING-THING, AD-ADD, AND TRANS

WRITING PRINCIPLES

Sounds of ng-ing-thing

Write a long curved stroke to express the combinations *ing* and *thing*, and the *ng* sound in words like *long*. Some words ending in *nk* also have an *ng* sound before the hard *c*. For such words write the letter *c* joined to the *ng-ing* ending (see *bank*, *think*, *blank*).

meeting	during	following	asking	reading
building	hearing	billing	looking	coming
taking	returning	concerning	bank	operating
showing	single	long	beginning	bring
think	bringing	blank	getting	thing
something	rank	nothing		

Cover the printed words and read the outlines until you can read them without hesitating. Then build your shorthand writing speed by scribble-writing the words in your notebook.

Prefix ad-add

Write a capital *a* to express the prefix *ad-add*.

ad-add | added | adding | address | advise

advice | adopt | admit

As you read each word containing the prefix *ad-add*, write the outline several times. When you have completed all words, you should be able to read and write them rapidly and accurately.

Prefix trans

Write a disjoined capital *T* to express the prefix *trans*.

transfer | transferred | transmit | transmitted | transit

transform | translate

Try to read from the shorthand outlines as fast as you can read from the print. Then write the outlines from the print and read them back. If any of your notes are difficult to read, rewrite them and read them again.

Learning tip:

Some writers prefer to join the *T* for speed.

Example: transfer *Tfr* or *Tfr*

New vocabulary

Cover the print and read the outlines until you can read them as fast as you can read from the print. Then cover the outlines and write them from print until you can write all of the outlines rapidly.

advertise | business | has | secretary | Tuesday

advertised | advertising | having | writing | being

shipping doing author counted counting

account accounted accounting

BUILDING TRANSCRIPTION SKILLS

Spelling review

The shorthand outlines which follow are for commonly misspelled words. Transcribe the outlines in your notebook. You may use a dictionary, a standard word reference list, or the *Forkner Shorthand Dictionary for Beginners* to verify the spelling. If an outline may be spelled in more than one way, give all of the spellings. Compare your answers with the key located at the end of the chapter. Write correctly any words that you may have misspelled. Then, write the shorthand outlines for each word until you can write them without hesitation.

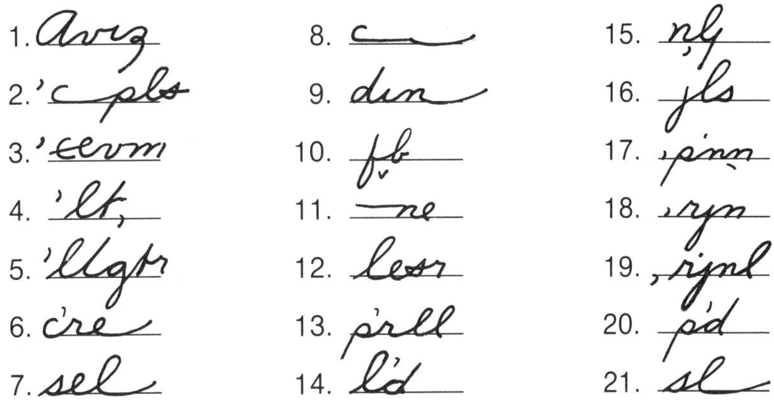

Word usage

Study the following groups of commonly misused words. Notice that within the groups, the words sound similar or alike, but have different meanings. Learn the meaning of each word.

Words Commonly Misused	Definition
capitol	legislative government building
capital	upper case letter; money

advice	suggestion; counsel
advise	to counsel
eraser	instrument for deleting written material
erasure	act of erasing
pare	to peel
pear	a fruit
pair	a couple; two

Application — **Word usage.** Use each of the words defined above in a sentence, writing as many of the words as you can in shorthand. Use a dictionary to clarify further any definition. Compare your work with the sample sentences located in Appendix G at the back of the text.

APPLYING NEW PRINCIPLES

Follow these procedures in learning to read and write the sentences on page 75.

1. Read the shorthand outlines for each of the sentences until you can read all of the sentences without hesitation.
2. Using the Transcript of Shorthand Sentences, write the shorthand outlines for each sentence in your notebook.
3. Check your outlines.
4. Write correctly three times each outline that you may have written incorrectly.
5. Rewrite the shorthand outlines as you read the sentences once again from the Transcript of Shorthand Sentences.
6. Transcribe the sentences from your own notes. Compare your transcript with the text transcript and circle any errors you may have made, including spelling and punctuation errors.

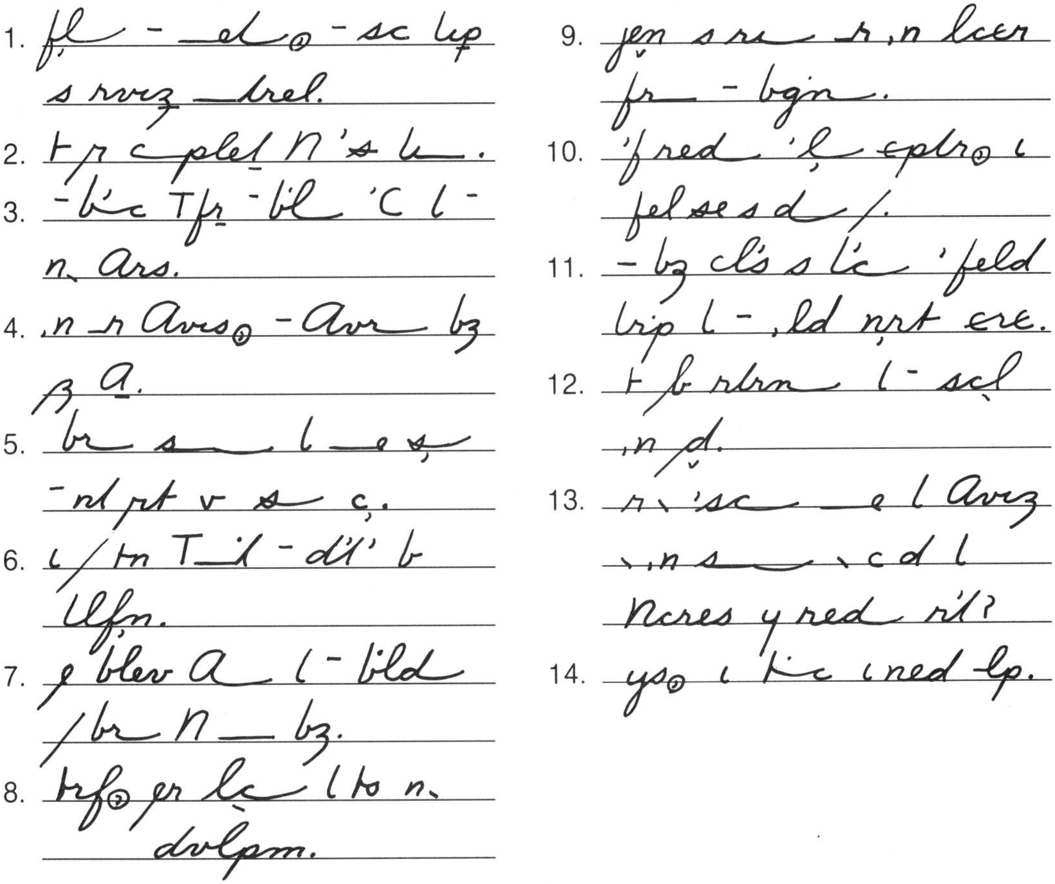

TRANSCRIPT OF SHORTHAND SENTENCES

1. Following the meeting, the secretary typed his revised material.
2. They were completed in a short time. (20)
3. The bank transferred the billing account to the new address.
4. On her advice, the advertising business was added. (40)
5. Bring something to me showing the net worth of the shipping company.
6. I will then transmit the data by telephone. (60)
7. We believe adding to the building will bring in more business.
8. Therefore, we are looking at this new development. (80)
9. Jean is writing her own lecture from the beginning.

10. After reading a long chapter, I feel she is doing well. (100)
11. The business class is taking a field trip to the Old North Church.
12. They will be returning to the school on Wednesday. (120)
13. Are you asking me to advise you on something you can do to increase your reading rate?
14. Yes, I think I need help. (140)

DICTATION AND TRANSCRIPTION

Write from dictation the Transcript of Shorthand Sentences. Your instructor will dictate each group of 20 words to you at various speeds. Select one set of notes, and transcribe it quickly and accurately.

BUILDING WRITING AND TRANSCRIPTION SPEEDS

New vocabulary

Read and write the following words and phrases until you can do so easily.

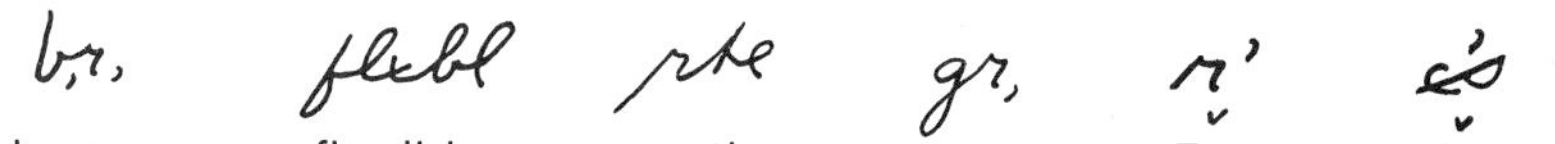

borrow flexible worthy grow Rae Chase

Manhattan to be able to help at any time we are ready

Letter 1

Read the following letter until you can do so fluently. Then using the self-dictation method, write the letter in shorthand as you read from the transcript. Check your outlines. Write the letter a second time and transcribe it at your best typing rate.

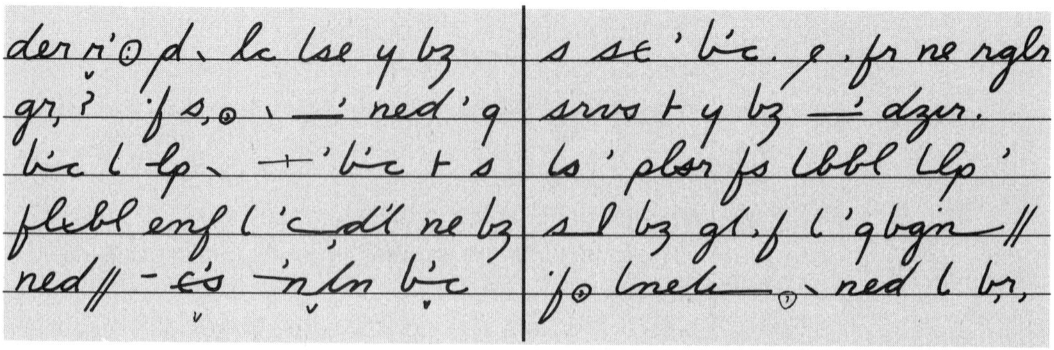

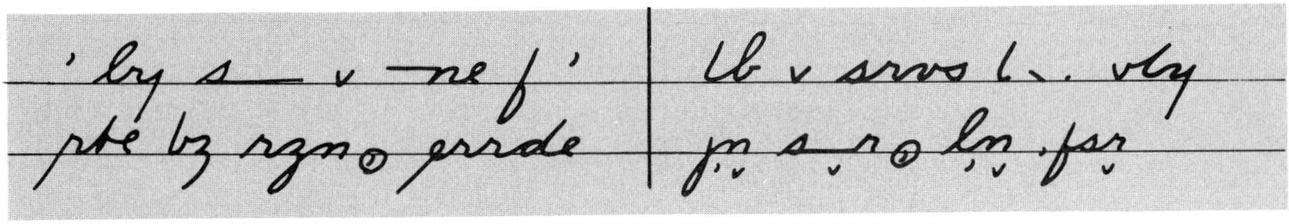

Learning tip:
Note that —+— in Forkner Shorthand indicates a dash.

Letter 1 transcript

Dear Rae: Would you like to see your business grow? If so, you may need a good bank to help you—a bank that is (20) flexible enough to accommodate any business need.

The Chase Manhattan Bank is such a bank. We offer any (40) regular service that your business may desire. It is a pleasure for us to be able to help a small business get (60) off to a good beginning.

If, at any time, you need to borrow a large sum of money for a worthy (80) business reason, we are ready to be of service to you. Very truly yours, John Summer, Loan Officer (99)

SKILL-BUILDING ASSIGNMENTS

1. Complete Unit 11 in *Forkner Shorthand Skill Builder for Colleges*.
2. Select Cassette 11 Side A of the *Theory and Speed-Building Tapes for Colleges* and follow the directions on the tape.
3. If instructed to do so, read, write, and transcribe the supplementary letter for this chapter found in Appendix A, Supplementary Dictation and Transcription.
4. Take additional live dictation as provided by your instructor.

Spelling review key

1. advise 2. accomplish 3. achievement 4. although
5. altogether 6. carrying 7. sealing, ceiling 8. coming
9. dining 10. February 11. many 12. leisure
13. parallel 14. lad, laid, laud 15. knowledge 16. jealous
17. opinion 18. origin 19. original 20. pad, paid
21. selling

Chapter 12

BUSINESS DICTATION AND TRANSCRIPTION

BUILDING TRANSCRIPTION SKILLS

Punctuating appositives

Use a comma to set off words or phrases that identify a preceding noun or phrase. These words or phrases are called *appositives*. Some authorities do not use commas to set off a one-word appositive. Study the examples which follow.

1. He kept his car, a 1924 Nash, in superb condition.

2. My nieces, Celeste and Lori, flew to New York City.

3. Mr. Wilson, our lawyer, traveled* to Canada, his native country, last fall.

Learning tip:

*Variant spelling traveled/travelled. Your instructor will indicate the spelling preferred in your community.

Punctuating dates, addresses, geographic locations, and titles

Use a comma to set off elements in dates, addresses, geographic locations, and titles. Study the examples which follow.

1. It was on October 12, 1492, that Columbus first saw the New World.

2. Our offices at 38 Arden Avenue, Winnipeg, Manitoba, are being renovated.

3. Dr. Roberts, our president, was also program chairperson.

Application—**Punctuating appositives, dates, addresses, and titles.** In your notebook number from 1-5. If a sentence requires one or more commas, write the preceding element(s) followed by a comma opposite the appropriate number. If the sentence is correctly punctuated, write OK opposite the appropriate number. Check your work with the key located in Appendix G at the back of this text.

1. Thursday September 30 is the last day of our fiscal period.

2. Wanda Mallory our vocational counselor was advisor to our club.

3. On February 15 1977 a new Citizenship Act became law.

4. His office was at 2039 West Lewis Avenue Phoenix Arizona.

5. Our officers for next year are Betty Bracken, President, and William Lyon, Secretary.

Spelling review

The outlines which follow have been selected from words you have reviewed in previous chapters. Transcribe the words in your shorthand notebook. Check your spelling with a dictionary, a standard word reference list, or the *Forkner Shorthand Dictionary for Beginners*. Compare your answers with the key located at the end of the chapter. Rewrite correctly any words that you may have misspelled. Write each of the shorthand outlines three times for speed development.

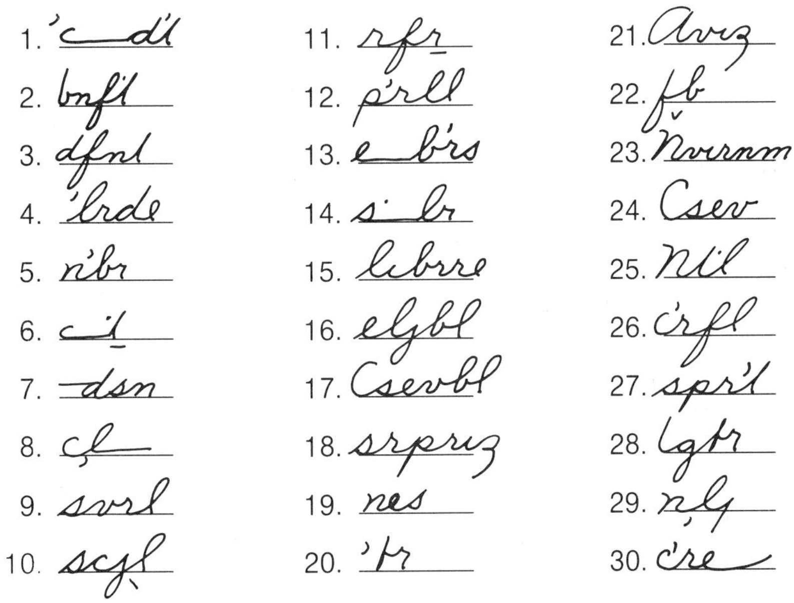

BUILDING WRITING AND TRANSCRIPTION SPEEDS

Letter 1 vocabulary review

Transcribe the following shorthand outlines in your notebook. Check your transcript and spelling with the vocabulary review key. Write each outline several times for speed development.

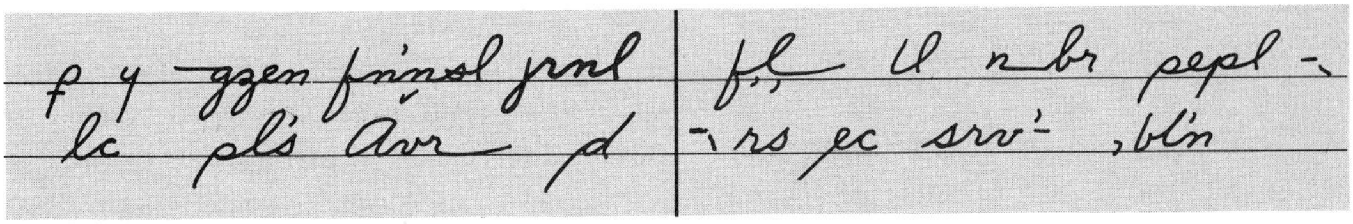

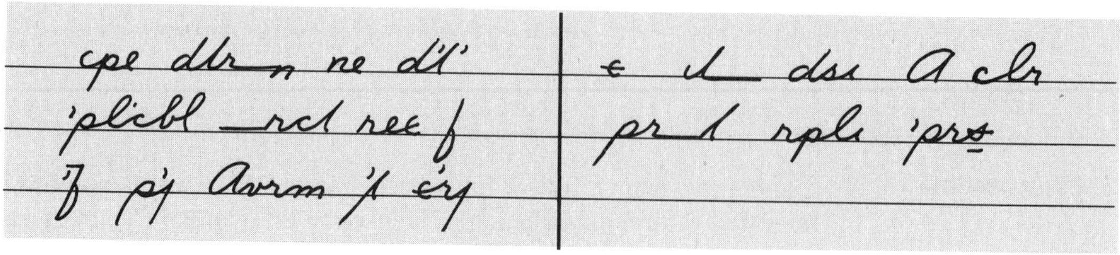

Vocabulary review key

pleased, your, magazine, Financial, Journal, like, place, advertising, would, following, tell, number, people, who, receive, week, surveyed, obtain, copy, determine, any, data, applicable, market, reach, for, half, page, advertisement, what, charge, each, item, decide, ad-add, color, prompt, reply, appreciated

Letter 1

Read the following letter until you can read it without hesitating. Then, using the transcript, write the shorthand for the letter in your notebook, making certain your outlines are readable. Read them back to be sure. Correct any errors you may have made.

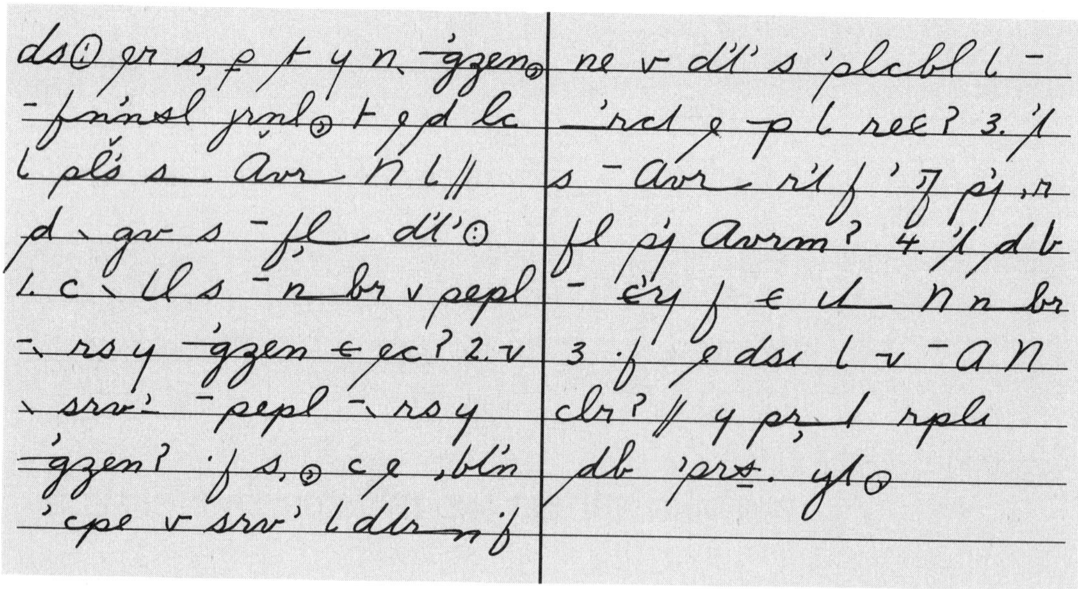

Letter 1 transcript

Dear Sir: We are so pleased with your new magazine, The Financial Journal, that we would like to place some advertising (20) in it.

Would you give us the following data:
1. Can you tell us the number of people who receive your (40) magazine each week?
2. Have you surveyed the people who receive your magazine? If so, can we obtain a (60) copy of the survey to determine if any of the data is applicable to the

FORT MYERS NATIONAL COMMUNITY BANK

MAIN BRANCH
27 Corbett Road, Fort Myers, FL 33903
(813) 334-4245

Current date

Managing Editor
Financial Book Company
375 Bank Street
Lansing, MI 48924-1140

Dear Sir:

We are so pleased with your new magazine, The Financial Journal, that we would like to place some advertising (20) in it.

Would you give us the following data:

1. Can you tell us the number of people who receive your (40) magazine each week?

2. Have you surveyed the people who receive your magazine? If so, can we obtain a (60) copy of the survey to determine if any of the data is applicable to the market we hope to reach?

3. What is the advertising rate for a half-page or full-page advertisement?

4. What would be the charge for (100) each item in No.3 if we decide to have the ad in color?

Your prompt reply would be appreciated. (120)

Yours truly, (123)

Thomas S. Elliott

Thomas S. Elliott

js

market we hope to (80) reach?

3. What is the advertising rate for a half-page or full-page advertisement?

4. What would be the charge for (100) each item in No. 3 if we decide to have the ad in color?

Your prompt reply would be appreciated. (120) Yours truly, (123)

Learning tips:

1. In a block style letter, enumerations are treated as separate paragraphs, with the numbers typed flush with the left margin. Two spaces follow the period.

2. Titles of publications are either underscored or typed in all capital letters.

Letter 2 new vocabulary

Read and write each word until you can do so quickly and accurately.

Paul improving popular

Letter 2

Read and write the following letter until you can do so without hesitation.

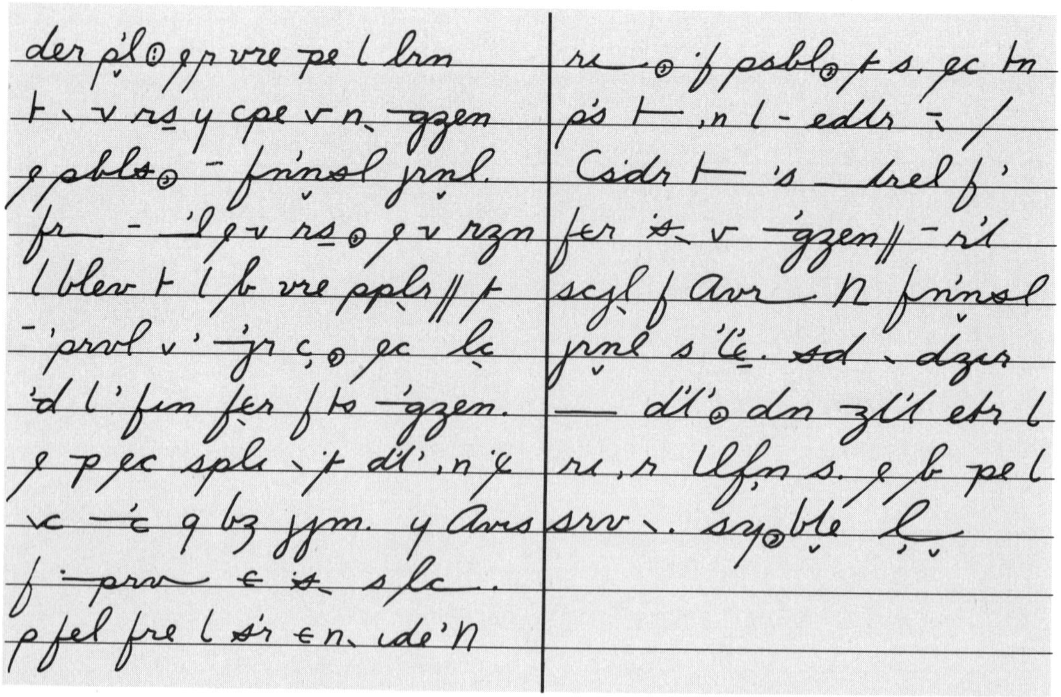

Letter 2 transcript

Dear Paul: We were very happy to learn that you have received your copy of the new magazine we publish, The (20) Financial Journal. From the mail we have received, we have reason to believe that it will be very popular. (40)

With the approval of a major company, we can look ahead to a fine future for this magazine. We (60) hope we can supply you with data on which you can make good business judgment. Your advice for improving each (80) issue is welcome. Please feel free to share each new idea in writing, if possible, with us. We can then pass them (100) on to the editor who will consider them as material for a future issue of the magazine. (120)

The rate schedule for advertising in The Financial Journal is attached. Should you desire more data, do not (140) hesitate either to write or telephone us. We will be happy to serve you. Sincerely yours, Betty Long (160)

DICTATION AND TRANSCRIPTION

Write from dictation the transcripts of Letters 1 and 2. Your instructor will dictate each letter to you at various speeds.

Using your own notes, transcribe both letters using the block style illustrated in this chapter. Use your own name and address for the inside address. Use your name for the typed signature line in Letter 1.

SKILL-BUILDING ASSIGNMENTS

1. Complete Unit 12 in *Forkner Shorthand Skill Builder for Colleges*.
2. Select Cassette 12 Side A of the *Theory and Speed-Building Tapes for Colleges* and follow the directions on the tape.
3. If instructed to do so, read, write, and transcribe the supplementary letter for this chapter found in Appendix A, Supplementary Dictation and Transcription.
4. Take additional live dictation as provided by your instructor.

PREVIEW EXAMINATION 3

Remove Preview Examination 3 from your *Forkner Shorthand Skill Builder for Colleges*. It follows Unit 32. This informal preview examination will help you in assessing your understanding of the Forkner principles presented in Chapters 9–12. It is similar to

Examination 3 which may be administered at a later date by your instructor.

Complete Preview Examination 3 and then check your answers carefully with the key in your *Forkner Shorthand Skill Builder for Colleges*. Correct any errors you may have made.

Spelling review key

1. accommodate 2. benefit 3. definite 4. already 5. neighbor 6. committed 7. medicine 8. column 9. several 10. schedule 11. referred 12. parallel 13. embarrass 14. similar 15. library 16. eligible 17. conceivable 18. surprise* 19. niece 20. author 21. advise 22. February 23. environment 24. conceive 25. until 26. careful 27. separate 28. together 29. knowledge 30. carrying

Learning tip:

Variant spelling *surprise/surprize*. Your instructor will indicate the spelling preferred in your community.

Chapter 13

WRITING NT-ND, AN, AND DIS-DES

WRITING PRINCIPLES

Combinations *nt-nd* Write a curved stroke to express the combinations *nt-nd*.

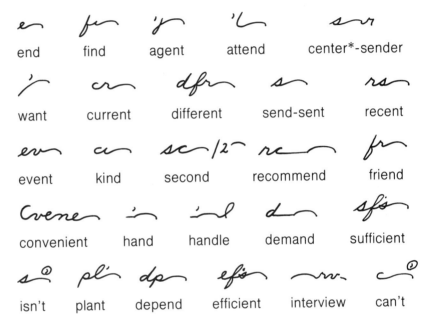

end find agent attend center*-sender

want current different send-sent recent

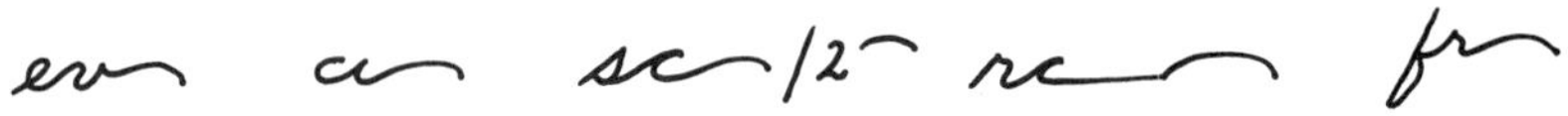

event kind second recommend friend

convenient hand handle demand sufficient

isn't plant depend efficient interview can't

Read the first line of outlines until you can read each word fluently. Then cover the shorthand, and write each outline as you read from the print. Write each outline rapidly and accurately. Follow the same procedure for each line.

Learning tips:

1. The word *interview* is written with the *nt* combination rather than the *in* prefix because the word is pronounced *int-er-view*.

2. Notice that a circled apostrophe has been added to the outline for *isn't*. If time permits, add the apostrophe when taking dictation as an aid in transcribing. For example, *aisle-isle* is written . *I'll* is written .

*3. The American spelling is *center*; the preferred Canadian spelling is *centre*.

Prefix *an* Write a small longhand *a* to express the prefix *an*.

an answer answering annual-annul annuity

animal analyze annex

As you read each outline, write it three times in your notebook. When you have finished writing all the words, you should be able to read and write them rapidly and accurately. Now cover the outlines and write them from the print. Read your notes, and correct any errors you may have made.

Prefixes *dis-des*

Write a capital *D* to express the prefixes *dis* and *des*.

discuss display desperate dispute discover

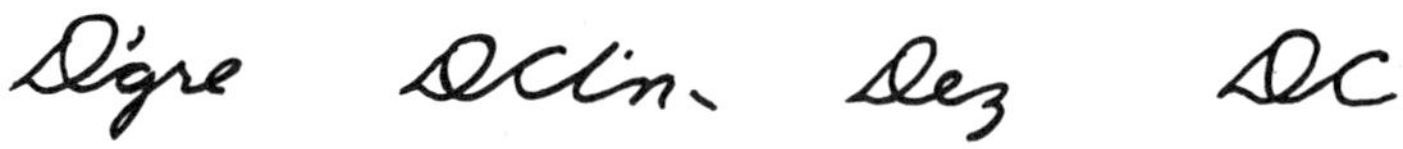

disagree discontinue disease discount

As you read each outline, write it several times. Do this for all the words. When you can read all the words fluently, cover the print and write each outline once. Read your own notes. If you have difficulty reading your notes, rewrite them and read them again.

New vocabulary

Read and write each of the following words until you have them memorized. Note how easy it is to write derivatives once you have learned the base word.

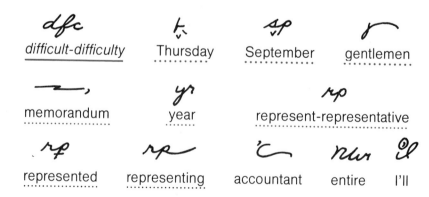

difficult-difficulty Thursday September gentlemen

memorandum year represent-representative

represented representing accountant entire I'll

BUILDING TRANSCRIPTION SKILLS

Spelling review

The shorthand outline in each sentence is for a word that is commonly misspelled. Transcribe the shorthand outline in your notebook. You may use a dictionary, a standard word reference list, or the *Forkner Shorthand Dictionary for Beginners* to verify the spelling. Compare your answers with the key located at the end of the chapter. Write correctly any words you may have misspelled. Then write the shorthand outlines for each word several times in your notebook.

1. Elephants and whales are ____ the largest animals in the world.
2. We hope the dispute dz ____ cause a delay in the work.
3. She has a pclr habit of blinking her eyes when talking.
4. Mary didn't rliz how late it was because her watch had stopped.
5. You will get a rsel each time you make a payment.
6. Did you rs an invitation to the party?
7. Teachers rcgniz that students have individual differences.
8. The doctor gave her medicine to rlev the pain.
9. Your rljs beliefs are not the same as mine.
10. He wore a rdicls outfit to the masquerade party.
11. He sez the opportunity for advancement.
12. The troops helped to sprs the rebellion.
13. We are having nsl weather for this time of the year.
14. Will you be ____ the car tonight?
15. My vc cleaner is broken.

16. We stopped at a ______ stand on the way home from work.
17. The rainy ______ is very depressing.
18. Please decide ______ you are taking the train or the bus.
19. ______ turn is it to drive to school?
20. The attorney will be ______ you soon about the lease.

The apostrophe

One important use of the apostrophe is to mark the omission of a letter or letters in contracted words. Omission of figures may also be indicated by an apostrophe.

Examples: *she'll* for *she will* or *she shall*
can't for *cannot*
isn't for *is not*
hasn't for *has not*
'62 for *1962*

A special problem for many students is the contraction of *it is* — *it's*. Remember that *it's* means *it is*, and *its* is a possessive.

Application — **The apostrophe**. In your notebook number from 1-10. Write the contraction for each of the following opposite the appropriate number. Check your work with the key located in Appendix G at the back of this text.

1. he is
2. were not
3. I have
4. Class of 1970
5. they are
6. of the clock
7. there is
8. you are
9. will not
10. let us

APPLYING NEW PRINCIPLES

Follow these procedures in learning to read and write the sentences on page 89.

1. Read the shorthand outlines for each of the sentences until you can read all the sentences without hesitation.

2. Using the Transcript of Shorthand Sentences, write the shorthand outlines for each sentence in your notebook.

3. Check your outlines.

4. Write correctly three times each outline that you may have written incorrectly.

5. Rewrite the shorthand outlines as you read the sentences once again from the Transcript of Shorthand Sentences.

6. Transcribe the sentences from your own notes. Compare your transcript with the text transcript and circle any errors you may have made, including spelling and punctuation errors.

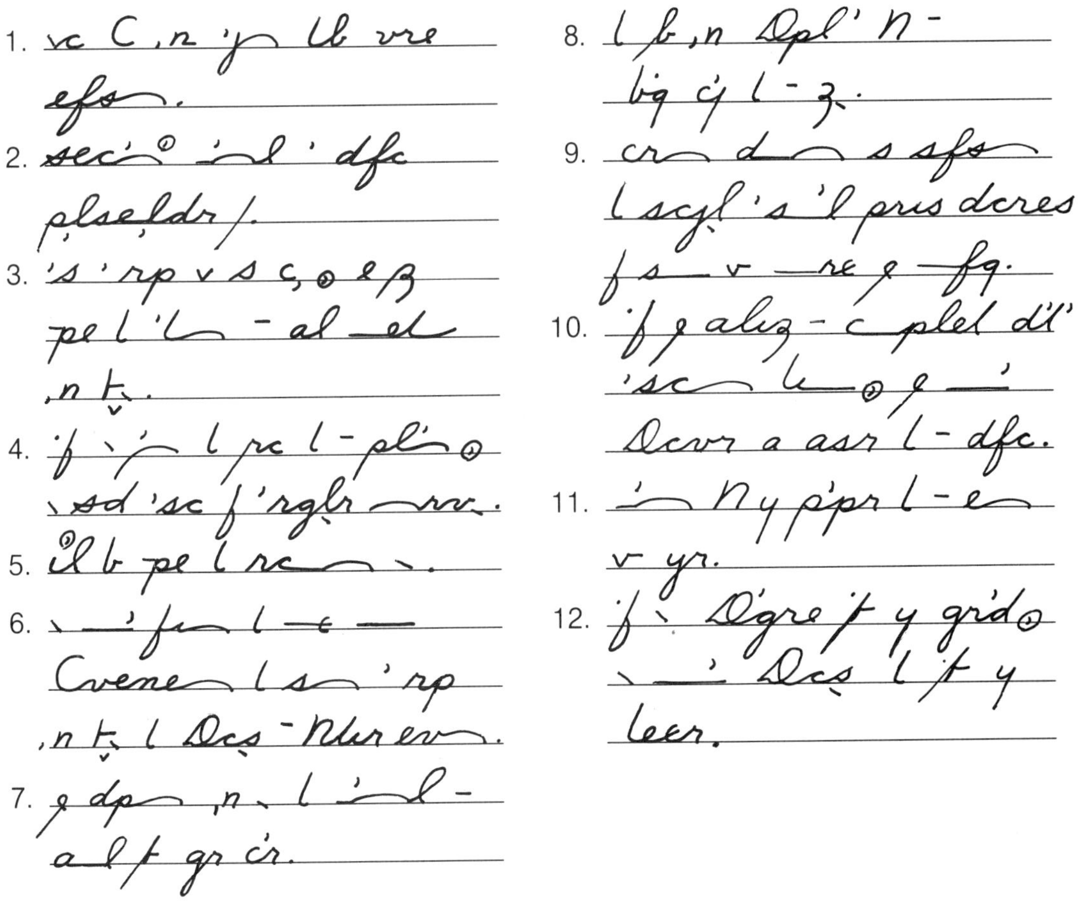

TRANSCRIPT OF SHORTHAND SENTENCES

1. You can count on the agent to be very efficient.
2. She can't handle a difficult policyholder well. (20)
3. As a representative of his company, he was happy to attend the annual meeting on Thursday. (40)
4. If you want to work at the plant, you should ask for a regular interview.
5. I'll be happy to recommend you. (60)
6. You may find it much more convenient to send a representative on Thursday to discuss the entire event. (80)
7. We depend on you to handle the animal with great care.
8. It will be on display in the big cage at the zoo. (100)
9. Current demand is sufficient to schedule a small price decrease for some of the merchandise we manufacture. (120)
10. If we analyze the complete data a second time, we may discover an answer to the difficulty. (140)
11. Hand in your paper at the end of the year.
12. If you disagree with your grade, you may discuss it with your teacher. (160)

DICTATION AND TRANSCRIPTION

Write from dictation the Transcript of Shorthand Sentences. Your instructor will dictate each group of 20 words to you at various speeds. Select one set of notes, and transcribe it quickly and accurately.

BUILDING WRITING AND TRANSCRIPTION SPEEDS

New vocabulary

Read and write the following words and phrases until you can do so easily.

graduated

Broadway

worked

applicant

could not

would like to be

I am looking

this matter

Yours sincerely

Letter 1

Read the following letter until you can read it fluently. Scribble-write the letter twice for speed building. Using the shorthand in the text, transcribe the letter once. Check your transcript with the text transcript.

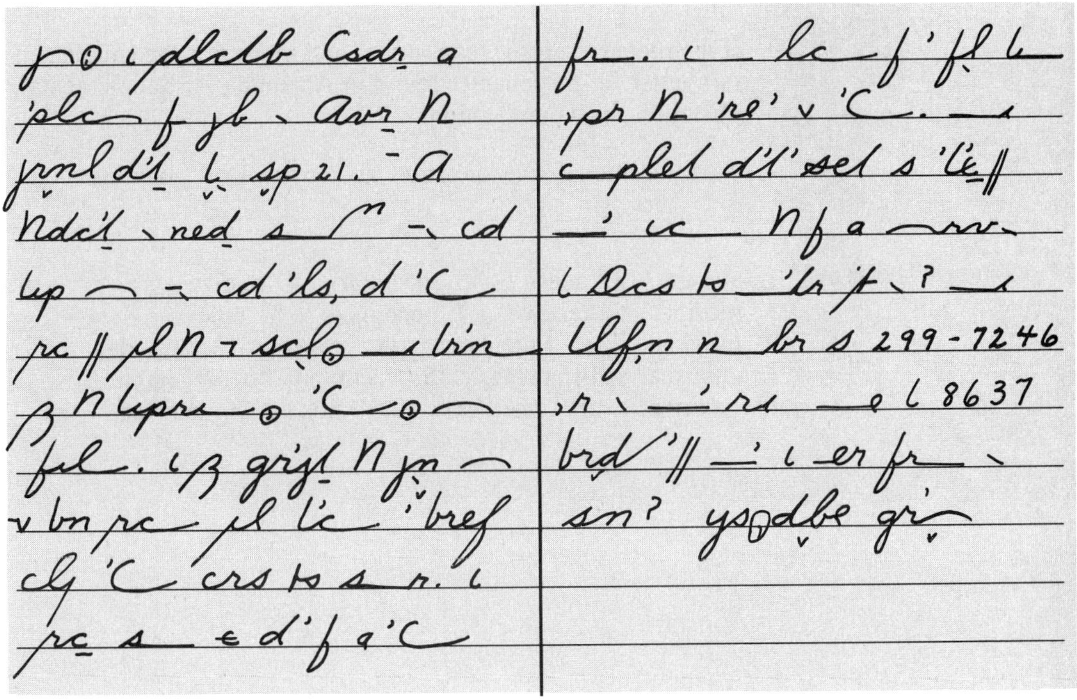

Letter 1 transcript

Gentlemen: I would like to be considered an applicant for the job you advertised in the Journal dated (20) Tuesday, September 21. The ad indicated you needed someone who could type and who could also do accounting (40) work.

While in high school, my training was in typewriting, accounting, and filing. I was graduated in June (60) and have been working while taking a brief college accounting course this summer. I worked some each day for an accounting (80) firm. I am looking for a full-time opportunity in the area of accounting. My complete data (100) sheet is attached.

May I come in for an interview to discuss this matter with you? My telephone number (120) is 299-7246 or you may write me at 8637 Broadway.

May I hear from you soon? Yours (140) sincerely, Debby Grant (144)

SKILL-BUILDING ASSIGNMENTS

1. Complete Unit 13 in *Forkner Shorthand Skill Builder for Colleges*.

2. Select Cassette 13 Side A of the *Theory and Speed-Building Tapes for Colleges* and follow the directions on the tape.

3. If instructed to do so, read, write, and transcribe the supplementary letter for this chapter found in Appendix A, Supplementary Dictation and Transcription.

4. Take additional live dictation as provided by your instructor.

Spelling review key

1. among 2. doesn't 3. peculiar 4. realize
5. receipt 6. receive 7. recognize 8. relieve
9. religious 10. ridiculous 11. seized 12. suppress
13. unusual 14. using 15. vacuum 16. vegetable
17. weather 18. whether 19. Whose 20. writing

Chapter 14

WRITING QU, INCL-ENCLOSE, AND LY

WRITING PRINCIPLES

Qu

Write only *q* for the combination *qu*.

quote equip equipment quality frequent

acquaint quite-quiet

Cover the print and as you read each word, write the outline several times in your notebook.

Incl-enclose

Write a capital longhand *I* to express *incl* and the following vowel, and the word *enclose*. The capital *I* must be written so that it cannot be confused with the longhand *l*.

include including incline enclose enclosed

enclosing enclosure

Cover the printed words and read the outlines until you can read each one rapidly. Then cover the shorthand, and write the outline for each word as you read it from the print. Check your notes, and correct any errors you may have made.

Ending *ly*

Write a short, disjoined dash - close to the word to which it belongs to express the *ly* ending. Write the final *l* in words that end in *l* and then add the *ly* dash, as in carefully *crfl-* and really *rel-* .

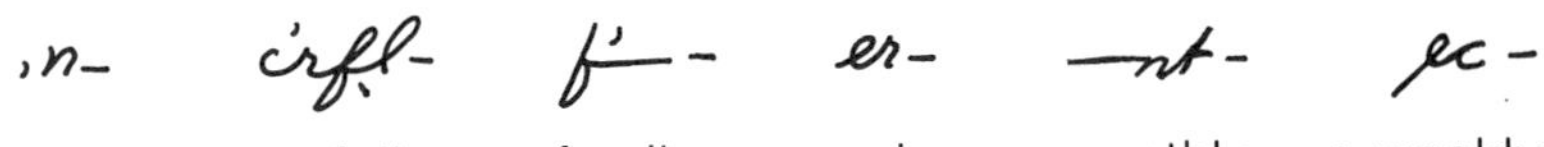

only carefully family early monthly weekly

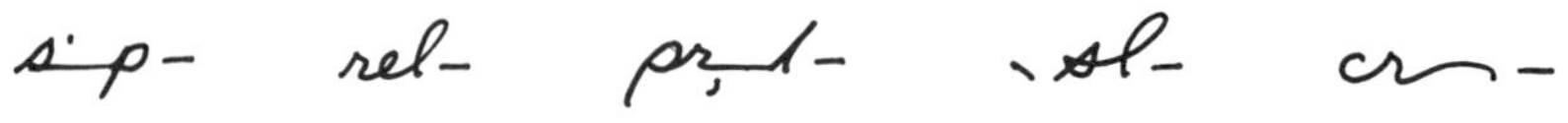

simply really promptly usually currently

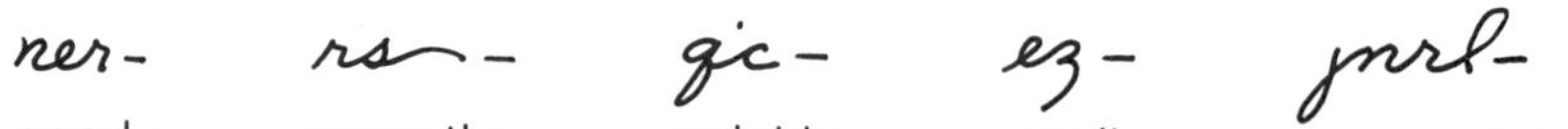

nearly recently quickly easily generally

Cover the print of the first line of words and read the outlines until you can read them easily. Then quickly write the outline for each word several times in your notebook. Follow the same procedure for each line of words. Now cover the outlines and write them from the print. Read your notes and correct any errors you may have made.

New vocabulary

Read and write the following outlines until you can do so easily. Note how the word *we* can be phrased with many other words. Remember to phrase only if the phrase comes naturally to you.

quantity question require approximate department

required requiring requirement questionnaire likely

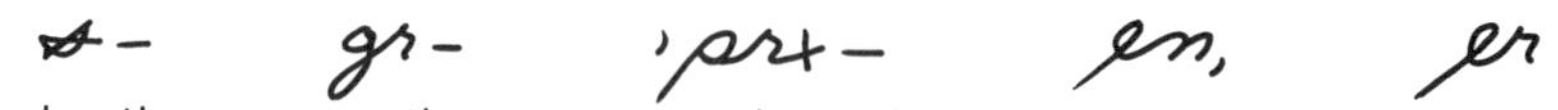

shortly greatly approximately we know we are

we can be we should we have we have not

BUILDING TRANSCRIPTION SKILLS

Possessives

The apostrophe is used to show the possessive case, or ownership, as well as to indicate a contraction. Study the following rules and examples that relate to possessives.

1. Add an apostrophe and an *s* to most words to form the **singular possessive**.
   a. The boy's coat was in the closet.
   b. Linda's birthday is in October.

2. Add an *s* followed by an apostrophe to form most **plural possessives**.
   a. The boys' coats were in the closet.
   b. Both doctors' offices were located in the same building.

3. The possessive of words that are **already plural** is formed by adding an apostrophe and an *s*.
   a. Some of the children's toys were broken.
   b. Women's fashions change from year to year.

Application — **Possessives**. In your notebook number from 1-5. If a sentence requires an apostrophe, write the word with the apostrophe opposite the appropriate number. If the sentence is correct, write OK opposite the number. Check your work with the key located in Appendix G at the back of this text.

1. Both girls dresses were very colorful.
2. Maries dress was very chic.
3. All of the children's toys were quite new.
4. The dog was nursing its paw.
5. Three weeks vacation is not adequate for the long trip.

Spelling review

Follow these procedures in reviewing a few more commonly misspelled words.

1. Transcribe each of the shorthand outlines in your notebook.
2. Use a dictionary, a standard word reference list, or the *Forkner Shorthand Dictionary for Beginners* to verify the spelling. Some outlines represent more than one word; therefore, your transcription should include all spellings. Compare your transcript with the key located at the end of the chapter.
3. Write each shorthand outline several times in your notebook.
4. Write each sentence below in your notebook, completing the missing words.

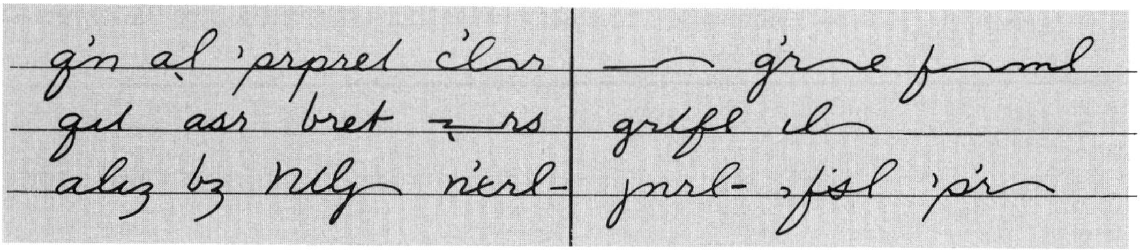

1. N________y, the quality of your work is more important than the q_______y.
2. It is a_______t that the a_____r was both i___________t and a___________e.
3. F___________l to any well-run b_______s is an a_____l report.
4. A_____e your g________e to be sure it is q___e satisfactory.
5. G________y, the o_______l c_______r is prepared a month in advance.
6. We are g_______l for the q___t i_____d where we can b______e fresh air.
7. His remarks were m___t to be h________s.

Learning tip:
Have you ever had difficulty trying to decide whether the word ending should be *ful* or *full*? If you have, try to remember this spelling tip. There is only *one* word in which *full* has *two l's*, and that is the word *full*. All other words ending with that sound are spelled with only *one l*.

APPLYING NEW PRINCIPLES

Follow these procedures in learning to read and write the sentences on page 97.

1. Read the shorthand outlines for each of the sentences until you can read all the sentences without hesitation.

2. Using the Transcript of Shorthand Sentences, write the shorthand outlines for each sentence in your notebook.
3. Check your outlines.
4. Write correctly three times each outline that you may have written incorrectly.
5. Rewrite the shorthand outlines as you read the sentences once again from the Transcript of Shorthand Sentences.
6. Transcribe the sentences from your own notes. Compare your transcript with the text transcript and circle any errors you may have made, including spelling and punctuation errors.

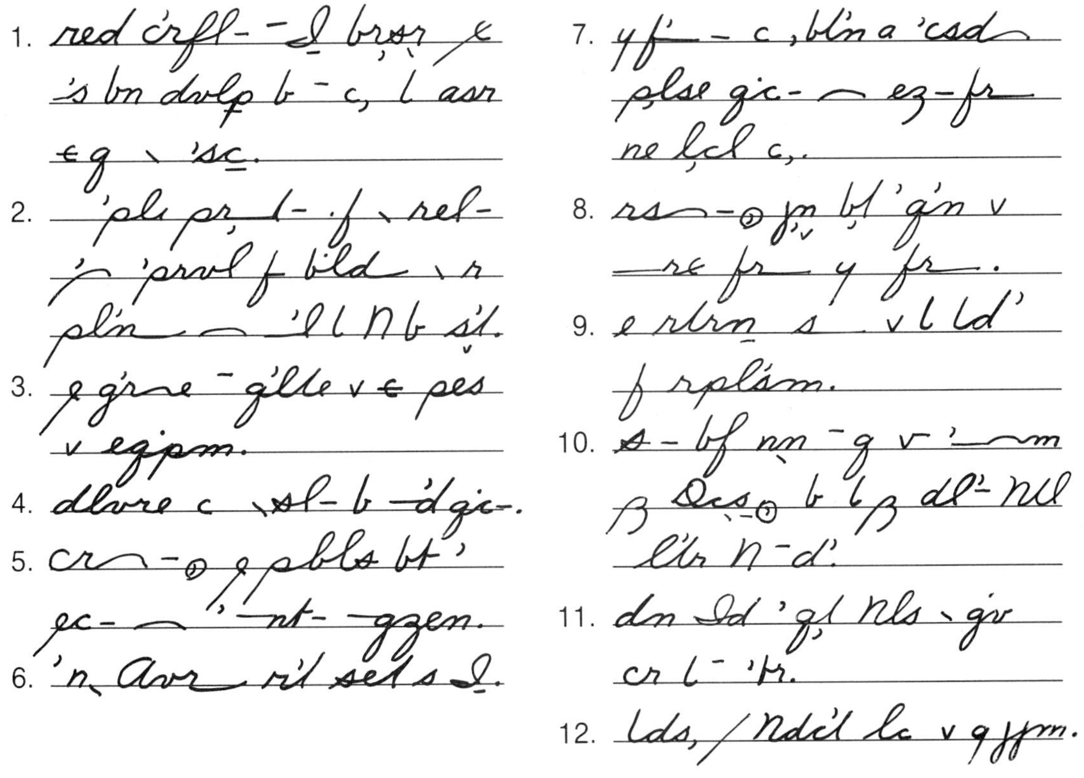

TRANSCRIPT OF SHORTHAND SENTENCES

1. Read carefully the enclosed brochure which has been developed by the company to answer each question you asked. (20)

2. Apply promptly if you really want approval for the building you are planning, and mail it in by Saturday. (40)
3. We guarantee the quality of each piece of equipment.
4. Delivery can usually be made quickly. (60)
5. Currently, we publish both a weekly and a monthly magazine.
6. A new advertising rate sheet is enclosed. (80)
7. Your family can obtain an accident policy quickly and easily from any local company. (100)
8. Recently, John bought a quantity of merchandise from your firm.
9. He returned some of it today for replacement. (120)
10. Shortly before noon the question of the amendment was discussed, but it was delayed until later in the day. (140)
11. Do not include a quote unless you give credit to the author.
12. To do so will indicate lack of good judgment. (160)

DICTATION AND TRANSCRIPTION

Write from dictation the Transcript of Shorthand Sentences. Your instructor will dictate each group of 20 words to you at various speeds. Select one set of notes, and transcribe it quickly and accurately.

BUILDING WRITING AND TRANSCRIPTION SPEEDS

New vocabulary

Read and write the following new words until you can do so easily.

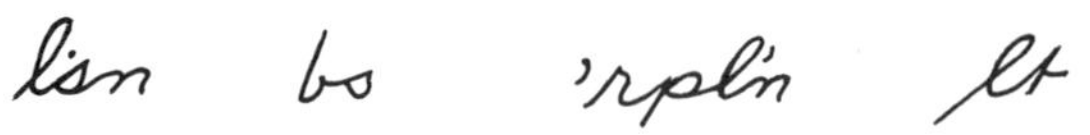

listen bus airplane wealth

Passage 1

The following paragraph has 110 words. Read the paragraph twice and calculate your reading rate each time. The second reading should be faster than the first. When finished reading and calculating, scribble-write the paragraph twice for speed development.

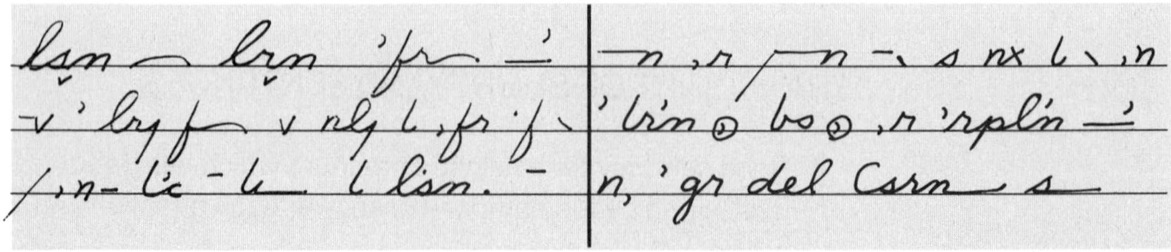

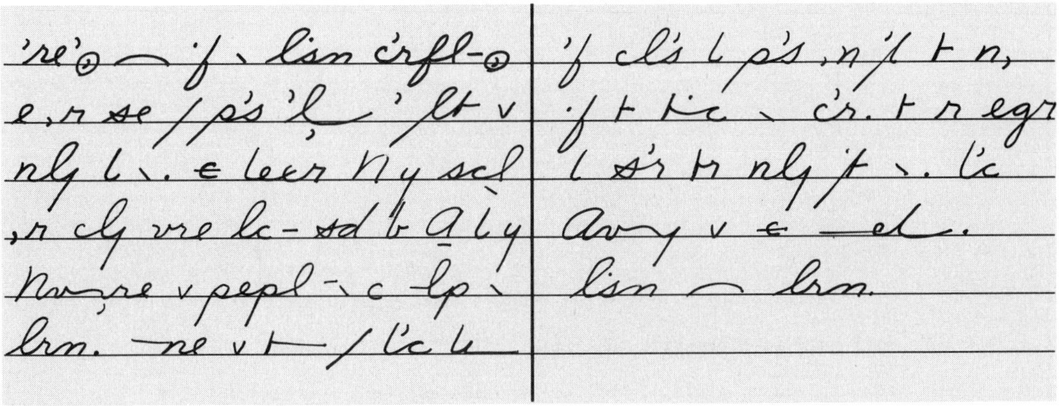

Calculating reading rate

Divide the time (to the nearest quarter of a minute) it takes you to read the paragraph into the number of words in the paragraph. Example: A letter contains 201 words and is read in $2^1/_2$ minutes. Divide the time, 2.5 minutes, into the number of words, 201, to calculate a reading rate of 80.4 words a minute.

Passage 1 transcript

The transcript for Passage 1 appears on the next page as a sample of an unbound, one-page manuscript.

Learning tips:

1. The title is centered and typed in all capitals 2 inches (50 mm) from the top of the page. Triple space after the title.
2. Allow for left and right margins of $1^1/_2$ inches (40 mm).
3. Indent all paragraphs 5 spaces.
4. Leave a bottom margin of 1 inch (25 mm).

SKILL-BUILDING ASSIGNMENTS

1. Complete Unit 14 in *Forkner Shorthand Skill Builder for Colleges* before you proceed to Chapter 15.
2. Select Cassette 14 Side A of the *Theory and Speed-Building Tapes for Colleges* and follow the directions on the tape.
3. If instructed to do so, read, write, and transcribe the supplementary passage for this chapter found in Appendix A, Supplementary Dictation and Transcription.
4. Take additional live dictation as provided by your instructor.

LISTEN AND LEARN

A friend may have a large fund of knowledge to offer if you will only take the time to listen. (20) The man or woman who is next to you on a train, bus, or airplane may know a great deal concerning some area, (40) and if you listen carefully, he or she will pass along a wealth of knowledge to you. Each teacher in your (60) school or college very likely should be added to your inventory of people who can help you learn. Many (80) of them will take time after class to pass on what they know if they think you care. They are eager to share their knowledge (100) with you. Take advantage of each meeting. Listen and learn. (110)

Spelling review key

1. naturally, quantity 2. apparent, answer, intelligent, appropriate 3. Fundamental, business, annual 4. Analyze*, guarantee, quite 5. Generally, official, calendar 6. grateful, quiet, island, breathe 7. meant, humorous

Learning tips:

* Variant spellings *analyze/analyse*. Your instructor will indicate the spelling preferred in your community.

Chapter 15

ADDING S TO ROOT WORDS AND WRITING EVER-EVERY

WRITING PRINCIPLES

Adding s to root words

Join an upward, slanted, straight stroke / to the last letter or symbol of a word to add *s* to a root word. This same stroke is used to add *s* to a root word to form the possessive. When a word ends in a vowel symbol, some writers prefer to *double* the vowel symbol to indicate the plural form.

Examples: says s" or s/; ideas ide" or ide/.

Use whichever form is easiest for you to write.

As you read each word illustrating this principle, write the root word first. Then write the root word again, adding the *s* stroke.

Example: 

Prefix *ever-every* and suffix *ever*

Write a capital V for the words *ever* and *every* and a disjoined V for the prefixes and suffixes *ever-every*.

ever-every   everybody   everyone   everything

everywhere   whatever   whenever

Read the outlines quickly with the print covered. Then write each outline once and read back your notes.

New vocabulary

Read and write the following words until you can do so easily.

immediate   important-importance   principal-principle

November   immediately   importantly   yours   thanks

questions   companies   years   receives   puts

requires   requirements   ships   represents-representatives

its   departments   quantities   accounts   news

BUILDING TRANSCRIPTION SKILLS

Word usage

Study the following groups of commonly misused words. Notice that within the groups, the words sound similar or alike, but have different meanings. Learn the meaning of each word.

Words Commonly Misused	Definition
ad	short form for advertisement
add	to find the sum of
complement	something that completes or makes perfect; make a whole
compliment	to praise
for	with the purpose of
fore	in front of; prior to
four	a number
no	opposite of yes
know	to be aware of
piece	a portion
peace	freedom from conflict or war
scene	something viewed
seen	past participle of see
principal	a governing person
principle	a fundamental truth or value

> *Application*—**Word usage**. Use each of the words defined above in a sentence, writing as many of the words as you can in shorthand. Use a dictionary to clarify further any definition. Compare your work with the sample sentences located in Appendix G at the back of the text.

Spelling review 1

You should be able to write all of the commonly *misused words* in the previous word-usage application in shorthand. Write each of the words in shorthand in your notebook. Check your outlines with those in the key located at the end of the chapter. Transcribe each word into longhand, and write the definition opposite the word. Remember that each of your shorthand outlines will represent more than one word. Include all spellings and a definition for each.

Spelling review 2

Remember to write *i* before *e* except after *c* and in words in which the combination is pronounced ā as in neighbor n'br and weigh /'.

Transcribe the following words in your notebook. Use a dictionary, a standard word reference list, or the *Forkner Shorthand Dictionary for Beginners* to verify the spelling. Compare your answers with the key located at the end of the chapter. Write correctly any words that you may have misspelled. Then write the shorthand outlines for each word until you can write them without hesitation.

1. yeld	5. blev	8. v'l
2. rsel	6. cef	9. Csel
3. fr'l	7. nes	10. 'cev
4. rs		

APPLYING NEW PRINCIPLES

Follow these procedures in learning to read and write the sentences on page 106.

1. Read the shorthand outlines for each of the sentences until you can read all the sentences without hesitation.
2. Using the Transcript of Shorthand Sentences, write the shorthand outlines for each sentence in your notebook.
3. Check your outlines.

4. Write correctly three times each outline that you may have written incorrectly.

5. Rewrite the shorthand outlines as you read the sentences once again from the Transcript of Shorthand Sentences.

6. Transcribe the sentences from your own notes. Compare your transcript with the text transcript and circle any errors you may have made, including spelling and punctuation errors.

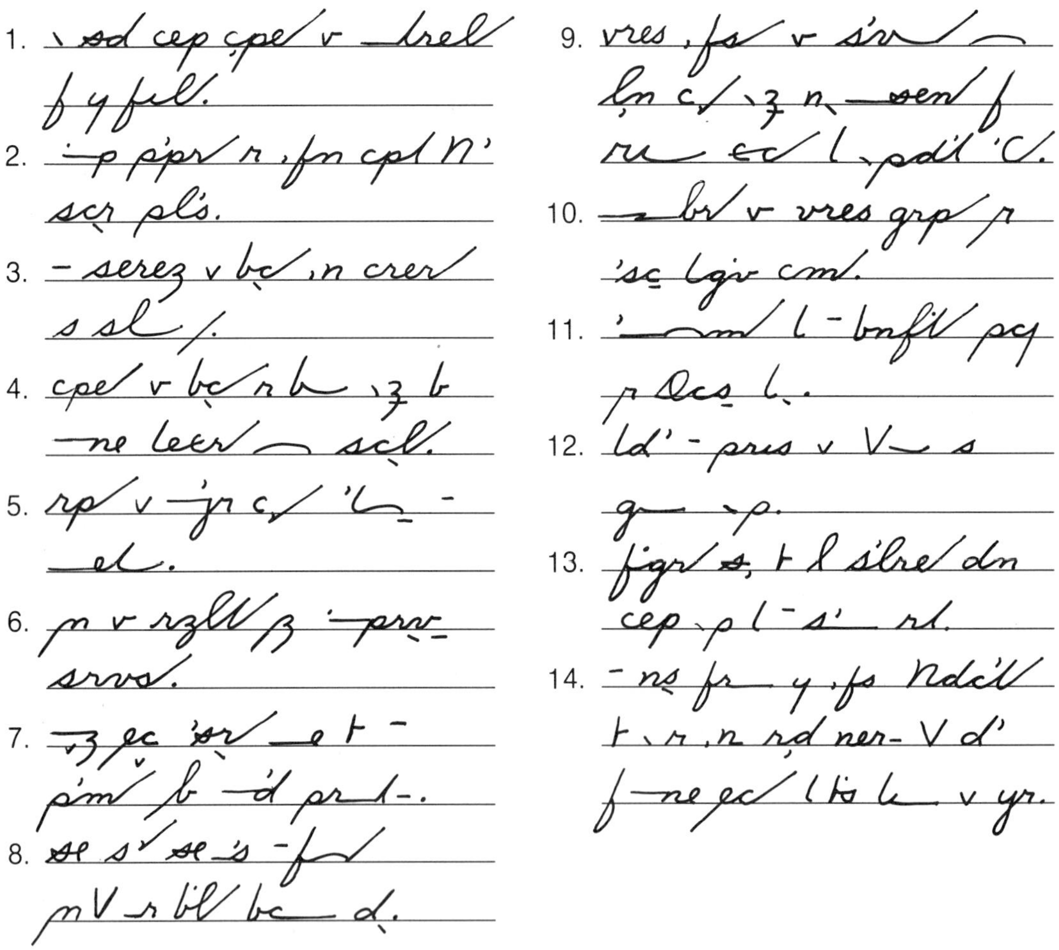

TRANSCRIPT OF SHORTHAND SENTENCES

1. You should keep copies of the materials for your files.
2. Important papers are often kept in a secure place. (20)
3. The series of books on careers is selling well.

4. Copies of the books are being used by many teachers and schools. (40)
5. Representatives of major companies attended the meeting.
6. One of the results was improved services. (60)
7. Ms. Week assures me that the payments will be made promptly.
8. She says she has the funds whenever her bills become due. (80)
9. Various offices of the savings and loan companies used new machines for writing checks* to update accounts. (100)
10. Members of the various groups were asked to give comments.
11. Amendments to the benefits package were discussed too. (120)
12. Today, the price of everything is going up.
13. Figures show that all salaries do not keep up at the same rate. (140)
14. The news from your office indicates that you are on the road nearly every day for many weeks at this time of year. (160)

DICTATION AND TRANSCRIPTION

Write from dictation the Transcript of Shorthand Sentences. Your instructor will dictate each group of 20 words to you at various speeds. Select one set of notes, and transcribe it quickly and accurately.

BUILDING WRITING AND TRANSCRIPTION SPEEDS

New vocabulary

Read and write the following words until you can do so easily.

heads

improvements

dealings

trained

plans

facilities

Memorandum 1

As you read the memorandum from print, write the shorthand outlines in your notebook. Check your outlines with those which follow, and transcribe your own notes as an attractively arranged memorandum.

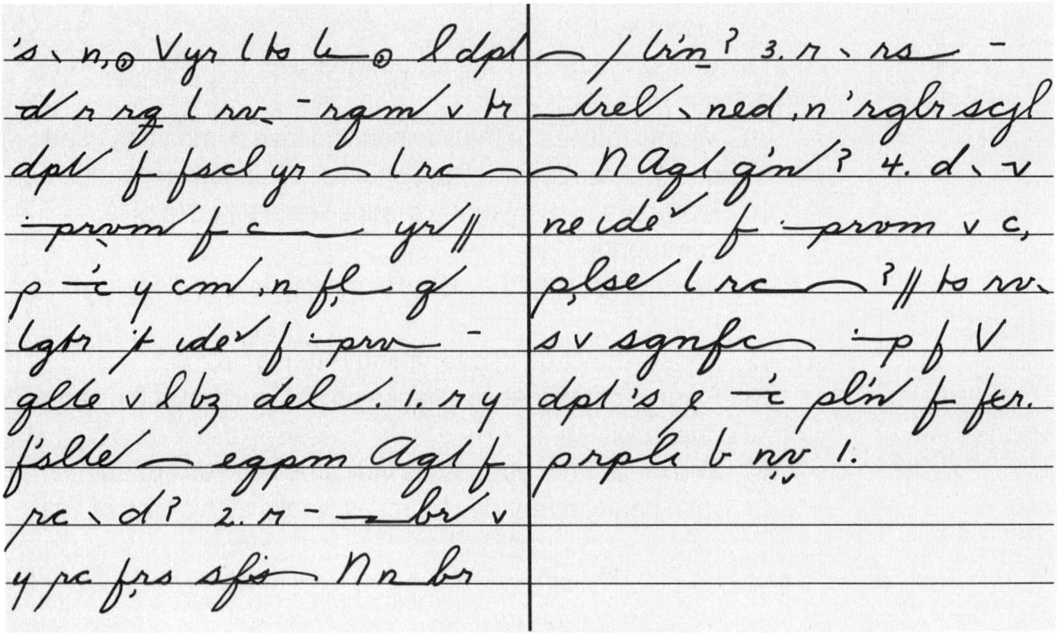

Memorandum 1 transcript

The transcript for Memorandum 1 appears on the next page as a sample of a typed memorandum.

Learning tips:

Most businesses use pre-printed or round-trip memo forms for internal correspondence. The sample memo form shown on the next page may be followed when pre-printed forms are not available.

1. The word MEMORANDUM is centered and typed in all capitals 1 inch (25 mm) from the top of the page. Triple space after the heading.
2. Allow for left and right margins of $1^1/_2$ inches (40 mm).
3. Type the TO:, FROM:, SUBJECT:, and DATE: lines flush with the left margin after setting one tab stop two spaces following the colon in the SUBJECT line. Double space between each line.
4. Triple space after the special lines.
5. Single space the body, leaving a double space between paragraphs. Treat enumerations as separate paragraphs, and align as illustrated in the sample.
6. Leave a bottom margin of no less than 1 inch (25 mm).
7. Timing of dictation begins with the body of the memorandum.

MEMORANDUM

TO: All Department Heads

FROM: John Grant, General Manager

SUBJECT: Annual Review

DATE: Current Date

As you know, every year at this time all department heads are required to review the requirements of their (20) departments for the fiscal year and to recommend improvements for the coming years.

Please make your comments on the (40) following questions together with ideas for improving the quality of all business dealings.

1. Are your (60) facilities and equipment adequate for the work you do?

2. Are the members of your work force sufficient (80) in number and well trained?

3. Are you receiving the materials you need on a regular schedule and in (100) adequate quantities?

4. Do you have any ideas for the improvement of company policies to (120) recommend?

This review is of significant importance for every department as we make plans for the (140) future. Please reply by November 1. (147)

iti

SKILL-BUILDING ASSIGNMENTS

1. Complete Unit 15 in *Forkner Shorthand Skill Builder for Colleges*.
2. Select Cassette 15 Side A of the *Theory and Speed-Building Tapes for Colleges* and follow the directions on the tape.
3. If instructed to do so, read, write, and transcribe the supplementary memorandum for this chapter found in Appendix A, Supplementary Dictation and Transcription.
4. Take additional live dictation as provided by your instructor.

Spelling review 1 key

Spelling review 2 key

1. yield 2. receipt 3. freight 4. receive 5. believe
6. chief 7. niece 8. vale, veil 9. conceit 10. achieve

Chapter 16

BUSINESS DICTATION AND TRANSCRIPTION

BUILDING TRANSCRIPTION SKILLS

The hyphen

The hyphen has many uses. In addition to being used to divide words at the end of a line of type, it is used to form compound words, to write out fractions, to join certain prefixes, and in several other ways. Many rules for hyphenating words, however, are inconsistent and subject to change over time. Therefore, when in doubt, always consult a dictionary or standard reference work.

The following rule for using the hyphen is consistent, however, and you should know how to apply it when transcribing. Use a hyphen to join two or more words used as a single descriptive word *before* a noun. Study the examples which follow.

1. Can he read college-level textbooks?
2. The well-known actor was featured in the show.
3. The troops engaged in hand-to-hand combat.
4. Plan to come to our end-of-the-season sale.
5. She reported up-to-date information.

Do not hyphenate two or more descriptive words when they *follow* the noun. Study the examples which follow.

1. Can he read textbooks at the college level?
2. The actor featured in the show is well known.
3. The troops engaged in combat hand to hand.
4. Plan to come to our sale at the end of the season.
5. She reported information that is up to date.

Application— **Hyphenation**. In your notebook number from 1-10. If a sentence requires a hyphen, write the hyphenated words opposite the appropriate number. If the sentence is correct, write OK opposite the number. Check your work with the key located in Appendix G at the back of this text.

1. An up to date filing system would be of great help.
2. The files should be kept up to date.
3. The bill was passed by the required two thirds majority.
4. We should make a city wide survey before starting the program.
5. Dr. Miller was a well known surgeon.
6. The actress was well known throughout the world.
7. Elizabeth was an above average student.
8. Use a high grade oil in your automobile to avoid wear.
9. Our one way streets run north and south.
10. We purchased our food for the picnic at the last minute.

Word division

Another common use of the hyphen is to mark the division of a word at the end of a line of type or printing. A growing number of companies and government agencies, possibly as a result of the increased use of word processing equipment, have discontinued the practice of dividing words at the end of a typewritten line. This is also a time-saver. Find out the preferred usage in your area, and if you are instructed to hyphenate and must do so, follow these simple guidelines or consult a standard reference work.

1. Do not divide words of one syllable, regardless of length.

   Examples: *roamed, through, talked, shipped*

2. Do not divide the names of persons, dates, numbers, or abbreviations.

3. Do not divide a beginning or ending syllable of one or two letters.

Application — **Word division**. In your notebook number from 1 – 10. If the word or item divided is correct, write OK opposite the appropriate number. If the word or item is divided incorrectly, write the correction opposite the appropriate number. Check your work with the key located in Appendix G at the back of this text.

1. Can you buy a gift for a-
   bout $10?

2. We celebrate Christmas on December 25.
3. She went to the party and then went straight home.
4. The 1000 m race was won easily by Virginia Sanchez.
5. The twins were born on November 30, 1972.
6. Mark Twain's real name was Samuel Clemens.
7. A large crowd attended the display — over 950.
8. If the present trend continues, school population will soon drop below 800.
9. If possible, the order should be shipped today.
10. Be sure to indicate it has been sent c. o.d.

BUILDING WRITING AND TRANSCRIPTION SPEEDS

You have now reached the half-way point in your instruction in beginning shorthand. Do you realize that you have already studied over 1500 words? With this vocabulary, you can already take a great deal of dictation. In the dictation passages in this chapter, see if you can apply the principles you have already learned. There are many new words in the passages—words which you have never before written in shorthand.

Passage 1—a *letter*—is divided into two parts; Passage 2—*memorandum*—into three parts. Follow this procedure for studying the parts in both passages.

1. Read through the transcript of each part, and, as you are reading, try to write the underscored words in shorthand in your notebook. Each is a new word.

2. When you have written the new words in each part, check your outlines with the new vocabulary key.
3. Then write the entire part from self-dictation until you can write it easily. Check all your outlines with the text shorthand.
4. After you have studied all the parts, you will be ready to take both passages from dictation.

Passage 1, Part 1
transcript

Dear Resident: The Federal Mortgage Company has several parcels of farm land which it is selling. The (20) Senior Citizens Club, knowing of this opportunity, is trying to secure funding through cash gifts or loans (40) to build a nursing home with approximately forty rooms.

New vocabulary key

resident, mortgage, parcels, farm, citizens, knowing, trying, funding, gifts, loans, build, nursing, forty, rooms

Passage 1, Part 1

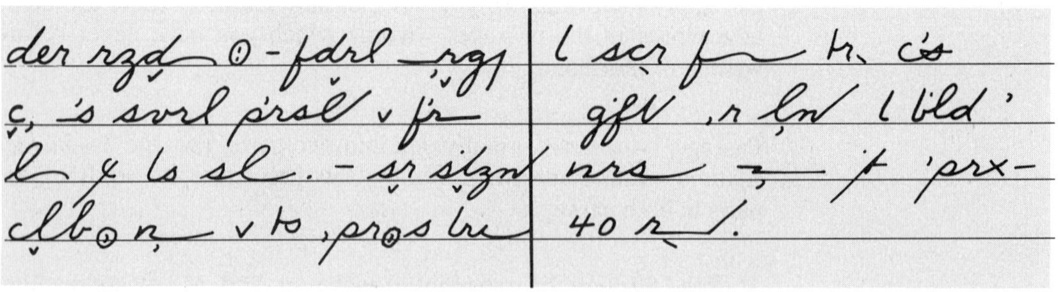

Passage 1, Part 2
transcript

Would you be willing to help us in this campaign? (60) Detailed data, which has been checked by the economic advisor, is contained in the enclosed manual.

These people (80) need help. Can we count on you? Mail in the enclosed form right away. Yours sincerely, (96)

New vocabulary key

willing campaign detailed checked economic

contained manual

Passage 1, Part 2

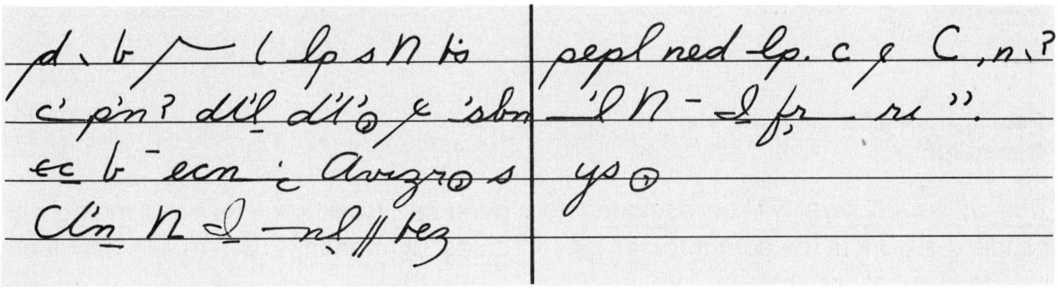

Passage 2, Part 1
transcript

To Faculty Members: Many new unique opportunities await us this coming year. We are delighted (20) that Modern Associates has already agreed to let us use their computer facilities at a (40) discount rate.

They are determined to get maximum earnings from their new models, so they are teaching their managers (60) to train new computer operators.

New vocabulary key

opportunities faculty unique delighted modern

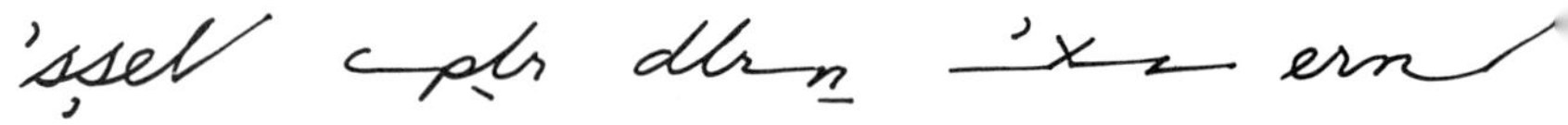

associates computer determined maximum earnings

models teaching managers operators

Passage 2, Part 1

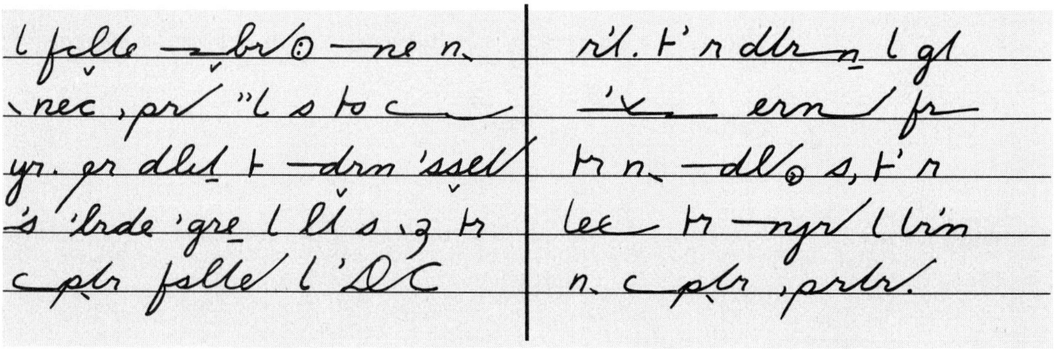

Passage 2, Part 2
transcript

Two office workers will be assigned to handle the work at the computer (80) facility. Do you realize that this will help us eliminate or reduce the volume of paper work (100) we do? Many of the duplicate forms can be done away with. The computer facility will send us a (120) memo with dates of meetings where we can learn more of the technical features of the machines. Anyone wishing (140) to attend may do so.

New vocabulary key

memo two workers assigned eliminate

volume duplicate dates meetings technical

features wishing

Passage 2, Part 2

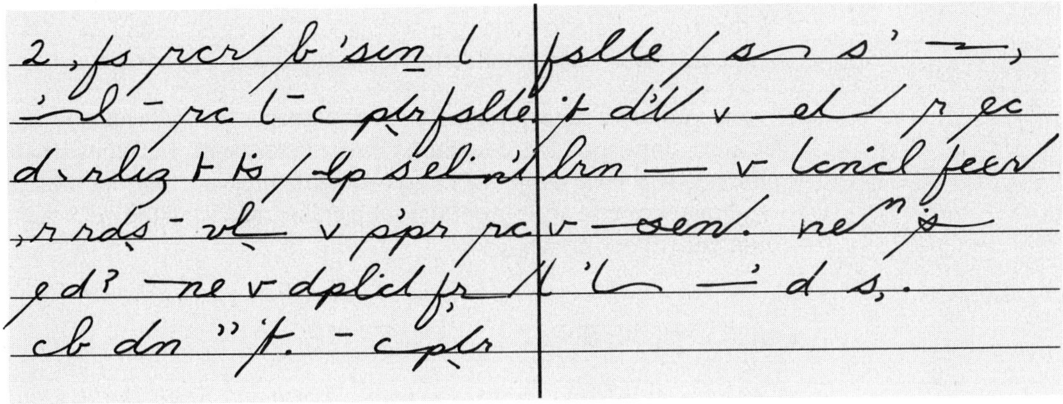

Passage 2, Part 3
transcript

New rules have also been devised to help eliminate parking difficulties in the (160) areas near the physical plants. Unless things improve, parking tickets will have to be issued to those who have (180) failed to pay parking fees. Before school begins, you may get your reserved parking-place ticket in the main office. This (200) term will begin June 5. (204)

New vocabulary key

Passage 2, Part 3

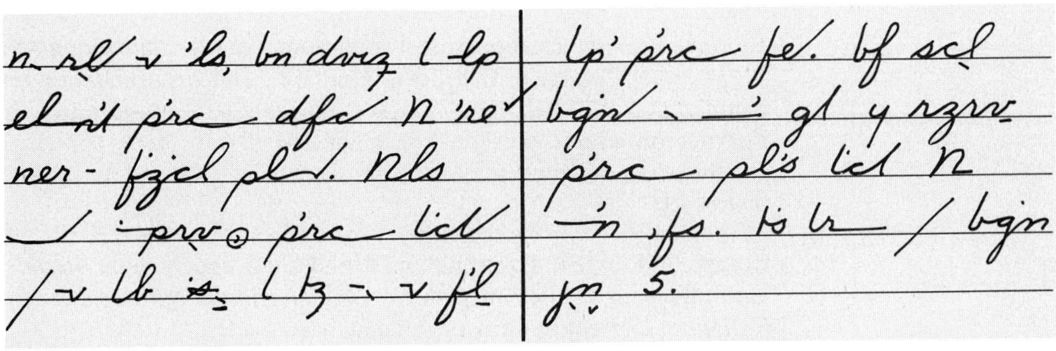

DICTATION AND TRANSCRIPTION

Write from dictation the transcripts of Passages 1 and 2. Your instructor will dictate each letter to you at various speeds.

Using your own notes, transcribe both passages using an appropriate business correspondence format. For the letter, use a fictitious inside address, and your name for the typed signature line. For the memorandum, compose an appropriate subject line, and send the memorandum under your name.

SKILL-BUILDING ASSIGNMENTS

1. Complete Unit 16 in *Forkner Shorthand Skill Builder for Colleges*.

2. Select Cassette 16 Side A of the *Theory and Speed-Building Tapes for Colleges* and follow the directions on the tape.

3. If instructed to do so, read, write, and transcribe the supplementary passage for this chapter found in Appendix A, Supplementary Dictation and Transcription.

4. Take additional live dictation as provided by your instructor.

REVIEWING THE WRITING PRINCIPLES

All the writing rules, abbreviated words, and standard abbreviations you have learned in Chapters 9 through 16 are reviewed on Cassette 17 Side B of the *Theory and Speed-Building Tapes for Colleges*. Take dictation from this tape before completing Preview Examination 4.

PREVIEW EXAMINATION 4

Remove Preview Examination 4 from your *Forkner Shorthand Skill Builder for Colleges*. It follows Unit 32. This informal preview examination will help you in assessing your understanding of the Forkner principles presented in Chapters 13–16. It is similar to Examination 4 which may be administered at a later date by your instructor.

Complete Preview Examination 4 and then check your answers carefully with the key in your *Forkner Shorthand Skill Builder for Colleges*. Correct any errors you may have made.

Chapter 17

WRITING ST AND CITY-SITY

WRITING PRINCIPLES

Combination *st*

Write a capital S to express the *st* combination.

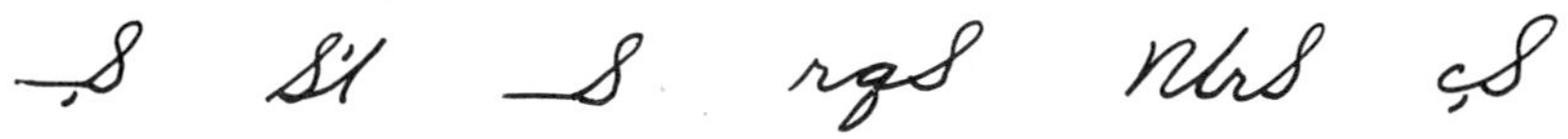

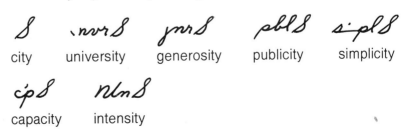

most state must request interest cost

best just study semester customer staff

latest last list history store past

test student against trust still students

industry almost register studies

As you read each outline, write it three times in your notebook. When you have written all the words, you should be able to read and write them rapidly and accurately. Now cover the outlines and write them from the print. Read your notes and correct any errors you may have made.

Combinations *city-sity*

Write a disjoined capital S to express the word *city* and the combinations *city-sity* and the preceding vowel.

city university generosity publicity simplicity

capacity intensity

As you read each outline, write it several times. Do this for all the words. When you can read all the shorthand fluently, cover the outlines and write each of them once. Then read your own notes. If you have difficulty reading your notes, rewrite them and read them again.

New vocabulary

Read and write each of the following words until you can read and write them without hesitation. Remember to memorize the abbreviated words.

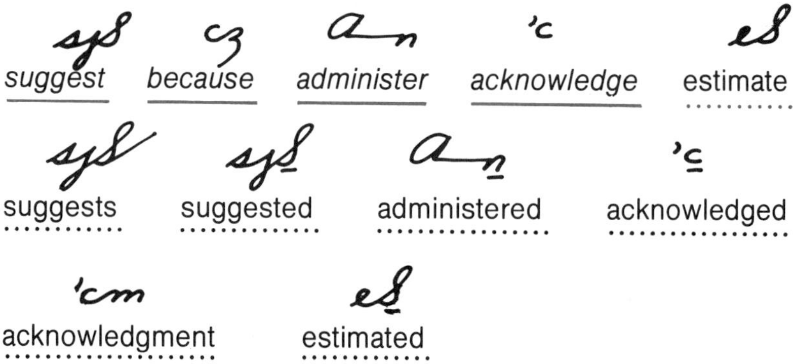

suggest because administer acknowledge estimate

suggests suggested administered acknowledged

acknowledgment estimated

BUILDING TRANSCRIPTION SKILLS

Spelling review

The shorthand outlines for a number of commonly misspelled words have been transcribed below. Is the transcript for each outline correct? If not, transcribe the outline correctly in your notebook. Check the accuracy of your work with a dictionary, a standard word reference list, or the *Forkner Shorthand Dictionary for Beginners*. Compare your answers with the key located at the end of the chapter. Then, write each shorthand outline several times until you can write all of them accurately.

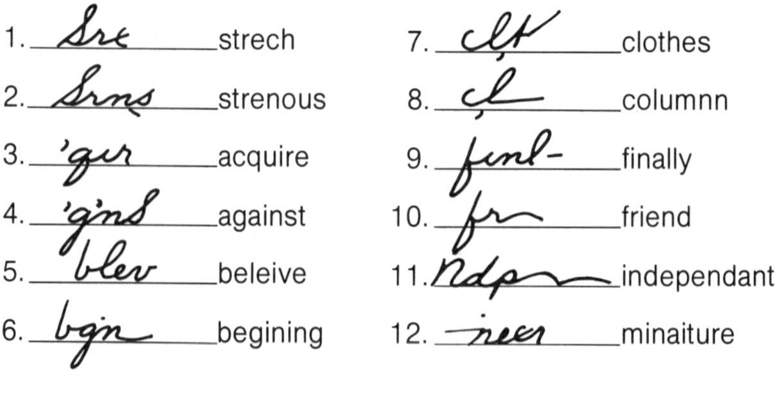

1. strech
2. strenous
3. acquire
4. against
5. beleive
6. begining
7. clothes
8. columnn
9. finally
10. friend
11. independant
12. minaiture

13. ,cr occur
14. ,fol official
15. ,pr opportunity
16. signific significent

Application— **Words that sound alike**. In your notebook number from 1-24. Then, match the words in Column A with their correct definitions by writing the letter from Column B beside the number of the word from Column A. Refer to a dictionary or any standard reference work, if necessary, to determine the correct definition for a word. Check your work with the key located in Appendix G at the back of this text.

Column A

1. allowed
2. aloud
3. born
4. borne
5. brake
6. break
7. buy
8. by
9. correspondence
10. correspondents
11. dew
12. do
13. due
14. leased
15. least

Column B

a. allot, distribute
b. beside, past and beyond
c. brought into life
d. carried
e. change, diversify
f. climate
g. communication by letter
h. device to slow down or slacken speed
i. extremely
j. flesh
k. fracture, abrupt change
l. expressing a choice or alternative
m. join, come together
n. letter writers, communicators
o. loudly
p. moisture
q. payable, expected

16. meat	r. perform
17. meet	s. permitted
18. mete	t. petitions, appeals
19. pleas	u. satisfy, gratify
20. please	v. purchase
21. vary	w. rented
22. very	x. smallest
23. weather	
24. whether	

Transcribing titles

Titles of books, magazines, newspapers, booklets, pamphlets, and other printed works may be typed in all capital letters or underlined with the first letters of the important words capitalized.

1. Have you read GONE WITH THE WIND? *or* Have you read Gone With the Wind?
2. The editorial appeared in THE LONDON TIMES. *or* The editorial appeared in The London Times.
3. The JOURNAL OF COMMERCE is essential reading. *or* The Journal of Commerce is essential reading.

Capitalize the important words in titles of *parts* of published works (chapters, articles, editorials, journalists' columns) and in names of movies, songs, lectures, and television shows. Enclose such titles in quotation marks.

1. “Building Your Writing Speed” is the title of Chapter 2 in NOTETAKING AND STUDY SKILLS. *or* “Building Your Writing Speed” is the title of Chapter 2 in Notetaking and Study Skills.
2. Our neighborhood movie theatre is rerunning “Star Wars” for the third time.

3. She wrote "Don't Get Hung Up on Your Hang Glider" for the HANG GLIDER QUARTERLY. *or* She wrote "Don't Get Hung Up on Your Hang Glider" for the Hang Glider Quarterly.

4. He reads the "Dear Abby" column every day.

APPLYING NEW PRINCIPLES

Follow these procedures in learning to read and write the sentences below.

1. Read the shorthand outlines for each of the sentences until you can read all the sentences without hesitation.
2. Using the Transcript of Shorthand Sentences, write the shorthand outlines for each sentence in your notebook.
3. Check your outlines.
4. Write correctly three times each outline that you may have written incorrectly.
5. Rewrite the shorthand outlines as you read the sentences once again from the Transcript of Shorthand Sentences.
6. Transcribe the sentences from your own notes. Compare your transcript with the text transcript, and circle any errors you may have made, including spelling and punctuation errors.

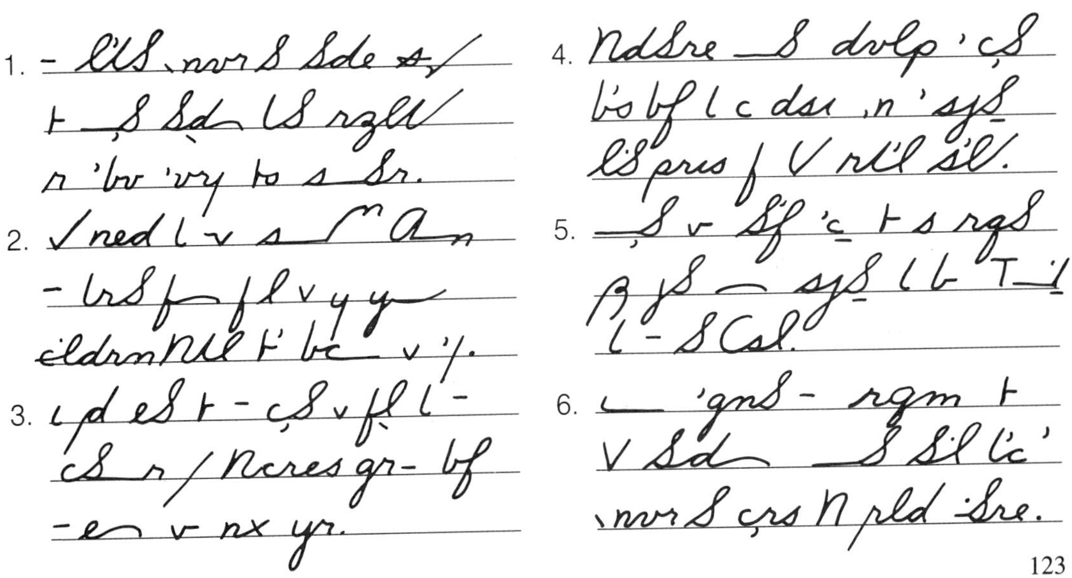

7. 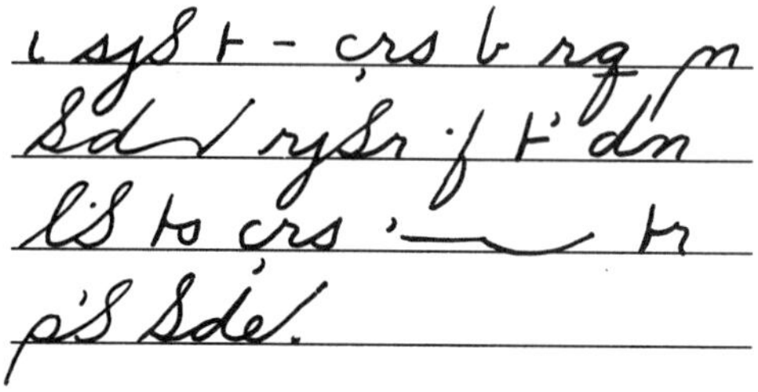

8. 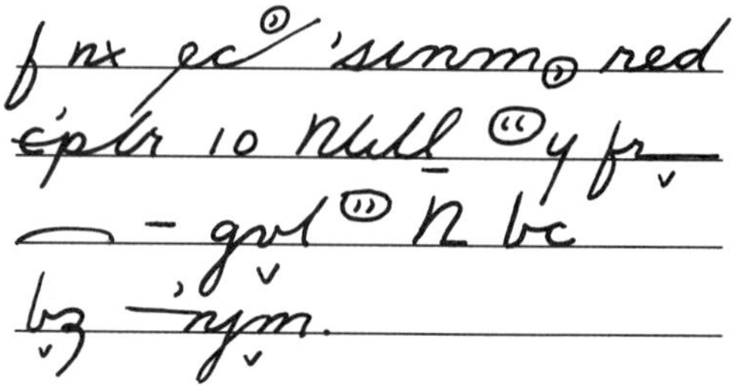

TRANSCRIPT OF SHORTHAND SENTENCES

1. The latest university study shows that most student test results are above average this semester. (20)
2. You will need to have someone administer the trust fund for all of your young children until they become of age. (40)
3. I would estimate that the cost of fuel to the customer will increase greatly before the end of the next year. (60)
4. Industry must develop a cost base before it can decide on a suggested list price for its retail sales. (80)
5. Most of the staff acknowledged that his request was just and suggested it be transmitted to the City Council. (100)
6. I am against the requirement that every student must still take a university course in world history. (120)
7. I suggest that the course be required when students register if they do not list this course among their past studies. (140)
8. For next week's assignment, read Chapter 10 entitled "Your Firm and the Government" in the book, Business Management. (160)

DICTATION AND TRANSCRIPTION

Write from dictation the Transcript of Shorthand Sentences. Your instructor will dictate each group of 20 words to you at various speeds. Select one set of notes, and transcribe it quickly and accurately.

BUILDING WRITING AND TRANSCRIPTION SPEEDS

New vocabulary

Read and write each of the following words until you can do so easily.

Masters pamphlet arise designated demonstrated

workmanship mails estate heirs fifty competent

Letter 1

Read Letter 1 under timed conditions. Calculate your reading rate. Then scribble-write the letter for speed building. Using the transcript of the letter, write it in shorthand in your notebook. Check your outlines with those which follow. Transcribe the letter and calculate your transcription rate.

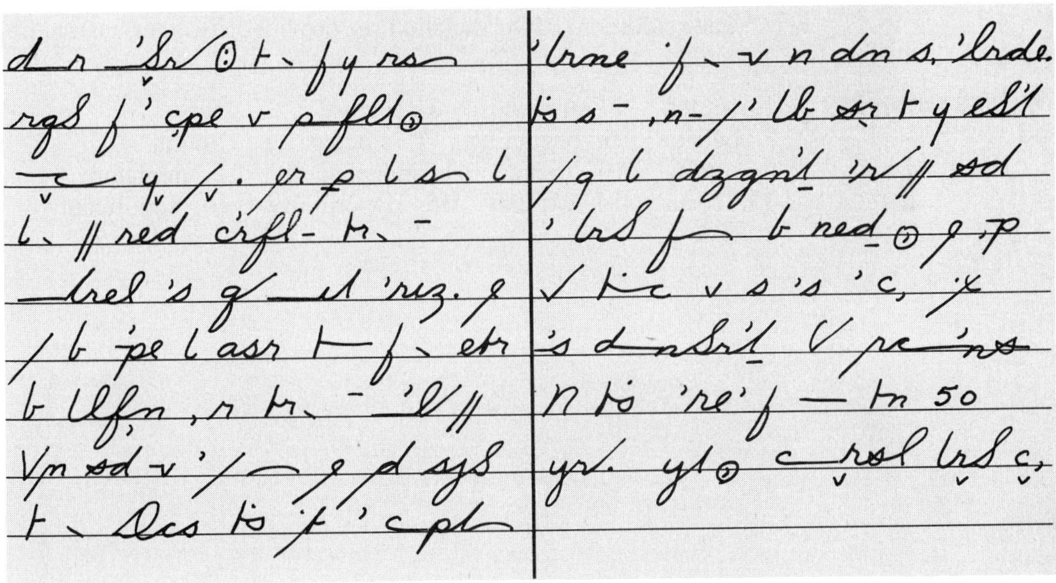

Letter 1 transcript

Dear Mr. Masters: Thank you for your recent request for a copy of the pamphlet, Making Your Will. We are pleased (20) to send it to you.

Read carefully through the material as questions might arise. We will be happy to answer (40) them for you either by telephone or through the mails.

Everyone should have a will, and we would suggest that you (60) discuss this with a competent attorney if you have not done so already. This is the only way to be sure (80) that your estate will go to designated heirs.

Should a trust fund be needed, we hope you will think of us as a (100) company which has demonstrated its workmanship in this area for more than fifty years. Yours truly, (120) Commercial Trust Company (124)

SKILL-BUILDING ASSIGNMENTS

1. Complete Unit 17 in *Forkner Shorthand Skill Builder for Colleges*.
2. Select Cassette 1 Side B of the *Theory and Speed-Building Tapes for Colleges* and follow the directions on the tape.
3. If instructed to do so, read, write, and transcribe the supplementary memorandum for this chapter found in Appendix A, Supplementary Dictation and Transcription.
4. Take additional live dictation as provided by your instructor.

Spelling review key

1. stretch 2. strenuous 3. acquire 4. against
5. believe 6. beginning 7. clothes 8. column
9. finally 10. friend 11. independent 12. miniature
13. occur 14. official 15. opportunity 16. significant

Chapter 18

WRITING SOUNDS OF OU-OW, OUT, AND SELF

WRITING PRINCIPLES

Sound of *ou-ow*

Write a small longhand *o* to express the sound *ou-ow*. Write the *o* in a clockwise direction  , so that you can write faster.

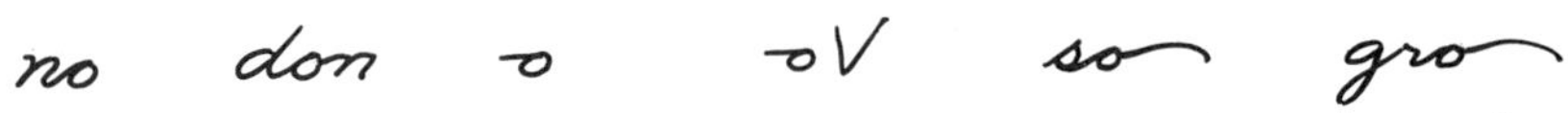

now down how however sound ground

town background found around power south

house warehouse allow amount allowed aloud

Cover the print of each line of words and read the outlines until you can read from shorthand as fast as you can read from the print. Then write the outline for each word once. Read your own notes back.

Prefix or suffix *out*

Write a small longhand *o* to express either the prefix or the suffix *out*.

outline outfit outcome without outstanding

throughout

As you read each outline, write it until you can do so accurately and rapidly. Say the word each time you write it.

Prefix or suffix *self*

Write a small disjoined longhand *s*  to express either the prefix or the suffix *self*. The suffix *selves* is expressed by adding the *s*-added stroke  to the suffix *self*  , as in themselves 

self-addressed self-service self-improvement

myself himself selfishness self-satisfied

herself self-government

Read the shorthand outlines until you can read them fluently. Then increase your writing rate on the words by scribble-writing each word three times.

New vocabulary

Use the Longhand/Shorthand (L/S) Recognition Drill to help you learn the new words. Refer to Chapter 9, page 59, for directions on how to rule your notebook. Be sure to fill in all the columns on your lined paper. Say each word as you write the shorthand.

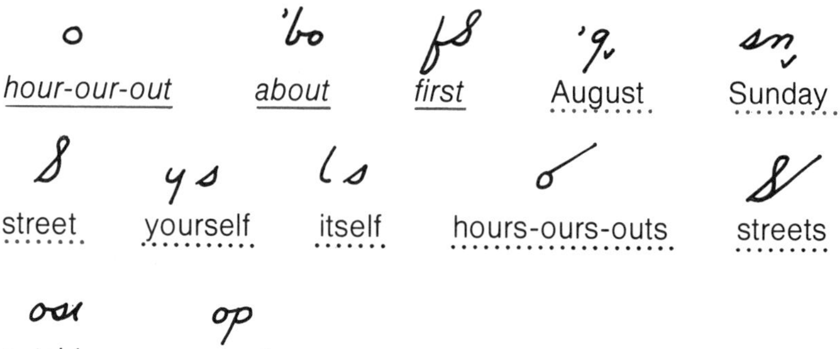

hour-our-out about first August Sunday

street yourself itself hours-ours-outs streets

outside output

BUILDING TRANSCRIPTION SKILLS

Spelling review

The shorthand outlines in each sentence are for words that are commonly misspelled. Transcribe the shorthand outlines in your notebook. You may use a dictionary, a standard word reference list, or the *Forkner Shorthand Dictionary for Beginners* to verify the spelling. Compare your answers with the key located at the end of the chapter. Write correctly any words that you may have misspelled. Then write the shorthand outlines for each word several times in your notebook.

1. That was a ______ ______ of art work.
2. I would ______ ______ in a ______ place.

3. The Lprer is ,sl- 'ro 20° at this time of year.
4. pr is the most dzrbl place for the dfr 'prts?
5. Ndot, you will dsi to seek Csl.
6. A horse-drawn carriage will 'roz cre8 today.
7. Do not p'nc : the Ntr8 rates will decline.
8. I met her csd-l in the hall.

APPLYING NEW PRINCIPLES

Follow these procedures in learning to read and write the sentences below.

1. Read the shorthand outlines for each of the sentences until you can read all the sentences without hesitation.
2. Using the Transcript of Shorthand Sentences, write the shorthand outlines for each sentence in your notebook.
3. Check your outlines.
4. Write correctly three times each outline that you may have written incorrectly.
5. Rewrite the shorthand outlines as you read the sentences once again from the Transcript of Shorthand Sentences.
6. Transcribe the sentences from your own notes. Compare your transcript with the text transcript, and circle any errors you may have made, including spelling and punctuation errors.

1. '-8 ,nec s -prvm crs b,fr l- ,nvr8 bgn f - 'q, tr-.

2. ,sd 'lo ys — trvl t- lts o0 oVO, -'b ,n t- f trfc s ltl ,n bz 8.

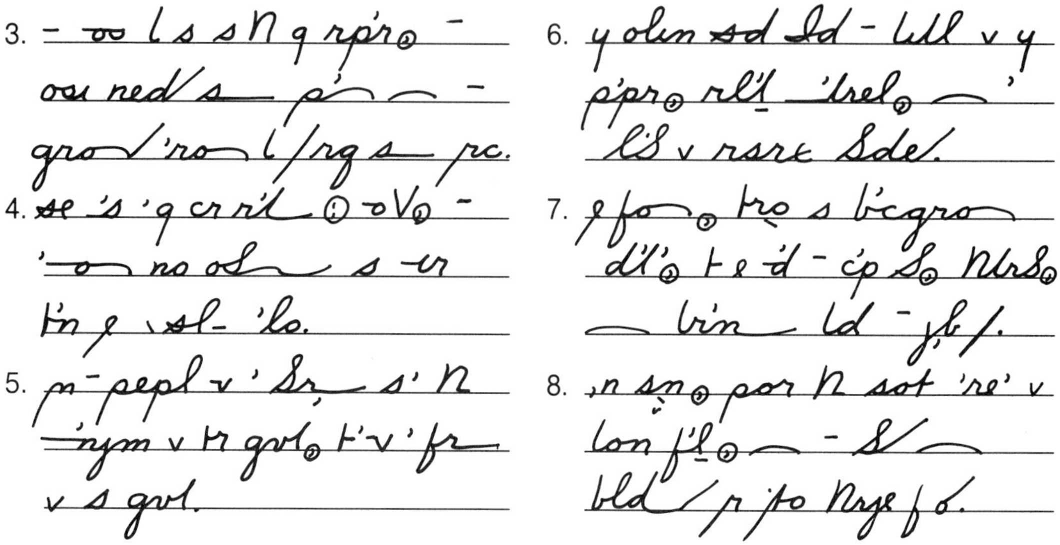

TRANSCRIPT OF SHORTHAND SENTENCES

1. A most unique self-improvement course will be offered at the university beginning with the August term. (20)
2. You should allow yourself more travel time at this hour; however, you may be on time if traffic is light on those streets. (40)
3. The house itself is in good repair; the outside needs some paint,and the grounds around it will require some work. (60)
4. She has a good credit rating; however, the amount now outstanding is higher than we usually allow. (80)
5. When the people have a strong say in the management of their government, they have a form of self-government. (100)
6. Your outline should include the title of your paper, related material, and a list of research studies. (120)
7. We found, throughout his background data, that he had the capacity, interest, and training to do the job well. (140)
8. On Sunday, power in the south area of town failed, and the streets and buildings were without energy for hours. (160)

DICTATION AND TRANSCRIPTION

Write from dictation the Transcript of Shorthand Sentences. Your instructor will dictate each group of 20 words to you at various speeds. Select one set of notes, and transcribe it quickly and accurately.

BUILDING WRITING AND TRANSCRIPTION SPEEDS

New vocabulary

Read and write the following words until you can do so easily.

comes residents aisles Bag labeled* enter

shopping operates ads telling mark helps

saved compare indicating feelings seven

seventeenth twenty-four

Learning tip:

* Variant spelling labeled/labelled. Your instructor will indicate the spelling preferred in your community.

Letter 1

You should be able to master the following letter easily. First, see if you can write quickly the underscored phrases in the transcript. All of these phrases should be familiar to you. Then, using the self-dictation method, write the letter in shorthand until you can write it quickly and accurately. You may also wish to have someone dictate the letter to you. Finally, make one good set of shorthand notes and read them back.

If your instructor prefers, transcribe the letter using a fictitious inside address, and your name for the typed signature line.

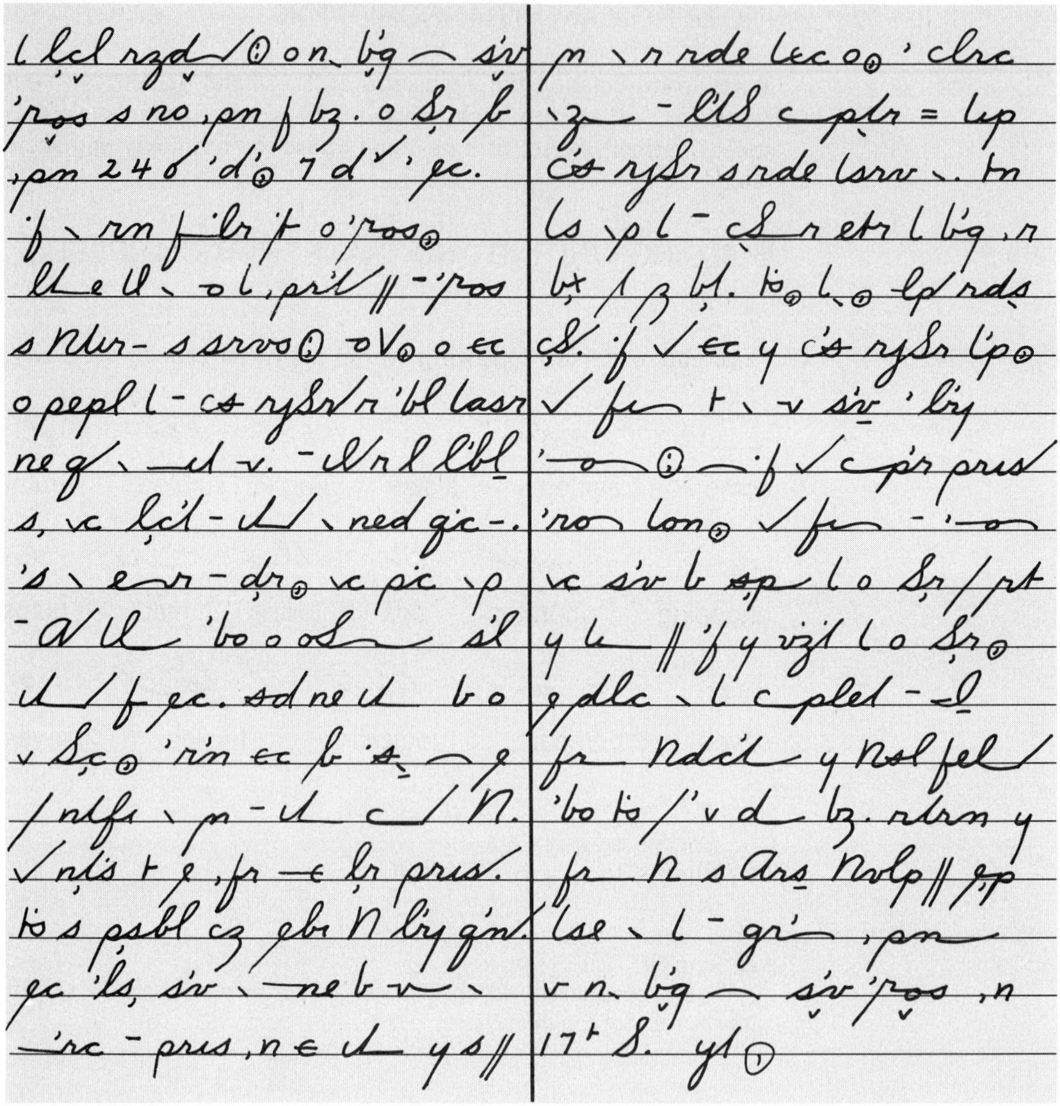

Letter 1 transcript

To Local Residents: Our new Bag-and-Save Warehouse is now open for business. Our store will be open twenty-four (20) hours a day, seven days a week. If you are not familiar with our warehouse, let me tell you how it operates. (40)

The Warehouse is entirely self-service; however, our check-out people at the cash registers are able to (60)answer any questions you might have. The aisles are all labeled so you can locate the items you need quickly. As (80) you enter the door, you can pick up the ads telling about our outstanding sale items for the week. Should any (100) item be out of stock, a rain check will be issued and we will notify you when the item comes in. You will (120) notice that we offer much lower prices. This is possible because we buy in large quantities. We can also (140) save you money by having you mark the price on each item yourself.

When you are ready to check out, a clerk (160) using the latest computer-type cash register is ready to serve you. Then it is up to the customer (180) either to bag or box what was bought. This, too, helps reduce costs. If you will check your cash-register tape, you will find (200) that you have saved a large amount; and if you will compare prices around town, you will find the amount you can save (220) by shopping at our store well worth your time.

After your visit to our store, we would like you to complete the enclosed (240) form indicating your initial feelings about this way of doing business. Return your form in the self-addressed (260) envelope.

We hope to see you at the grand opening of the new Bag-and-Save Warehouse on 17th Street. Yours truly, (280)

SKILL-BUILDING ASSIGNMENTS

1. Complete Unit 18 in *Forkner Shorthand Skill Builder for Colleges*.

2. Select Cassette 2 Side B of the *Theory and Speed-Building Tapes for Colleges* and follow the directions on the tape.

3. If instructed to do so, read, write, and transcribe the supplementary letter for this chapter found in Appendix A, Supplementary Dictation and Transcription.

4. Take additional dictation as provided by your instructor.

Spelling review key

1. brilliant, piece 2. recommend, studying, quiet 3. temperature, usually, around 4. Where, desirable, different, apparatus 5. Undoubtedly, decide, counsel 6. arouse, curiosity 7. panic, interest 8. accidentally

Chapter 19

WRITING THE SOUND OF SHUN

WRITING PRINCIPLES

Sound of *shun*

Write a short, vertical, downward stroke under the last letter or symbol of a word to express the *shun* sound and the *preceding* vowel. Note how additional endings are added to the *shun* symbol.

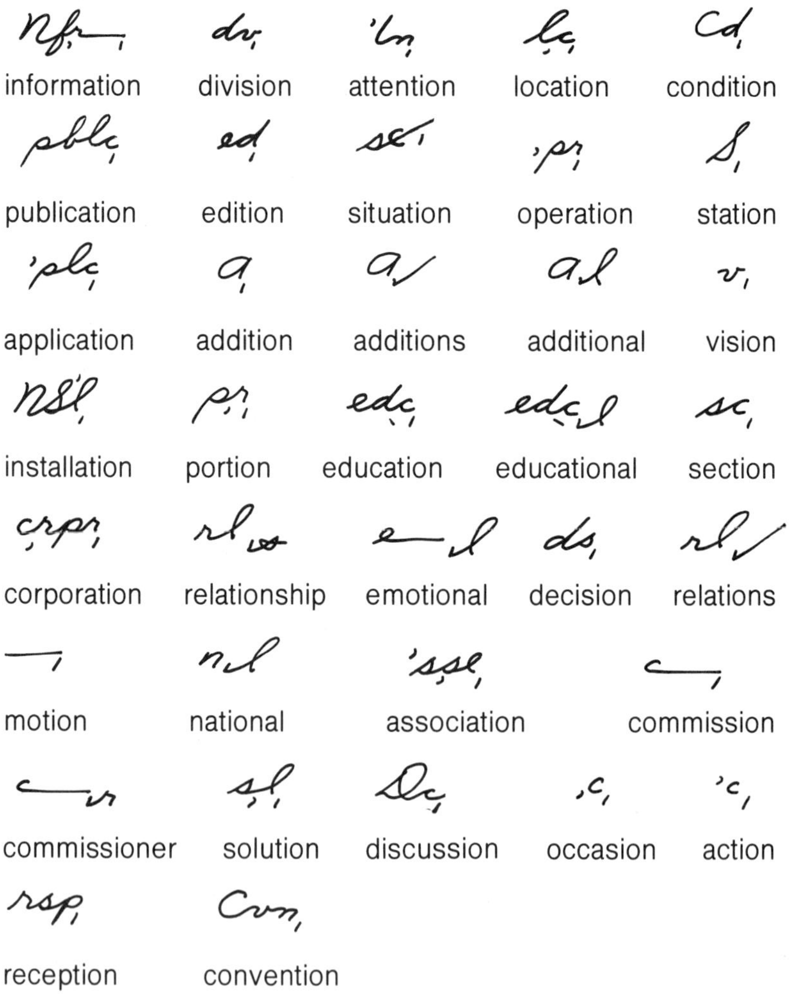

As you read each outline, write it three times in your notebook. When you have written all the words, you should be able to read and write them rapidly and accurately. Then cover the shorthand and write each outline as you read from the print. Read your notes and correct any errors you may have made.

New vocabulary

Read and write the following words until you can do so fluently and accurately. Notice how you can write many words after you have memorized the base word.

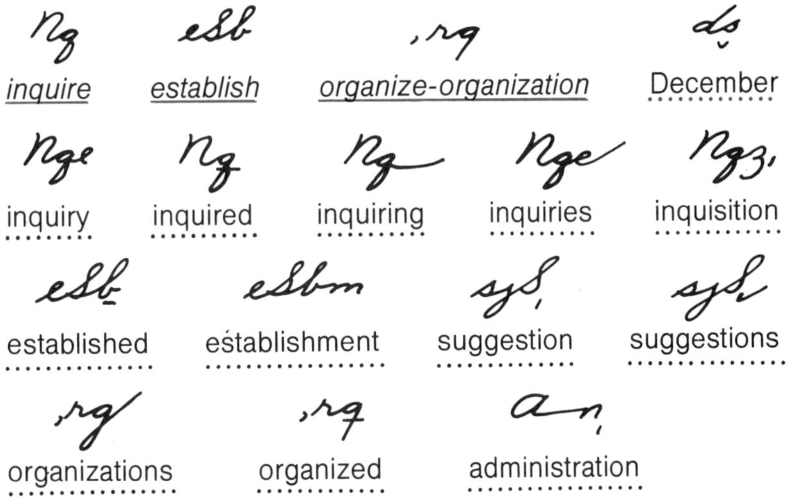

BUILDING TRANSCRIPTION SKILLS

Spelling review

The shorthand outlines in each sentence are for words that are commonly misspelled. Transcribe the shorthand outlines in your notebook. You may use a dictionary, a standard word reference list, or the *Forkner Shorthand Dictionary for Beginners* to verify the spelling. Compare your answers with the key located at the end of the chapter. Write correctly any words you may have misspelled. Then write the shorthand outlines for each word several times in your notebook.

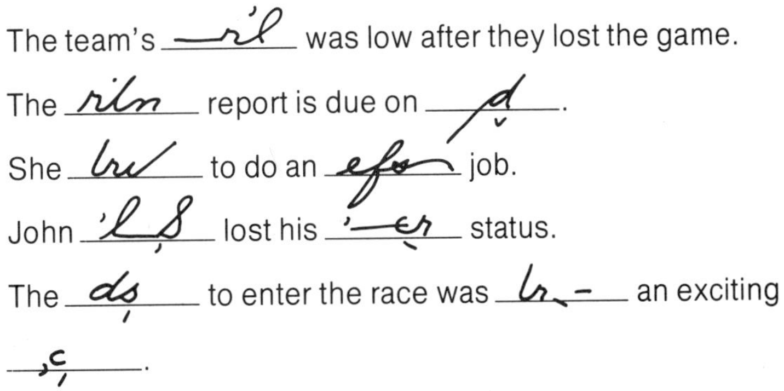

1. The team's ______ was low after they lost the game.
2. The ______ report is due on ______.
3. She ______ to do an ______ job.
4. John ______ lost his ______ status.
5. The ______ to enter the race was ______ an exciting ______.

6. The gymnast pulled a *sl* and was *Dsls* with his performance.
7. The *s tre* lot is in the new *dvlpm*.
8. *netr 'rgm* is valid.
9. We have *cprbv* few *Dpln* problems at our school.
10. The *vln* will *D'per* near the end of the play.

APPLYING NEW PRINCIPLES

Follow these procedures in learning to read and write the sentences below.

1. Read the shorthand outlines for each of the sentences until you can read all the sentences without hesitation.
2. Using the Transcript of Shorthand Sentences, write the shorthand outlines for each sentence in your notebook.
3. Check your outlines.
4. Write correctly three times each outline that you may have written incorrectly.
5. Rewrite the shorthand outlines as you read the sentences once again from the Transcript of Shorthand Sentences.
6. Transcribe the sentences from your own notes. Compare your transcript with the text transcript, and circle any errors you may have made, including spelling and punctuation errors.

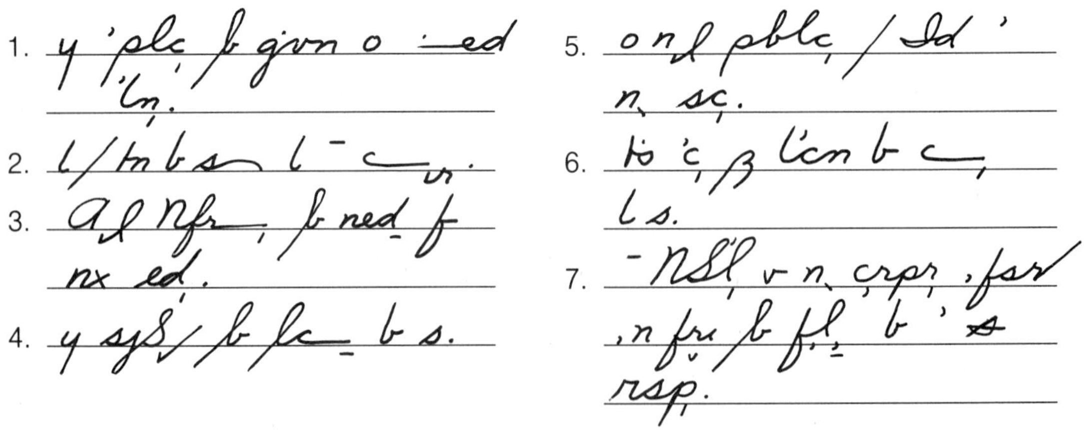

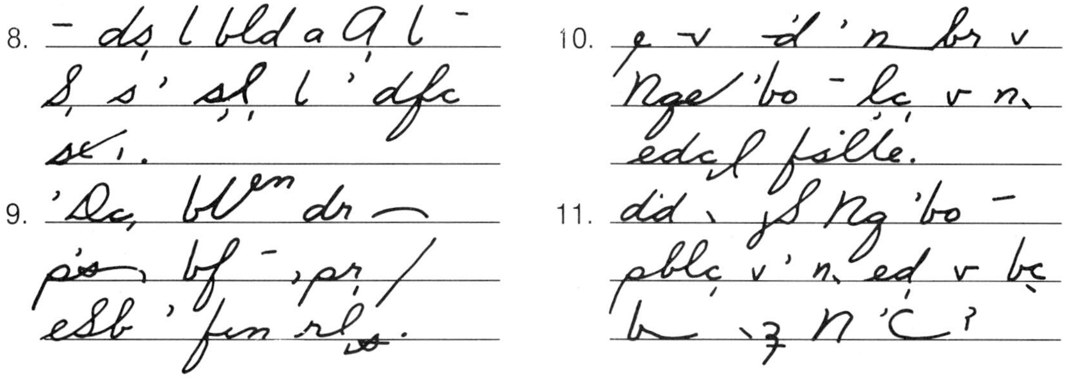

TRANSCRIPT OF SHORTHAND SENTENCES

1. Your application will be given our immediate attention.
2. It will then be sent to the commissioner. (20)
3. Additional information will be needed for the next edition.
4. Your suggestions will be welcomed by us. (40)
5. Our national publication will include a new section.
6. This action was taken by the commission itself. (60)
7. The installation of the new corporation officers on Friday will be followed by a short reception. (80)
8. The decision to build an addition to the station is a solution to a difficult situation. (100)
9. A discussion between doctor and patient before the operation will establish a fine relationship. (120)
10. We have had a number of inquiries about the location of the new educational facility. (140)
11. Did you just inquire about the publication of a new edition of the book being used in accounting? (160)

DICTATION AND TRANSCRIPTION

Write from dictation the Transcript of Shorthand Sentences. Your instructor will dictate each group of 20 words to you at various speeds. Select one set of notes, and transcribe it quickly and accurately.

BUILDING WRITING AND TRANSCRIPTION SPEEDS

New vocabulary

Read and write the following words until you can do so without hesitation.

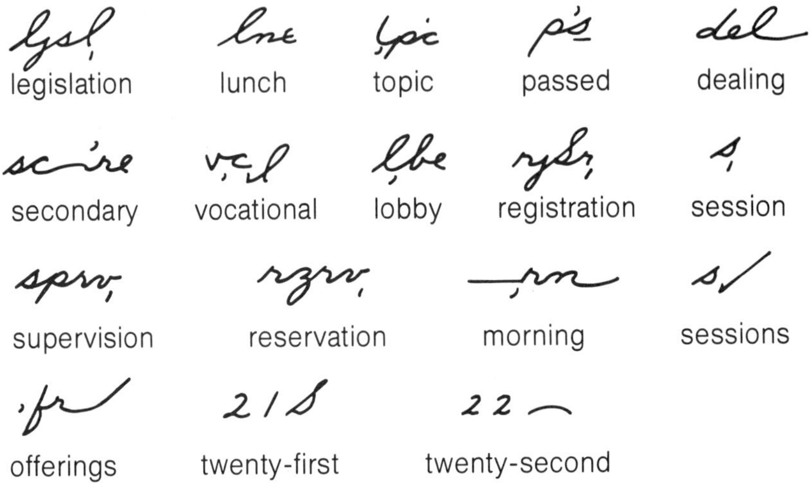

Letter 1

You should be able to read the following letter easily. Read the letter several times until you can read it without hesitation. Then, using the transcript, write the letter in shorthand as you read from the print. Read your notes. If there are any outlines you cannot read, look them up and rewrite them several times. Transcribe the letter according to directions given by your instructor.

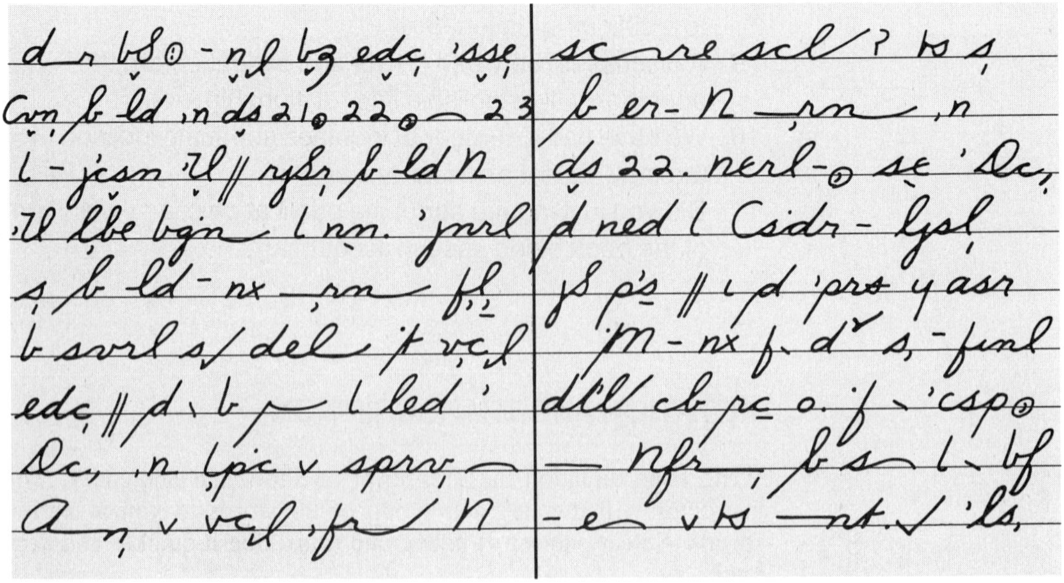

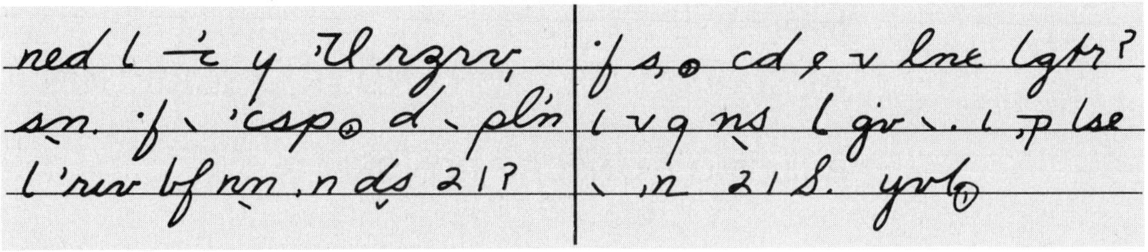

Letter 1 transcript

Dear Mr. Best: The National Business Education Association Convention will be held on December (20) 21, 22, and 23 at the Jackson Hotel.

Registration will be held in the hotel (40) lobby beginning at noon. A general session will be held the next morning followed by several sessions (60) dealing with vocational education.

Would you be willing to lead a discussion on the topic of (80) supervision and administration of vocational offerings in secondary schools? This session will be early (100) in the morning on December 22. Naturally, such a discussion would need to consider (120) the legislation just passed.

I would appreciate your answer within the next few days so the final details (140) can be worked out. If you accept, more information will be sent to you before the end of this month. You will also (160) need to make your hotel reservation soon. If you accept, do you plan to arrive before noon on December (180) 21? If so, could we have lunch together? I have good news to give you. I hope to see you on the (200) 21st. Yours very truly, (205)

SKILL-BUILDING ASSIGNMENTS

1. Complete Unit 19 in *Forkner Shorthand Skill Builder for Colleges*.
2. Select Cassette 3 Side B of the *Theory and Speed-Building Tapes for Colleges* and follow the directions on the tape.
3. If instructed to do so, read, write, and transcribe the supplementary letter for this chapter found in Appendix A, Supplementary Dictation and Transcription.
4. Take additional live dictation as provided by your instructor.

Spelling review key

1. morale 2. written, Wednesday 3. tries, efficient 4. almost, amateur 5. decision, truly, occasion 6. muscle, dissatisfied 7. cemetery, development 8. Neither, argument 9. comparatively, discipline 10. villain, disappear

Chapter 20

BUSINESS DICTATION AND TRANSCRIPTION

BUILDING TRANSCRIPTION SKILLS

Transcribing numbers

In this text, isolated numbers under eleven are spelled out and all numbers over ten are written in figures.

1. There were nine runners in the race.
2. The first five customers collected 53 stamps.

The above examples illustrate one common principle for transcribing numbers. Four additional principles are summarized below.

1. When they occur at the beginning of a sentence, all numbers should be spelled out. If this results in an awkward sentence, rewrite the sentence.

   Sixty-five of the 242 students were employed on a part-time basis.

2. Figures are used to express age, dates, and time of day.

   a. Renée will be 2 years old on November 6.
   b. The plane will arrive at 6:30 p.m.
   c. The plane will arrive at 18:30. (24-hour clock)

3. Figures preceded by a dollar sign are used to express sums of money. If the amount is in even dollars, omit the decimal and zeros.

   Estimated sales for the day were $925; the actual amount was $942.75.

4. Spell out ordinal numbers that are not a part of an address or a date. Ordinal numbers are forms of numbers that indicate order or succession such as first, tenth, seventy-fifth, etc.

   a. For the fourth time he ran for office and again came in second.
   b. She lives on East 42d Street.

Application— **Transcribing numbers**. Type the following sentences making any required corrections. If the sentence is correct as written, simply retype it. Check your work with the key located in Appendix G at the back of the text.

1. The new house will cost seventy thousand dollars.
2. The bill came to $250 and fifty-five cents.
3. 100 of the contest winners were awarded $50.00 each.
4. Our car will be 3 months old tomorrow; it has depreciated $865.
5. Unleaded gas now costs one dollar and sixty cents.
6. They celebrated their seventy-fifth anniversary on the tenth of December.
7. Lindbergh was the 1st man to fly the Atlantic Ocean alone.

Spelling review

Column A contains a list of commonly misspelled words that will really challenge your ability to spell. In your notebook number from 1–18. Complete each word and write it correctly opposite the appropriate number. Then, select the correct shorthand outline from Column B and write it in your notebook beside the appropriate transcribed word. Compare your answers with the key located at the end of the chapter. Write each outline three times in your notebook.

Column A

1. av_r_ge
2. al_ rig_t
3. con_ci__s
4. c_nt_n__us
5. _ylind_r
6. d_v_ne
7. ea_il_

Column B

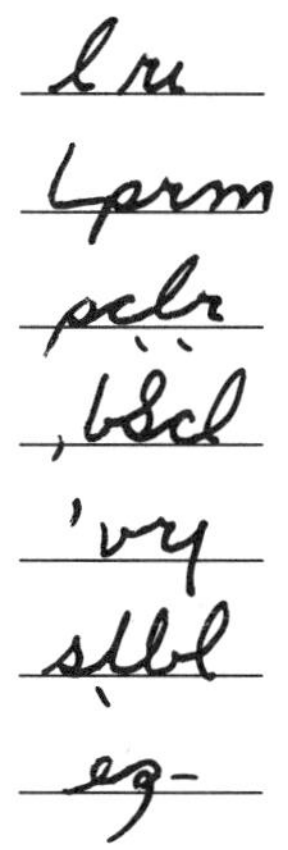

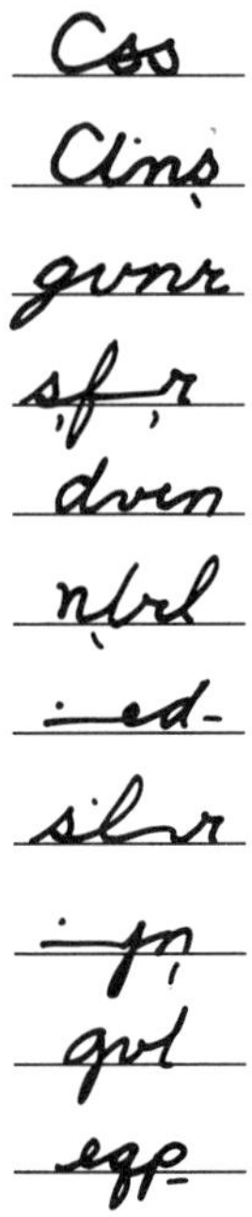

8. eq_ip_ed
9. pecul__r
10. go_ern_r
11. g_ver_m_nt
12. im_gin_t__n
13. i__ed__tely
14. n__tr_l
15. ob__acle
16. s_ph_m_re
17. su_t_ble
18. t_mp_r_ment

BUILDING WRITING AND TRANSCRIPTION SPEEDS

The following series of six letters (four in the text and two in *Forkner Shorthand Skill Builder for Colleges*) is correspondence that has developed between Carol Clark, a student at Freedom High School, and Ms. Mary Church, a fashion consultant.

New vocabulary

Read and write the following words and phrases until you can do so without hesitation.

Freedom fashion Carol Clark leaders

inasmuch as please let me know Yours very sincerely

Letter 1

Read Letter 1 following this procedure: Read sentence one. Then, go back and read sentences one and two. Then, go back to the beginning and read sentences one, two, and three. Follow this plan for reading the entire letter. By the time you have completed reading the letter, you should be able to transcribe the outlines easily.

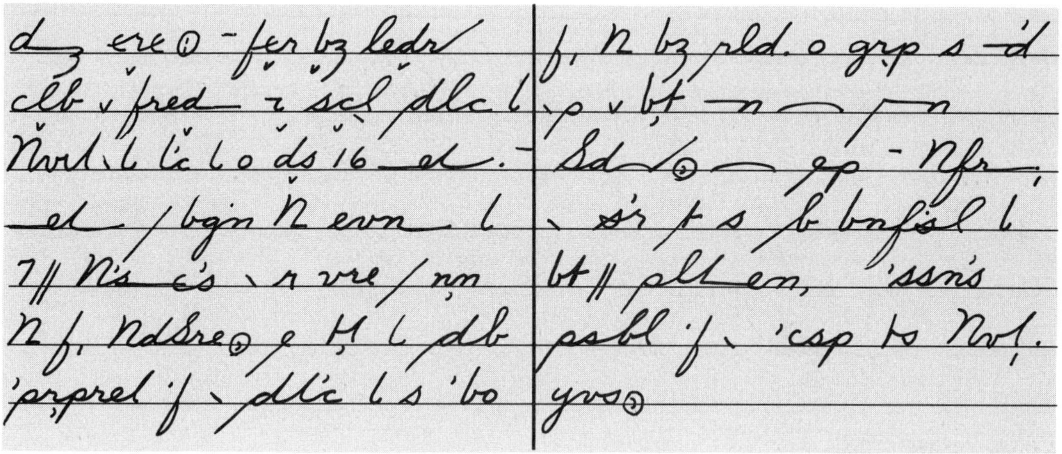

Letter 1 transcript

Dear Ms. Church: The Future Business Leaders Club of Freedom High School would like to invite you to talk at our December (20) 16 meeting. The meeting will begin in the evening at seven.

Inasmuch as you are very well known (40) in the fashion industry, we thought it would be appropriate if you would talk to us about fashion in the (60) business world. Our group is made up of both men and women students, and we hope the information you share with us (80) will be beneficial to both.

Please let me know as soon as possible if you accept this invitation. Yours (100) very sincerely, (104)

New vocabulary

As you read each of the words and phrases, write the corresponding outlines three times in your shorthand notebook.

fashions packet variety tips individuals

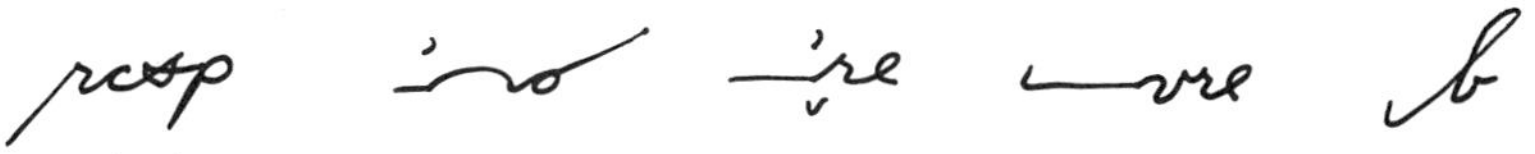

workshop handouts Mary I am very I will be

Letter 2

Read the following letter until you can read it without hesitation. Then, using the transcript of Letter 2, write the shorthand outlines for the letter in your notebook from self-dictation. Check the accuracy of your outlines and write the letter again. This time write the sentences as quickly as you can. Read your notes. Can you read them quickly?

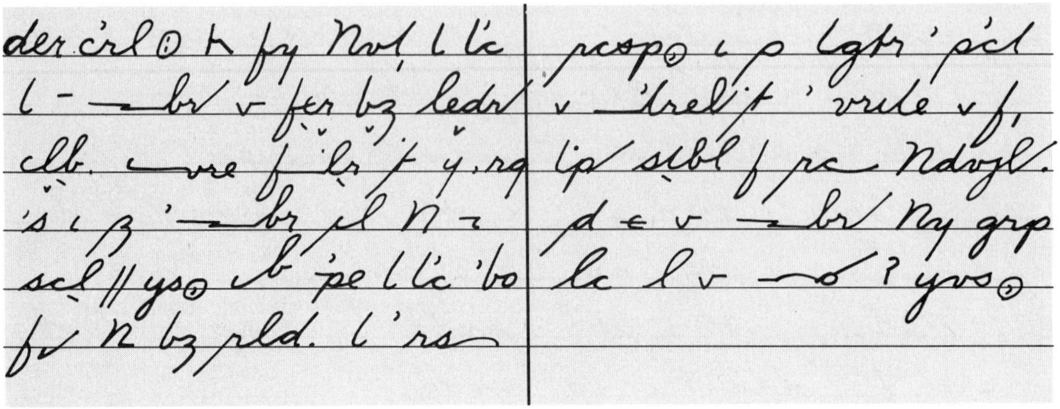

Letter 2 transcript

Dear Carol: Thank you for your invitation to talk to the members of the Future Business Leaders Club. I am (20) very familiar with your organization as I was a member while in high school.

Yes, I will be happy (40) to talk about fashions in the business world. At a recent workshop, I put together a packet of (60) materials with a variety of fashion tips suitable for working individuals. Would each of the (80) members in your group like all of the handouts? Yours very sincerely, (91)

New vocabulary

As you read each outline, scribble-write it for speed development.

photograph

newspaper

would like

we hope

in our

you can

Letter 3

As you read the following letter, scribble-write it in your notebook until you can both read and write the letter easily.

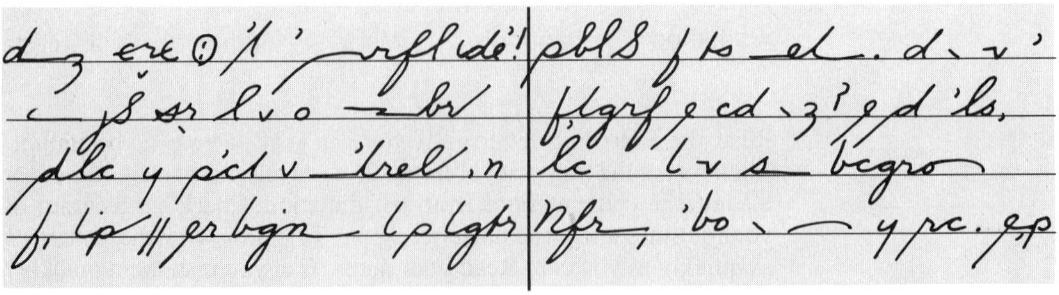

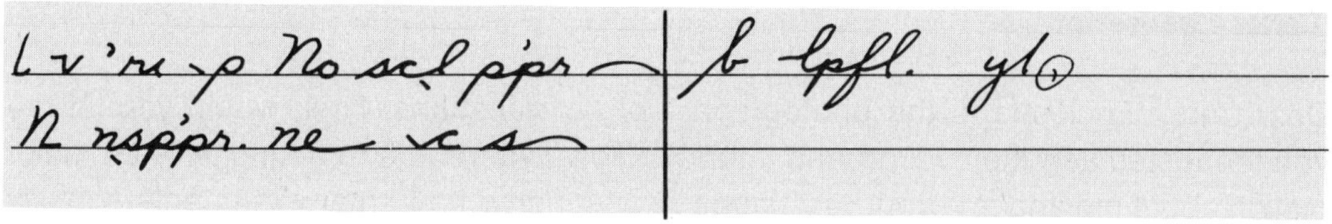

Letter 3 transcript

Dear Ms. Church: What a wonderful idea! I am just sure all of our members would like your packet of materials (20) on fashion tips.

We are beginning to put together publicity for this meeting. Do you have a (40) photograph we could use? We would also like to have some background information about you and your work. We hope (60) to have a write-up in our school paper and in the newspaper. Anything you can send will be helpful. Yours truly, (80)

New vocabulary

Read and write the following outlines until you can do so easily.

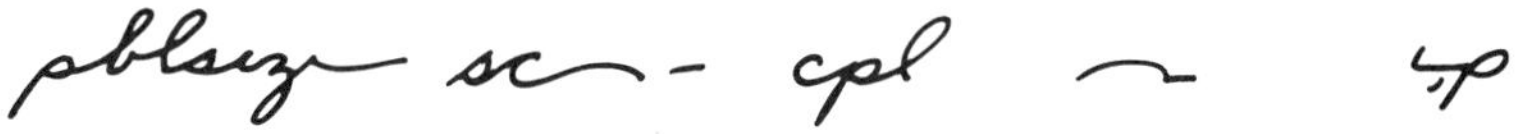

publicizing secondly couple and the I hope

by the I do to meet

Letter 4

Read the following letter until you can read it without hesitation. Then write the shorthand for the letter in your notebook, making certain your outlines are correct and readable. Read them back to be sure. Transcribe the letter from your own notes. Correct your transcript by referring to the text transcript.

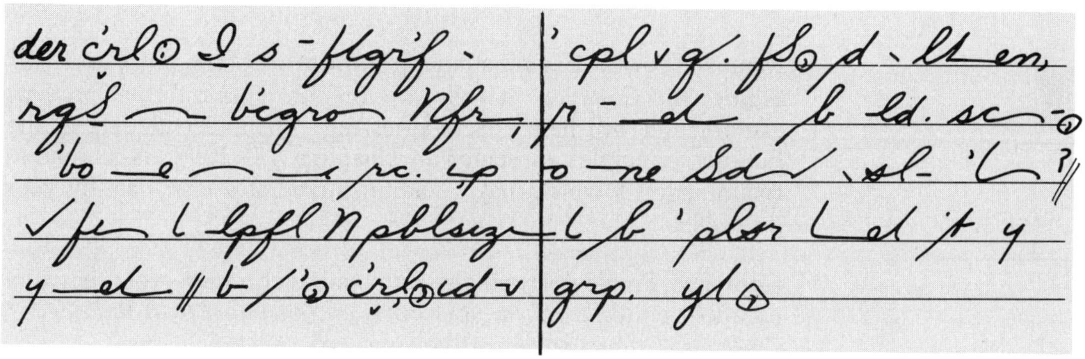

Letter 4 transcript

Dear Carol: Enclosed is the photograph you requested and the background information about me and my work. (20) I hope you will find it helpful in publicizing your meeting.

By the way, Carol, I do have a couple of (40) questions. First, would you let me know where the meeting will be held. Secondly, how many students usually attend? (60)

It will be a pleasure to meet with your group. Yours truly, (70)

DICTATION AND TRANSCRIPTION

Write from dictation Letters 1–4. Your instructor will dictate each letter to you at various speeds.

Using your own notes, transcribe the letters using an appropriate business correspondence format. Use fictitious addresses for Freedom High School and Ms. Mary Church.

SKILL-BUILDING ASSIGNMENTS

1. Complete Unit 20 in *Forkner Shorthand Skill Builder for Colleges*.
2. Select Cassette 4 Side B of the *Theory and Speed-Building Tapes for Colleges* and follow the directions on the tape.
3. If instructed to do so, read, write, and transcribe the supplementary letter for this chapter found in Appendix A, Supplementary Dictation and Transcription.
4. Take additional live dictation as provided by your instructor.

PREVIEW EXAMINATION 5

Remove Preview Examination 5 from your *Forkner Shorthand Skill Builder for Colleges*. It follows Unit 32. This informal preview examination will help you in assessing your understanding of the Forkner principles presented in Chapters 17–20. It is similar to Examination 5 which may be administered at a later date by your instructor.

Complete Preview Examination 5 and then check your answers carefully with the key in your *Forkner Shorthand Skill Builder for Colleges*. Correct any errors you may have made.

Spelling review key

1. average
2. all right
3. conscious
4. continuous
5. cylinder
6. divine
7. easily
8. equipped
9. peculiar

10. governor
11. government
12. imagination
13. immediately
14. neutral
15. obstacle
16. sophomore
17. suitable
18. temperament

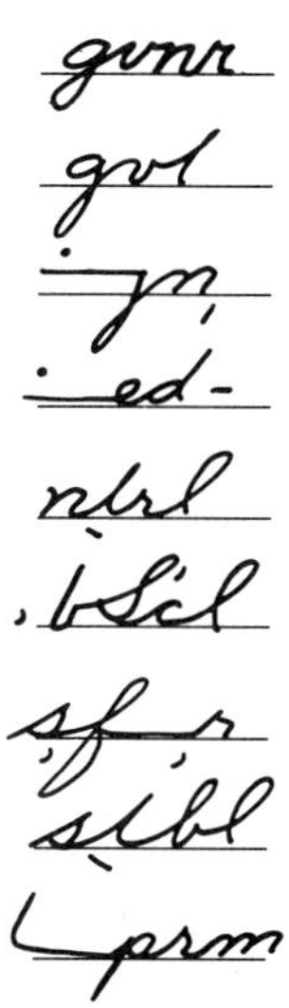

Chapter 21

WRITING SP, CT, AND INSTR

WRITING PRINCIPLES

Combination *sp*

Write a small printed *s* s to express the *sp* combination when no vowel occurs between the *s* and *p*.

Cover the print of the first line of words and read the outlines until you can read them easily. Then quickly write the outline for each word several times in your shorthand notebook. Follow the same procedure for all lines. When you can read the outlines fluently, cover them and write the outlines from the print. Verify the accuracy of your outlines.

Combination *ct*

Omit the *t* in the combination *ct* when *ct* ends a word. When the *ct* combination is followed by a common word ending such as *ing*, *ive*, *ed*, *ly*, or *s*, also omit the *t*.

active activity activities respect select district

subject connect fact deduct defects direct

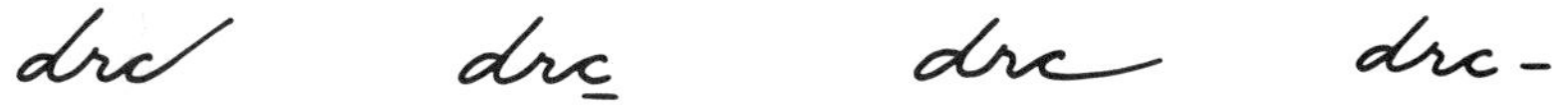

directs directed directing directly

director directive directors

As you read each word, write the correct outline several times in your notebook. When you have completed writing all words, you should be able to read and write them rapidly and accurately.

Combination *instr*

Write a disjoined capital *N*  to express the combination *instr* and the following vowel.

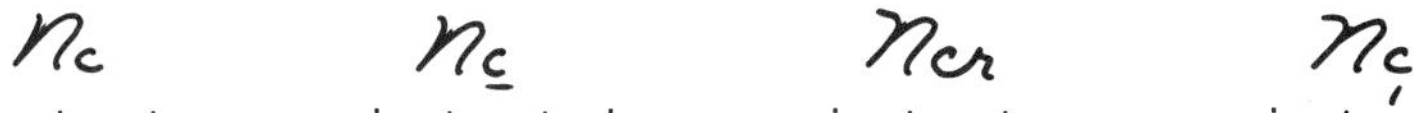

instruct instructed instructor instruction

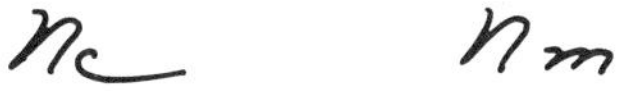

instructing instrument

As you read each outline write it three times in your notebook.

New vocabulary

Read and write the following words until you can do so easily.

correspond-correspondence March administrator

BUILDING TRANSCRIPTION SKILLS

Spelling review

The outlines which follow are for words commonly misspelled. Transcribe the words in your notebook. Check your spelling with a dictionary, a standard word reference list, or the *Forkner Shorthand Dictionary for Beginners*. Compare your answers with the key located at the end of the chapter. Write correctly any words you may have misspelled. Then write the shorthand outlines for all words until you can do so easily.

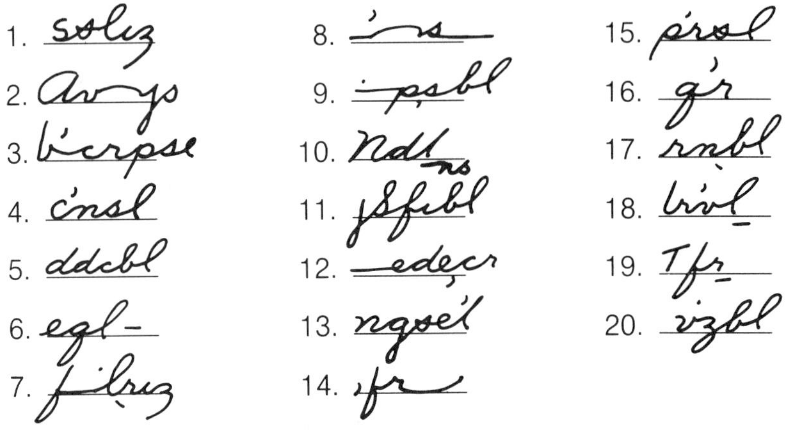

Titles used with personal names

1. Abbreviate the following titles when they are used with personal names: Dr., Mr., Mrs., and Ms. These abbreviations should be followed by a period. Miss and Misses are not abbreviations and should not be followed with periods.

2. In general, spell out all other titles when they are used with personal names: Professor, President, and Prime Minister.

APPLYING NEW PRINCIPLES

Follow these procedures in learning to read and write the sentences on page 151.

1. Read the shorthand outlines for each of the sentences until you can read all the sentences without hesitation.

2. Using the Transcript of Shorthand Sentences, write the shorthand outlines for each sentence in your notebook.

3. Check your outlines.

4. Write correctly three times each outline that you may have written incorrectly.

5. Rewrite the shorthand outlines as you read the sentences once again from the Transcript of Shorthand Sentences.

6. Transcribe the sentences from your own notes. Compare your transcript with the text transcript and circle any errors you may have made, including spelling and punctuation errors.

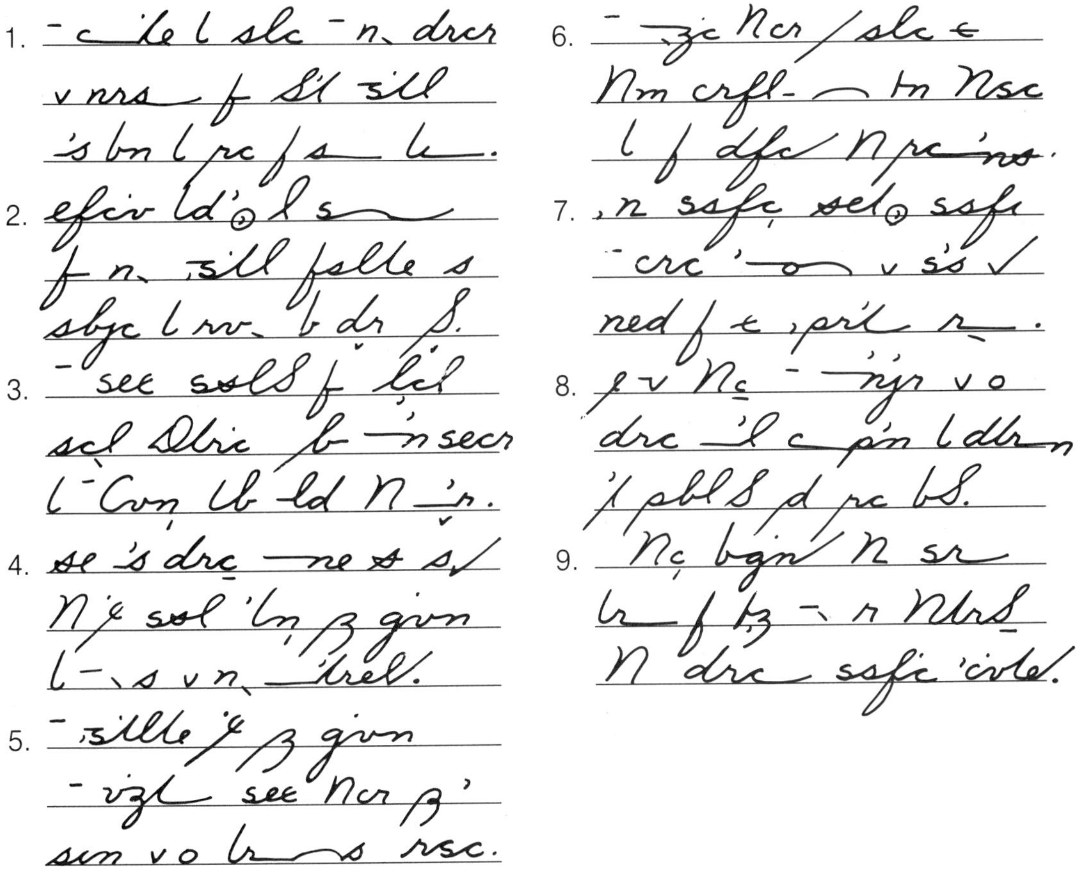

TRANSCRIPT OF SHORTHAND SENTENCES

1. The committee to select the new director of nursing for the state hospital has been at work for some time. (20)
2. Effective today, all spending for the new hospital facility is subject to review by Dr. West. (40)
3. The speech specialist for the local school district will be the main speaker at the convention to be held in March. (60)
4. She has directed many short sessions in which special attention was given to the use of new materials. (80)

5. The hospitality which was given the visiting speech instructor was a sign of our tremendous respect. (100)
6. The music instructor will select each instrument carefully and then inspect it for defects in workmanship. (120)
7. On the specification sheet, specify the correct amount of space you will need for each operating room. (140)
8. We have instructed the manager of our direct-mail campaign to determine what publicity would work best. (160)
9. Instruction begins in the spring term for those who are interested in directing specific activities. (180)

DICTATION AND TRANSCRIPTION

Write from dictation the Transcript of Shorthand Sentences. Your instructor will dictate each group of 20 words to you at various speeds. Select one set of notes, and transcribe it quickly and accurately.

BUILDING WRITING AND TRANSCRIPTION SPEEDS

New vocabulary

Read and write the following words and closing until you can do so easily.

Letter 1

Read the following letter from Walter Smith until you can read it fluently. Scribble-write the letter once for speed development. Then, as you read the letter from the transcript, make one good set of notes. Transcribe your notes. Use a fictitious inside address.

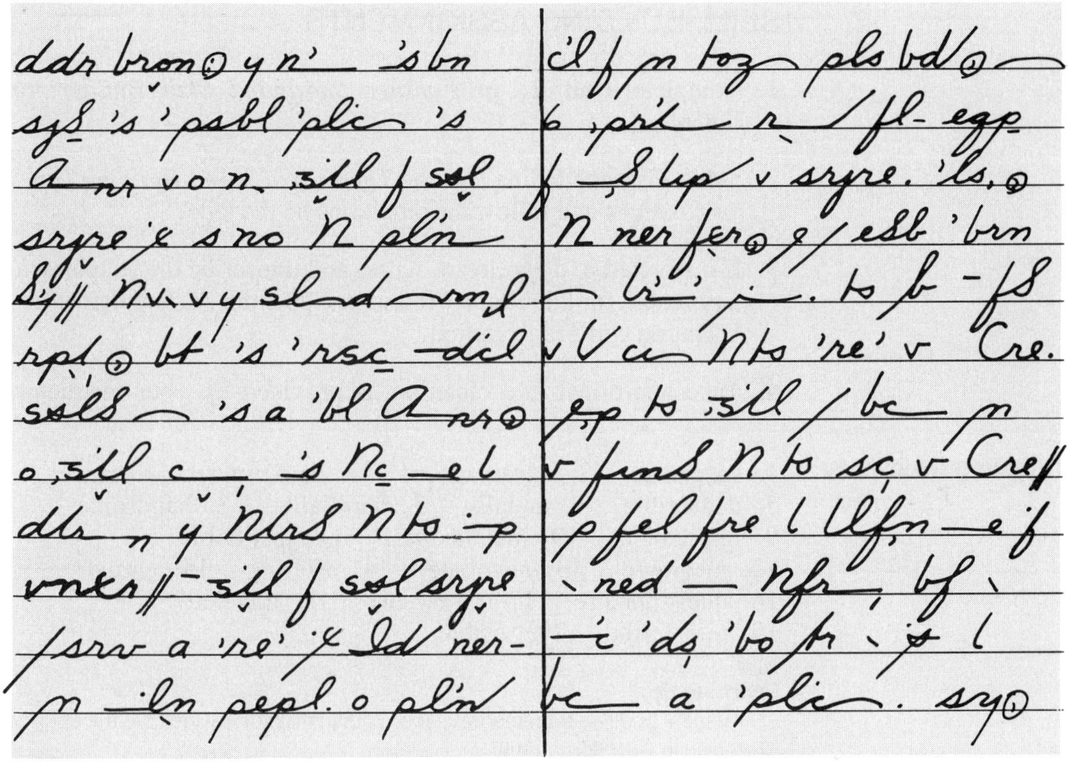

Letter 1 transcript

Dear Dr. Brown: Your name has been suggested as a possible applicant as administrator of our new (20) Hospital for Special Surgery which is now in the planning stage.

In view of your splendid international (40) reputation, both as a respected medical specialist and as an able administrator, our (60) Hospital Commission has instructed me to determine your interest in this important venture.

The Hospital (80) for Special Surgery will serve an area which includes nearly one million people. Our plans call for one (100) thousand plus beds, and six operating rooms fully equipped for most types of surgery. Also, in the near (120) future, we will establish a burn and trauma wing. This will be the first of its kind in this area of the (140) country. We hope this hospital will become one of the finest in this section of the country.

Please feel free to (160) telephone me if you need more information before you make a decision about whether you wish (180) to become an applicant. Sincerely yours, (186)

SKILL-BUILDING ASSIGNMENTS

1. Complete Unit 21 in *Forkner Shorthand Skill Builder for Colleges*.
2. Select Cassette 5 Side B of the *Theory and Speed-Building Tapes for Colleges* and follow the directions on the tape.
3. If instructed to do so, read, write, and transcribe the supplementary letters for this chapter found in Appendix A, Supplementary Dictation and Transcription.
4. Take additional live dictation as provided by your instructor.

Spelling review key

1. specialize 2. advantageous 3. bankruptcy 4. cancel
5. deductible 6. equally 7. familiarize 8. handsome
9. impossible 10. indebtedness 11. justifiable
12. mediocre 13. negotiate 14. offering 15. partial
16. questionnaire 17. renewable 18. traveled*
19. transferred 20. visible

Learning tip:

* Variant spelling traveled/travelled. Your instructor will indicate the spelling preferred in your community.

Chapter 22

WRITING RT-RD AND RITY

WRITING PRINCIPLES

Combinations *rt-rd*

Write a capital *R* to express the *rt-rd* combinations when no vowel occurs between the two letters.

report effort record quarter article accord

according quarterly part card board word

participate transportation toward certain third

start reported participation support reports

heard guard cardboard

Cover the printed words and read the outlines until you can read them rapidly. Then cover the shorthand and write each outline as you read it from the print. Check your outlines and correct any errors you may have made.

Combination *rity*

Write a disjoined capital *R* to express the combination *rity* and the preceding vowel.

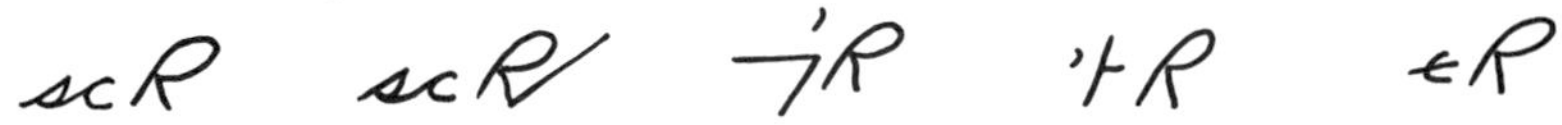

security securities majority authority charity

authorities familiarity

Read the outlines quickly with the print covered. Then, from the print, write each outline once. Read your notes back.

New vocabulary

As you read each word, write it three times in your notebook. After you have written all of the words, cover the print and as you say each word, write it once in your notebook. Transcribe your notes at your best typing rate.

BUILDING TRANSCRIPTION SKILLS

Introducing a series

Use a colon to introduce a series beginning with expressions such as *these*, *as follows*, and *the following*.

1. The following three countries sent representatives to the meeting: Canada, Mexico, and the United States.
2. Follow these directions in typing the letter:
   a. Use the block style.
   b. Use open punctuation.
   c. Make one carbon copy.

Learning tip:
When transcribing, remember to leave two spaces after the colon.

Application—**Introducing a series.** Type the following items. If a colon is required, type it in the appropriate place. If the sentence is correct, type it as is. Check your work with the key located in Appendix G at the back of the text.

1. Tickets are available at the following prices $4.75, $5.75, and $7.75.
2. Please type the following items a memo, a letter, and a short manuscript.

3. We were studying these three punctuation marks the comma, the colon, and the semicolon.
4. Type the following memo using these directions
   a. Use today's date.
   b. Do not indent paragraphs.
   c. Double space the body.
   d. Make one carbon copy.

Spelling review

The shorthand outlines in each sentence are for words that are commonly misspelled. Transcribe each outline in your notebook. Check your spelling with a dictionary, a standard word reference list, or the *Forkner Shorthand Dictionary for Beginners*. Compare your answers with the key located at the end of the chapter. Review any words you may have misspelled. Write the outlines until you can write them easily.

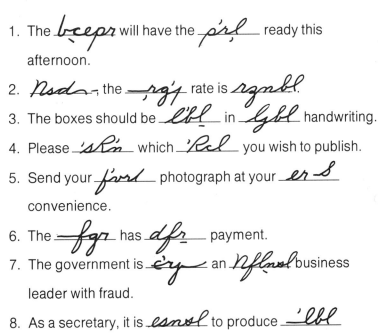

1. The  will have the  ready this afternoon.
2. , the 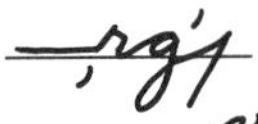 rate is .
3. The boxes should be  in  handwriting.
4. Please  which  you wish to publish.
5. Send your  photograph at your 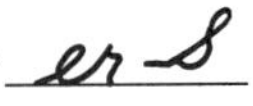 convenience.
6. The  has  payment.
7. The government is  an  business leader with fraud.
8. As a secretary, it is  to produce  letters.

9. A fvrbl yeld from investments is necessary.
10. The duplicator is not producing \zbl copy.

APPLYING NEW PRINCIPLES

Follow these procedures in learning to read and write the sentences below.

1. Read the shorthand outlines for each of the sentences until you can read all the sentences without hesitation.
2. Using the *Transcript of Shorthand Sentences*, write the shorthand outlines for each sentence in your notebook.
3. Check your outlines.
4. Write correctly three times each outline that you may have written incorrectly.
5. Rewrite the shorthand outlines as you read the sentences once again from the Transcript of Shorthand Sentences.
6. Transcribe the sentences from your own notes. Compare your transcript with the text transcript and circle any errors you may have made, including spelling and punctuation errors.

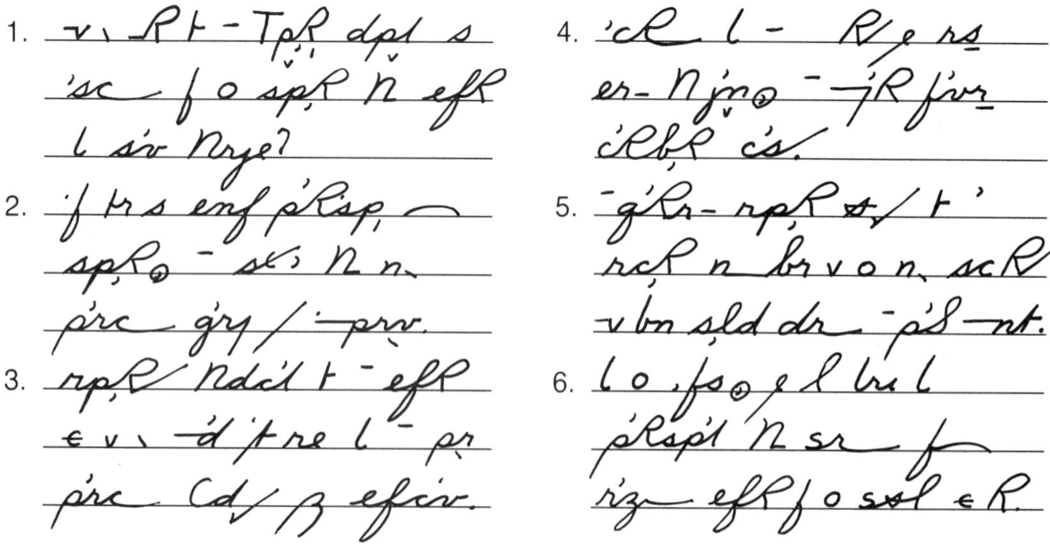

7. 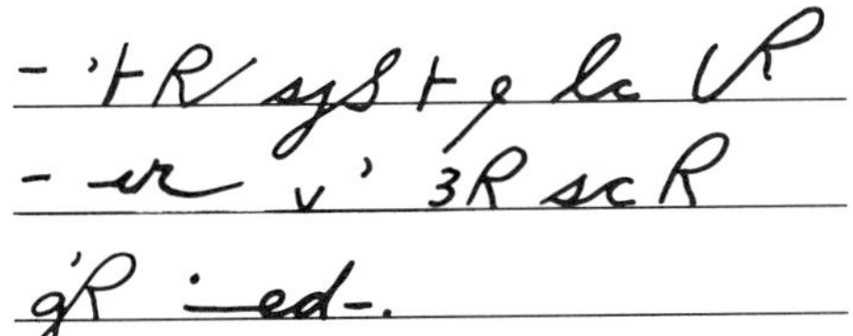

8. 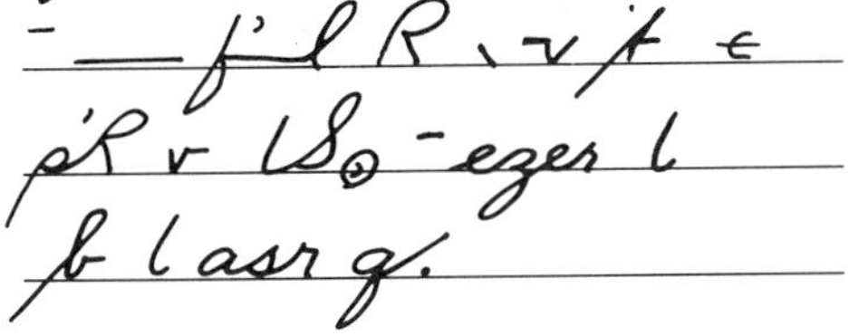

9. 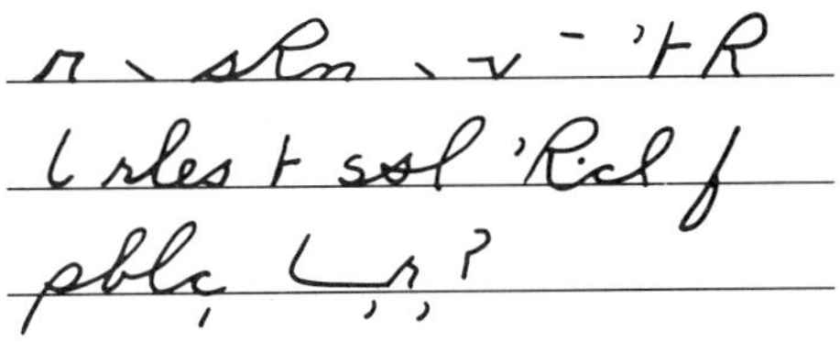

TRANSCRIPT OF SHORTHAND SENTENCES

1. Have you heard that the Transportation Department is asking for our support in the effort to save energy? (20)
2. If there is enough participation and support, the situation in the new parking garage will improve. (40)
3. Reports indicate that the effort each of you made with regard to the poor parking conditions was effective. (60)
4. According to the orders we received early in January, the majority favored cardboard cases. (80)
5. The quarterly report shows that a record number of our new securities have been sold during the past month. (100)
6. At our office, we all try to participate in the spring fund-raising effort for our special charity. (120)
7. The authorities suggest that we look toward the hiring of a third security guard immediately. (140)
8. The more familiarity you have with each part of the test, the easier it will be to answer questions. (160)
9. Are you certain you have the authority to release that special article for publication tomorrow? (180)

DICTATION AND TRANSCRIPTION

Write from dictation the Transcript of Shorthand Sentences. Your instructor will dictate each group of 20 words to you at various speeds. Select one set of notes, and transcribe it quickly and accurately.

BUILDING WRITING AND TRANSCRIPTION SPEEDS

New vocabulary

Read and write the following words until you can do so easily.

Sue Ford Shirley buyers women's planned

implemented maintained Burton Ace wardrobe

popularity articles records summary efforts

Memorandum 1

The following dictation is presented in the form of an interoffice memorandum. As you read the memorandum from the transcript, write the shorthand outlines in your notebook. Check your outlines with the text, and rewrite any outlines you may have written incorrectly. Reread your notes under timed conditions and calculate your reading rate. Keep your notes for use in Self-check 4 in *Forkner Shorthand Skill Builder for Colleges*.

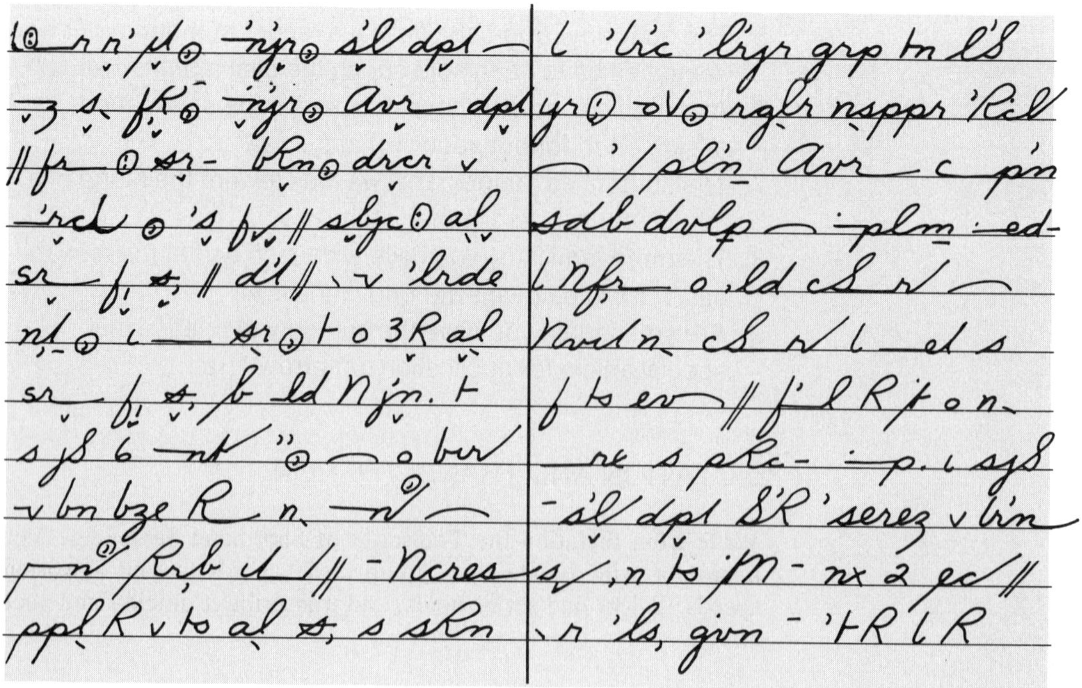

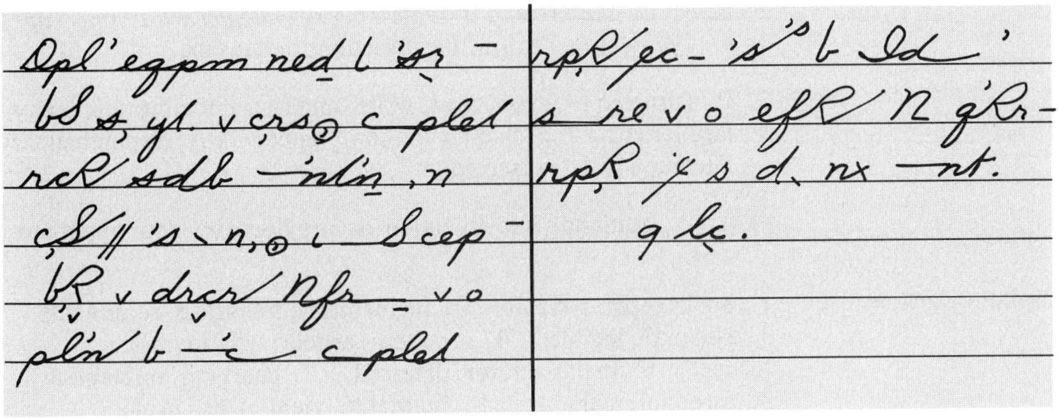

Memorandum 1
transcript

TO: Mr. Ray White, Manager, Sales Department and Ms. Sue Ford, Manager, Advertising Department
FROM: Shirley Burton, Director of Marketing, Ace Fashions
SUBJECT: Annual Spring Fashion Show
DATE: Use current date

You have already noted, I am sure, that our Third Annual Spring Fashion Show will be held in January. (20) That is just six months away, and our buyers have been busy ordering new men's and women's wardrobe items.

The (40) increasing popularity of this annual show is certain to attract a larger group than last year; (60) however, regular newspaper articles and a well-planned advertising campaign should be developed and (80) implemented immediately to inform our old customers and invite new customers to meet us for (100) this event.

Familiarity with our new merchandise is particularly important. I suggest the (120) Sales Department start a series of training sessions on this within the next two weeks.

You are also given the (140) authority to order display equipment needed to assure the best show yet. Of course, complete records should be (160) maintained on costs.

As you know, I must keep the Board of Directors informed of our plans by making complete reports (180) weekly as well as by including a summary of our efforts in the quarterly report which is due (200) next month. Good luck. (203)

SKILL-BUILDING ASSIGNMENTS

1. Complete Unit 22 in *Forkner Shorthand Skill Builder for Colleges*.

2. Select Cassette 6 Side B of the *Theory and Speed-Building Tapes for Colleges* and follow the directions on the tape.

3. If instructed to do so, read, write, and transcribe the supplementary letter for this chapter found in Appendix A, Supplementary Dictation and Transcription.

4. Take additional live dictation as provided by your instructor.

Spelling review key

1. bookkeeper, payroll 2. incidentally, mortgage, reasonable 3. labeled*, legible 4. ascertain, article 5. favorite, earliest 6. manufacturer, deferred 7. charging, influential 8. essential, mailable 9. favorable, yield 10. usable

Learning tip:

*Variant spelling labeled/labelled. Your instructor will indicate the spelling acceptable in your community.

Chapter 23

WRITING SOUNDS OF OI-OY, NCE-NSE, AND POST AND POSITION

WRITING PRINCIPLES

Sound of *oi-oy*

Write a dotted *i* *i* to express the sound of *oi-oy*.

point choice employee boys boy's voice

enjoy employment appoint employees

unemployment appointed avoid oil

join points

Cover the printed words and read the outlines until you can read them without hesitating. Then build your writing speed by scribble-writing the outlines in your notebook.

Combinations *nce-nse*

Write a small, disjoined *n* *n* to express the combinations *nce-nse* and the preceding vowel. Write the disjoined *n* close to the word to which it belongs.

insurance conference since-sense balance advance

agency chance ounce license reference

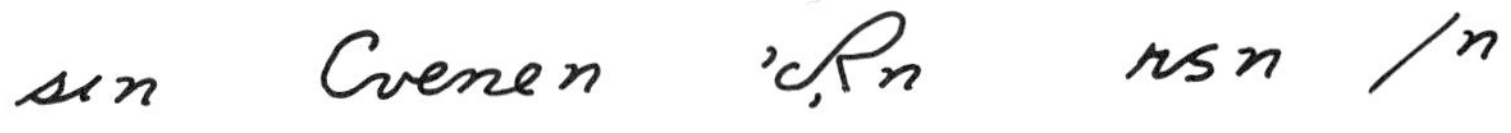

science convenience accordance response once

As you read each outline, write it three times in your notebook. When you have written all the words, you should be able to read and write them rapidly and accurately. Cover the outlines and write them from the print. Read your notes and correct any errors you may have made.

Prefix and suffix *post* and *position*

Write a capital *P*  to express the prefix and suffix *post* and *position*. Begin the first stroke of *P* on the line and write upward.

post-position posted postage postpone postdate

disposition imposition-impost post office post offices

As you read each outline, write it three times in your notebook. Then cover the print and write the outlines once. Read your notes and correct any errors you may have made.

New vocabulary

Read and write the following words until you can read and write them easily.

sincere-sincerely *remember* avenue October invoice

Incorporated invoices invoicing invoiced

Learning tip:

Remember when *sincerely* is used as part of a complimentary close, you use only the *s*. Examples: *Sincerely yours* 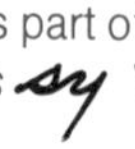 *Yours* sincerely .

BUILDING TRANSCRIPTION SKILLS

Spelling review

All of the words which follow are commonly misspelled. Write each of the words in shorthand in your notebook. Compare your outlines with those in the key located at the end of the chapter. Then, see if you can correctly spell all the words as you transcribe your own shorthand notes. Check the accuracy of your spelling.

1. destroy
2. appearance
3. absence
4. argument
5. difference
6. conscientious

7. guidance
8. guard
9. irrelevant
10. interfere
11. occasionally
12. occurrence
13. competent
14. disappoint
15. license
16. measurement
17. invoicing
18. totaling*
19. serviceable
20. responsible

Learning tip:
*Variant spelling totaling/totalling. Your instructor will indicate the spelling preferred in your community.

APPLYING NEW PRINCIPLES

Follow these procedures in learning to read and write the sentences below.

1. Read the shorthand outlines for each of the sentences until you can read all the sentences without hesitation.
2. Using the Transcript of Shorthand Sentences, write the shorthand outlines for each sentence in your notebook.
3. Check your outlines.
4. Write correctly three times each outline that you may have written incorrectly.
5. Rewrite the shorthand outlines as you read the sentences once again from the Transcript of Shorthand Sentences.
6. Transcribe the sentences from your own notes. Compare your transcript with the text transcript and circle any errors you may have made, including spelling and punctuation errors.

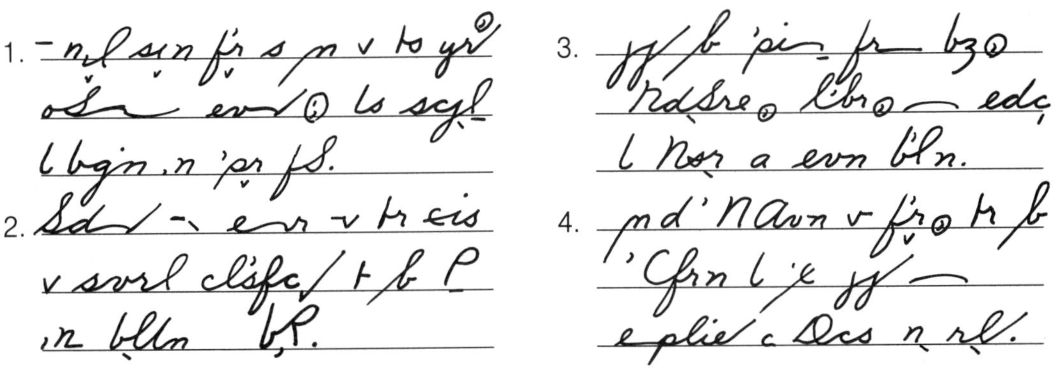

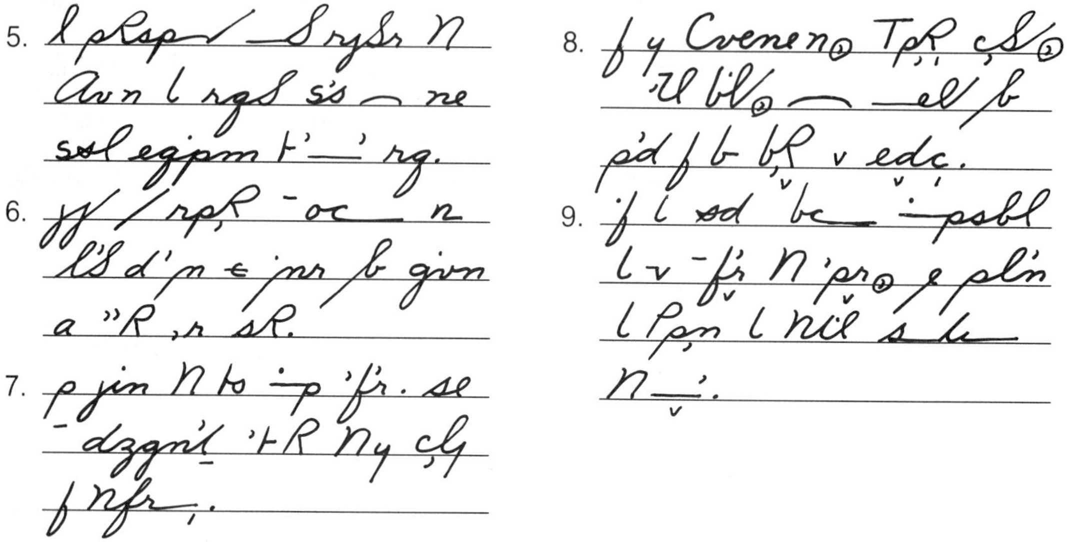

TRANSCRIPT OF SHORTHAND SENTENCES

1. The National Science Fair is one of this year's outstanding events; it is scheduled to begin on April first. (20)
2. Students who enter have their choice of several classifications that will be posted on the bulletin board. (40)
3. Judges will be appointed from business, industry, labor, and education to ensure an even balance. (60)
4. One day in advance of the Fair, there will be a conference at which judges and employees can discuss new rules. (80)
5. All participants must register in advance to request space and any special equipment they may require. (100)
6. Judges will report the outcome on the last day, when each winner will be given an award or certificate. (120)
7. Please join in this important affair. See the designated authority in your college for information. (140)
8. For your convenience, transportation costs, hotel bills, and meals will be paid for by the Board of Education. (160)
9. If it should become impossible to have the Fair in April, we plan to postpone it until sometime in May. (180)

DICTATION AND TRANSCRIPTION

Write from dictation the Transcript of Shorthand Sentences. Your instructor will dictate each group of 20 words to you at various speeds. Select one set of notes, and transcribe it quickly and accurately.

BUILDING WRITING AND TRANSCRIPTION SPEEDS

New vocabulary

Read and write the following words until you can do so easily.

discussing published textbook evaluate homeowner

homeowners classroom supplement twenty-five

Letter 1

After learning the new vocabulary words, you should find it quite easy to read the following letter from Ms. Debby Morris. Read the letter until you can read it without hesitation. Then using the transcript, write the shorthand outlines for the letter as you read from the print. Read your notes. If there are any outlines which cause you to hesitate, check them with the shorthand below, and rewrite them accurately several times. Transcribe the letter using a fictitious inside address.

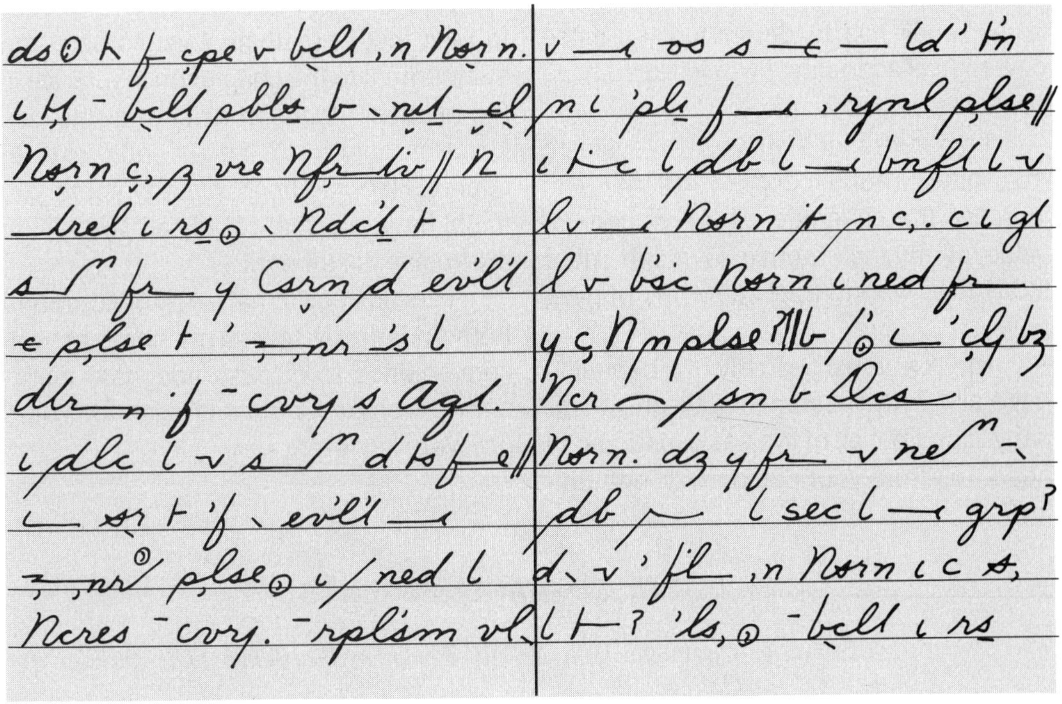

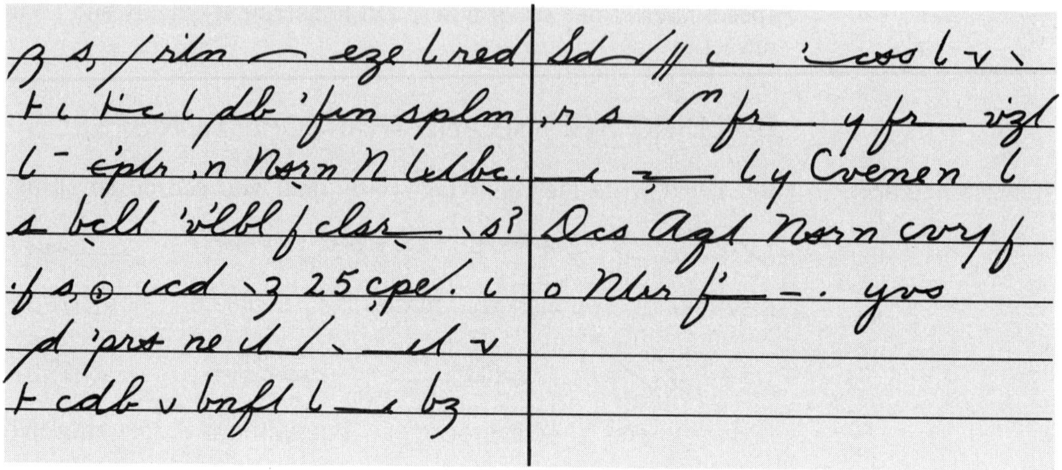

Letter 1 transcript

Dear Sir: Thank you for the copy of the booklet on insurance. I thought the booklet published by the United (20) Mutual Insurance Company was very informative.

In the material I received, you indicated (40) that someone from your Concern would evaluate each policy that a homeowner has to determine (60) if the coverage is adequate. I would like to have someone do this for me.

I am sure that after you (80) evaluate my homeowner's policy, I will need to increase the coverage. The replacement value of my (100) house is much more today than when I applied for my original policy.

I think it would be to my (120) benefit to have all of my insurance with one company. Can I get all of the basic insurance I need (140) from your company in one policy?

By the way, I am a college busines instructor and will soon be (160) discussing insurance. Does your firm have anyone who would be willing to speak to my group? Do you have a film on (180) insurance I can show to them? Also, the booklet I received was so well written and easy to read that I (200) think it would be a fine supplement to the chapter on insurance in the textbook. Is the booklet available (220) for classroom use? If so, I could use 25 copies. I would appreciate any items you might have (240) that could be of benefit to my business students.

I am anxious to have you or someone from your firm visit (260) my home at your convenience to discuss adequate insurance coverage for our entire family. Yours (280) very sincerely, (284)

SKILL-BUILDING ASSIGNMENTS

1. Complete Unit 23 in *Forkner Shorthand Skill Builder for Colleges*.

2. Select Cassette 7 Side B of the *Theory and Speed-Building Tapes for Colleges* and follow the directions on the tape.

3. If instructed to do so, read, write, and transcribe the supplementary letter for this chapter found in Appendix A, Supplementary Dictation and Transcription.

4. Take additional live dictation as provided by your instructor.

Spelling review key

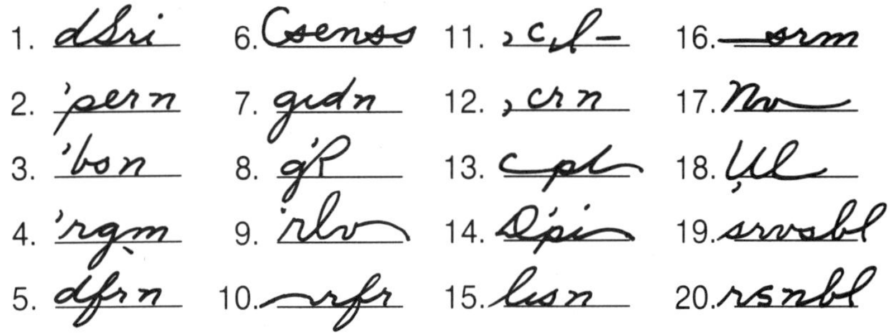

Chapter 24

BUSINESS DICTATION AND TRANSCRIPTION

BUILDING TRANSCRIPTION SKILLS

Making corrections

If you have not already begun to do so, you should now begin correcting any transcription errors you may have made. This is a major step toward producing mailable correspondence. You are probably familiar with, or have used, an eraser, correc-type, liquid paper, or the self-correcting typewriter. In correcting your errors, use the method your instructor prefers. Remember that a good correction is one that cannot be detected by the reader.

Enumerations in letters

When typing letters containing enumerations, follow these common guidelines:

1. Treat each enumeration as a separate paragraph.
2. Single space each enumeration, but leave a double space before and after the enumerated item.
3. If paragraphs are indented, indent each enumeration.
4. If paragraphs begin flush with the left margin, type the enumerations flush with the left margin.
5. If an enumeration is longer than one line, align the second and subsequent lines below the first letter of the first word in the enumeration.

Series of questions

Each question within a sentence should be followed by a question mark. Double space after each question mark.

Example: Will the books be colorful? well-illustrated? inexpensive?

BUILDING WRITING AND TRANSCRIPTION SPEEDS

New vocabulary

Read and write the following words until you can do so easily.

shorthand tests testing ways determining

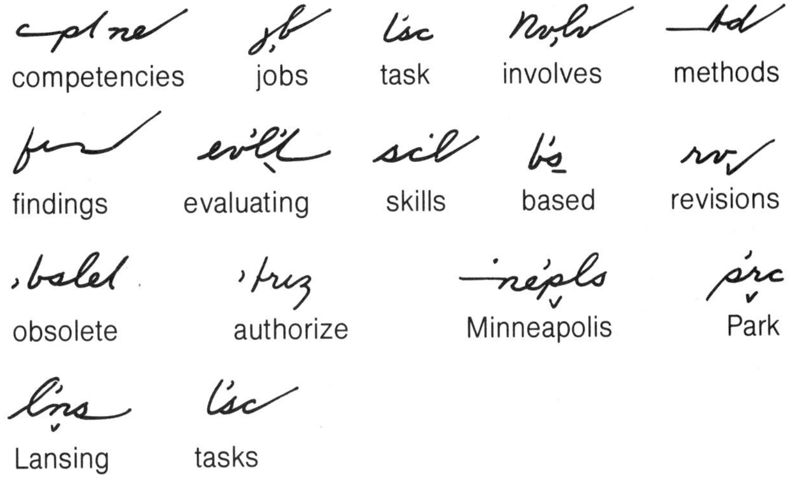

Letter 1

Read Letter 1 until you can read it fluently. Then using the self-dictation method, write the letter in shorthand until you can write it quickly and accurately. You may also wish to have someone dictate the letter to you. Finally, make one good set of notes and read them back.

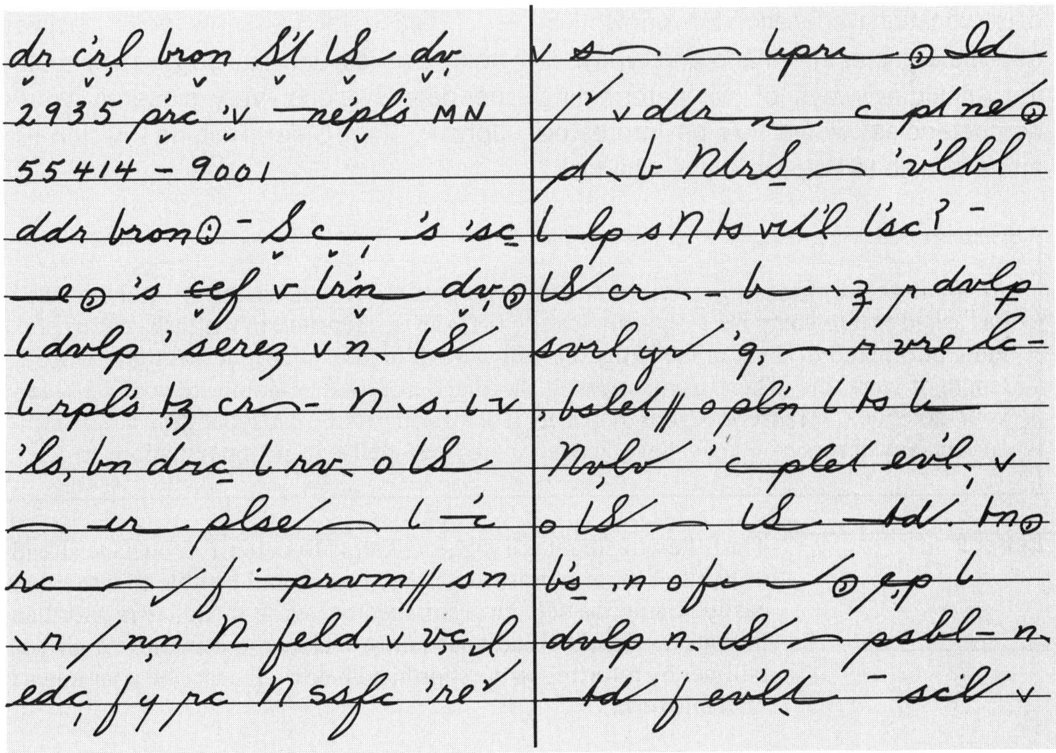

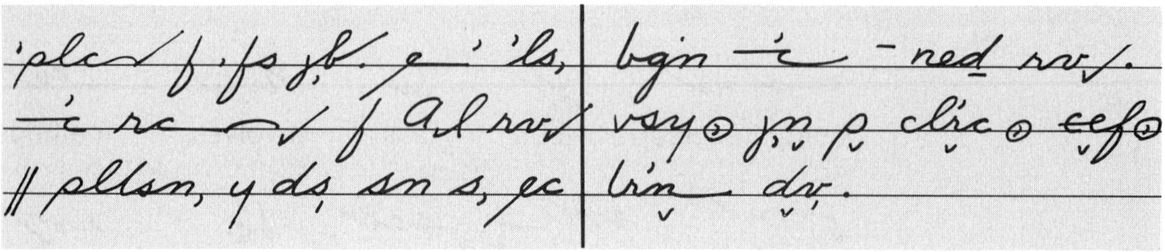

Letter 1 transcript

Dr. Carol Brown, State Testing Division, 2935 Park Avenue, Minneapolis, MN 55414-9001

Dear Dr. Brown: The City Commission has asked me, as Chief of the Training Division, to develop a (20) series of new tests to replace those currently in use. I have also been directed to review our testing and (40) hiring policies and to make recommendations for improvement.

Since you are well known in the field of (60) vocational education for your work in specific areas of shorthand and typewriting, including ways of (80) determining competencies, would you be interested and available to help us in this vital task? (100) The tests currently being used were developed several years ago and are very likely obsolete.

Our plan (120) at this time involves a complete evaluation of our tests and testing methods. Then, based on our findings, we hope (140) to develop new tests and possibly new methods for evaluating the skills of applicants for office (160) jobs. We may also make recommendations for additional revisions.

Please let us know your decision soon (180) so we can begin making the needed revisions. Very sincerely yours, John P. Clark, Chief, Training Division (200)

Application – **Composing a letter**. Assume you are Dr. Brown's secretary and that she has asked you to compose a reply indicating that she is interested in the task, but needs more information. Think of the items she will want to inquire about such as time, place, length of work, etc. Then, using as much shorthand as possible, compose your reply in your notebook. Transcribe your notes in letter form. Proofread your transcript and correct any errors you may have made, including spelling and punctuation errors.

Letter 2

The following letter is a suggested reply to Letter 1. You have already used all of these words; therefore, you should be able to write them easily. Using the self-dictation method, write the letter in shorthand in your notebook. Read your notes. Verify the accuracy of all your outlines by referring to the shorthand below. Transcribe your notes in mailable form.

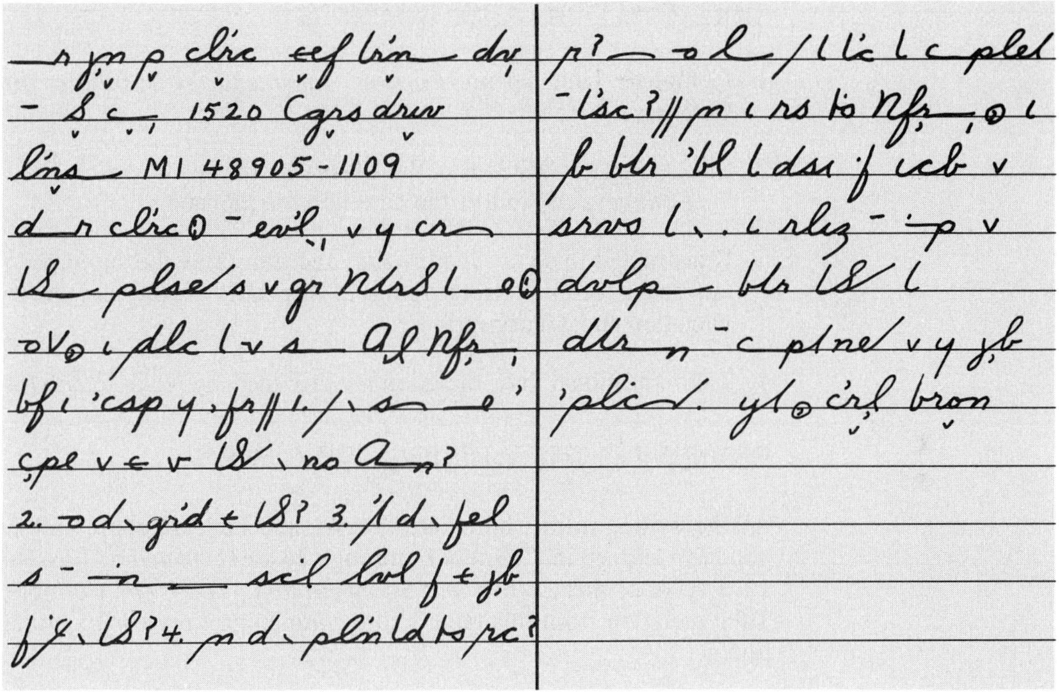

Letter 2 transcript

Mr. John P. Clark, Chief, Training Division, The City Commission, 1520 Congress Drive, Lansing, MI 48905-1109

Dear Mr. Clark: The evaluation of your current testing policies is of great interest to me; (20) however, I would like to have some additional information before I accept your offer.

1. Will you send (40) me a copy of each of the tests you now administer? 2. How do you grade each test? 3. What do you feel is (60) the minimum skill level for each job for which you test? 4. When do you plan to do this work? where? and how long will (80) it take to complete the task?

When I receive this information, I will be better able to decide if I (100) can be of service to you. I realize the importance of developing better tests to determine the (120) competencies of your job applicants. Yours truly, Carol Brown (131)

DICTATION AND TRANSCRIPTION

Write from dictation Letters 1 and 2. Your instructor will dictate each letter to you at various speeds.

Using your own notes, transcribe the letters using an appropriate business correspondence format.

SKILL-BUILDING ASSIGNMENTS

1. Complete Unit 24 in *Forkner Shorthand Skill Builder for Colleges*.

2. Select Cassette 8 Side B of the *Theory and Speed-Building Tapes for Colleges*, and follow the directions on the tape.

3. If instructed to do so, read, write, and transcribe the supplementary letter for this chapter found in Appendix A, Supplementary Dictation and Transcription.

4. Take additional live dictation as provided by your instructor.

REVIEWING THE WRITING PRINCIPLES

All the writing rules, abbreviated words, and standard abbreviations you have learned in Chapters 17 through 24 are reviewed on Cassette 18 Side A of the *Theory and Speed-Building Tapes for Colleges*. Take dictation from this tape before completing Preview Examination 6.

PREVIEW EXAMINATION 6

Remove Preview Examination 6 from your *Forkner Shorthand Skill Builder for Colleges*. It follows Unit 32. This informal preview examination will help you in assessing your understanding of the Forkner principles presented in Chapters 21–24. It is similar to Examination 6 which may be administered at a later date by your instructor.

Complete Preview Examination 6 and then check your answers carefully with the key in your *Forkner Shorthand Skill Builder for Colleges*. Correct any errors you may have made.

Chapter 25

WRITING FOR-FORE-FER-FUR, BILITY, AND LETTER-LITER

WRITING PRINCIPLES

Prefixes *for-fore-fer-fur*

Write a disjoined *f* for the prefixes *for-fore-fer-fur*. The disjoined *f* is used *only* when it represents a syllable.

Compare: *form* *formal*

further furnish formal forest former forget

fortunate forecast fertile furnished unfortunately

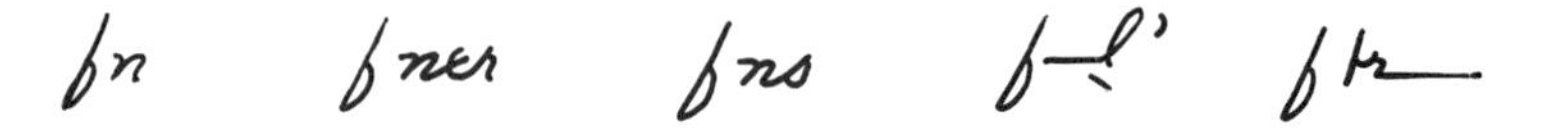

foreign furniture furnace formula furthermore

Read the first word and write its shorthand outline in your notebook. Then, read the first two words and write their shorthand outlines in your notebook. Follow this procedure until all words have been written. Your shorthand notebook should look like this:

Combination *bility*

Write a capital *B* to express the combination *bility* and the preceding vowel. Note how the *B* is joined to the preceding letter.

ability liability possibility responsibility dependability

flexibility capability desirability feasibility stability

eligibility   reliability   instability

Read the outlines quickly with the print covered. Then, from the print, write each outline once. Read your notes.

Combinations
letter-liter

Write a capital *L*  to express the combinations *letter-liter*

letter   letters   letterhead   literature   literary

newsletter   letterheads

Cover the printed words and read the outlines until you can read them rapidly. Then cover the outlines and write each word as you read it from the print. Check your notes, and correct any errors you may have made.

BUILDING TRANSCRIPTION SKILLS

Spelling review

The shorthand outlines in each sentence are for words that are commonly misspelled. Transcribe the shorthand outlines in your notebook. You may use a dictionary, a standard word reference list, or the *Forkner Shorthand Dictionary for Beginners* to verify the spelling. Compare your answers with the key located at the end of the chapter. If you spelled any of the words incorrectly, rewrite them accurately. Then write the shorthand outline for each word several times for speed building.

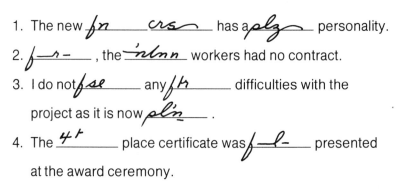

1. The new   has a  personality.
2. 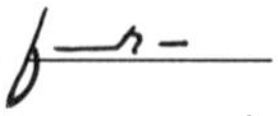, the  workers had no contract.
3. I do not  any 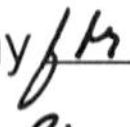 difficulties with the project as it is now 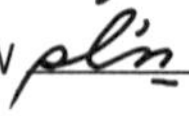.
4. The 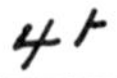 place certificate was  presented at the award ceremony.

5. A cRes receptionist will dvlp friendly relationships with our customers.
6. sRn Cvenen foods are very expensive.
7. We should do c p'rliv shopping in all dpl.
8. The [illegible] of your signature on the lease made it invalid.
9. Will it be Cvene for you to drive this week?
10. The staff has been 'rg about the type of Ld we should use.

Word usage

Study the following groups of words. Notice that within the groups the words sound similar or alike, but have different meanings. Learn the meaning of each word.

Word	Definition
lessen	decrease
lesson	assignment
know	understand
no	refusal
fair	equitable, pleasing
fare	price, to get along
ate	consumed
eight	a number, 8
your	belonging to you
you're	you are

Application — **Word Usage**. In your notebook number from 1 — 5. Complete each of the following sentences by writing the correct word opposite the appropriate sentence number. Check your work with the key located in Appendix G at the back of this text.

1. Please (lessen, lesson) the tension on the rope.
2. Do you (know, no) the distance from Seattle to Vancouver?
3. The (fair, fare) for the dinner seems (fair, fare).
4. We (ate, eight) dinner at (ate, eight) last evening.
5. If (your, you're) going to be on time, you'd better locate (your, you're) watch.

APPLYING NEW PRINCIPLES

Follow these procedures in learning to read and write the sentences below.

1. Read the shorthand outlines for each of the sentences until you can read all the sentences without hesitation.
2. Using the Transcript of Shorthand Sentences, write the shorthand outlines for each sentence in your notebook.
3. Check your outlines.
4. Write correctly three times each outline that you may have written incorrectly.
5. Rewrite the shorthand outlines as you read the sentences once again from the Transcript of Shorthand Sentences.
6. Transcribe the sentences from your own notes. Compare your transcript with the text transcript and circle any errors you may have made, including spelling and punctuation errors.

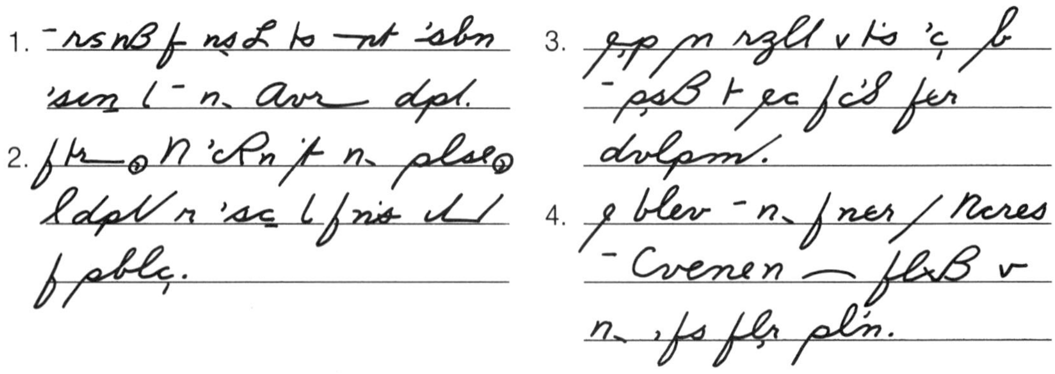

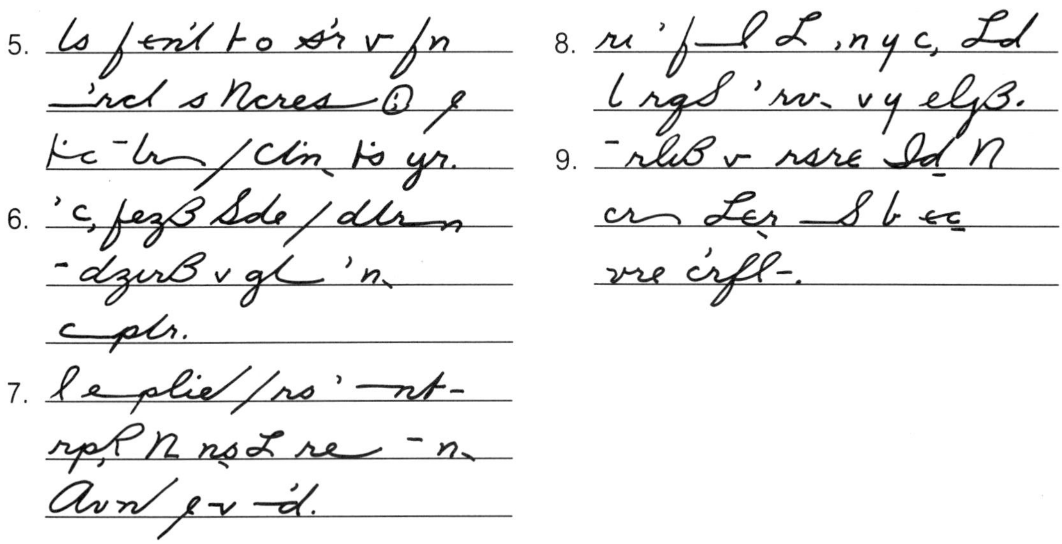

TRANSCRIPT OF SHORTHAND SENTENCES

1. The responsibility for the newsletter this month has been assigned to the new advertising department. (20)
2. Furthermore, in accordance with new policy, all departments are asked to furnish items for publication. (40)
3. We hope one result of this action will be the possibility that we can forecast future developments. (60)
4. We believe the new furniture will increase the convenience and flexibility of the new office floor plan. (80)
5. It is fortunate that our share of the foreign market is increasing; we think the trend will continue this year. (100)
6. A company feasibility study will determine the desirability of getting a new computer. (120)
7. All employees will receive a monthly report in the newsletter regarding the new advances we have made. (140)
8. Write a formal letter on your company letterhead to request a review of your eligibility. (160)
9. The reliability of the research included in current literature must be checked very carefully. (180)

DICTATION AND TRANSCRIPTION

Write from dictation the Transcript of Shorthand Sentences. Your instructor will dictate each group of 20 words to you at various speeds. Select one set of notes, and transcribe it quickly and accurately.

BUILDING WRITING AND TRANSCRIPTION SPEEDS

New vocabulary

Read and write the following words until you can do so easily.

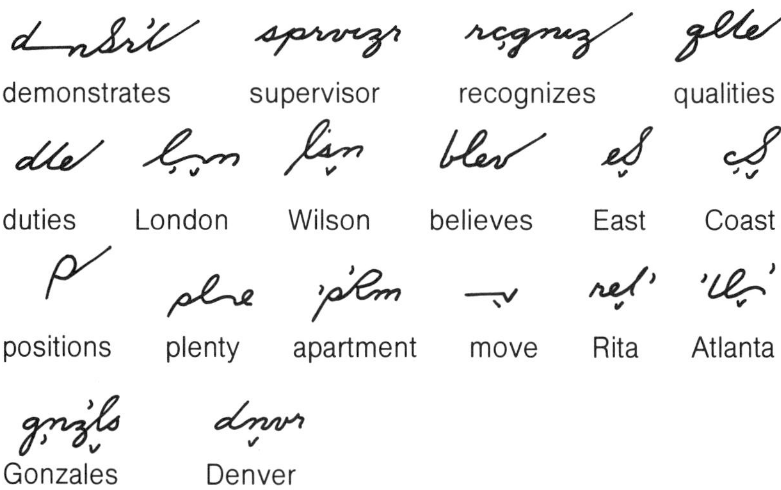

Letter 1

Read the following letter until you can do so fluently. Then, using the self-dictation method, write the letter as you read from the transcript. Finally, from the transcript, write the letter once and transcribe it, correcting any errors you may have made.

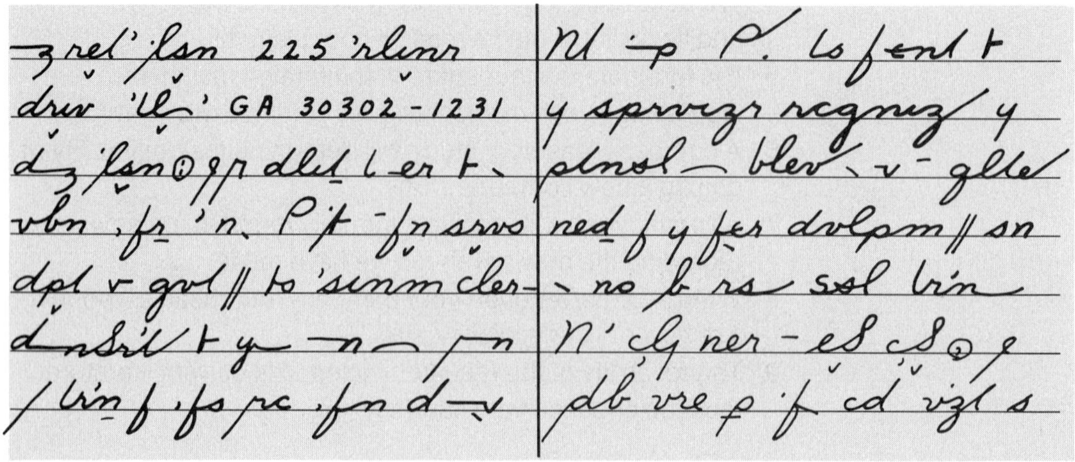

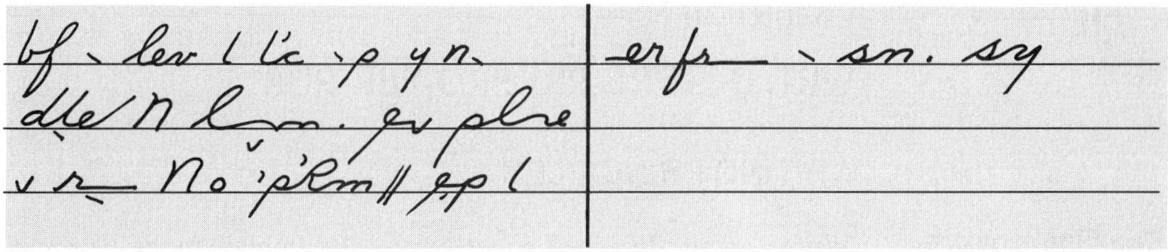

Letter 1 transcript

Ms. Rita Wilson, 225 Airliner Drive, Atlanta, GA 30302-1231 Dear Ms. Wilson: We were delighted to hear that you have been offered a new position with the Foreign Service (20) Department of the government.

This assignment clearly demonstrates that young men and women well trained for (40) office work often do move into important positions. It is fortunate that your supervisor recognizes (60) your potential and believes you have the qualities needed for your future development.

Since you now will (80) be receiving special training in a college near the East Coast, we would be very pleased if you could visit us (100) before you leave to take up your new duties in London. We have plenty of room in our apartment.

We hope to (120) hear from you soon. Sincerely yours, (126)

NOTE: Where addresses are provided, the word count begins with the salutation.

SKILL-BUILDING ASSIGNMENTS

1. Complete Unit 25 in *Forkner Shorthand Skill Builder for Colleges*.
2. Select Cassette 9 Side B of the *Theory and Speed-Building Tapes for Colleges* and follow the instructions on the tape.
3. If instructed to do so, read, write, and transcribe the supplementary letter for this chapter found in Appendix A, Supplementary Dictation and Transcription.
4. Take additional live dictation as provided by your instructor.

Spelling review key

1. foreign, correspondent, pleasant 2. Formerly, maintenance
3. foresee, further, planned 4. fourth, formally
5. courteous, develop 6. Certain, convenience
7. comparative, departments 8. omission 9. convenient
10. arguing, letterhead

Chapter 26

WRITING PRE-PRI-PRO-PER-PUR

WRITING PRINCIPLES

Combinations *pre-pri-pro-per-pur*

Write a small, disjoined *p* to express the combinations *pre-pri-pro-per-pur* when they begin a word containing more than one syllable.

Examples:

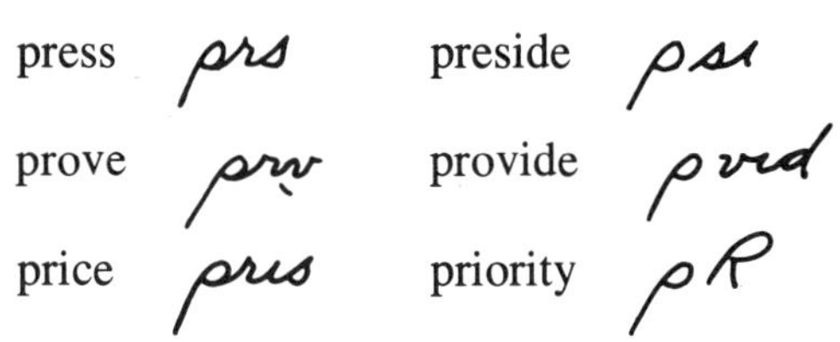

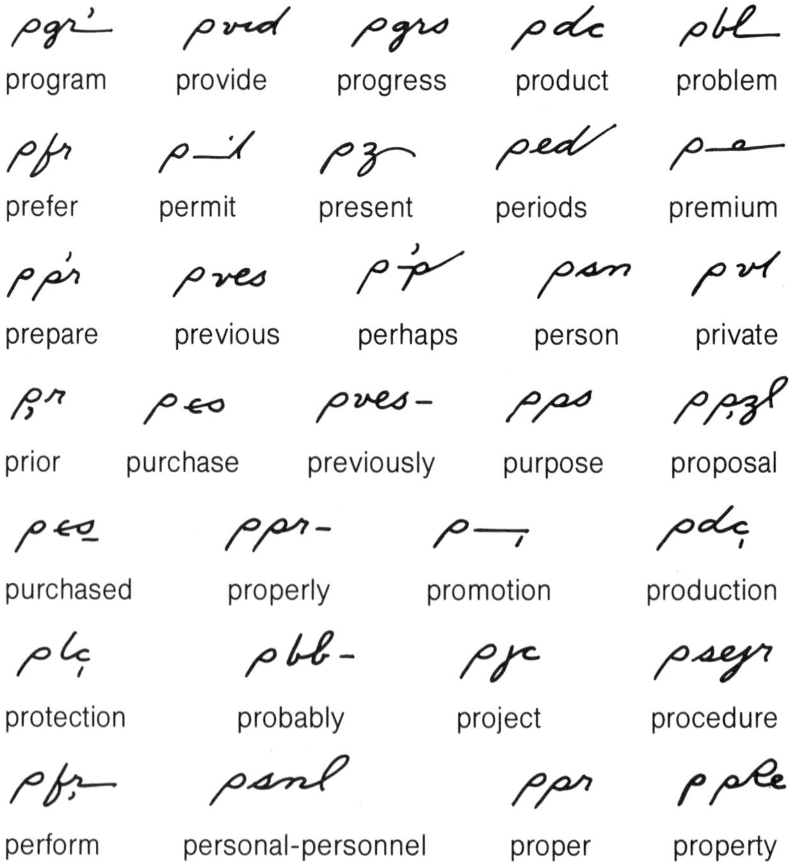

As you read each word, write the corresponding shorthand outline three times or until you can write it accurately without hesitation. Then, write each outline once. Transcribe your notes three times.

BUILDING TRANSCRIPTION SKILLS

Spelling review

The outlines which follow are for words that are commonly misspelled. Transcribe the outlines in your notebook. Check your spelling with a dictionary, a standard word reference list, or the *Forkner Shorthand Dictionary for Beginners*. If the shorthand outline represents more than one word, give all the spellings. Compare your answers with the key located at the end of the chapter. Write correctly any words you may have misspelled. Then, write the shorthand outlines for all the words until you can write them without hesitation.

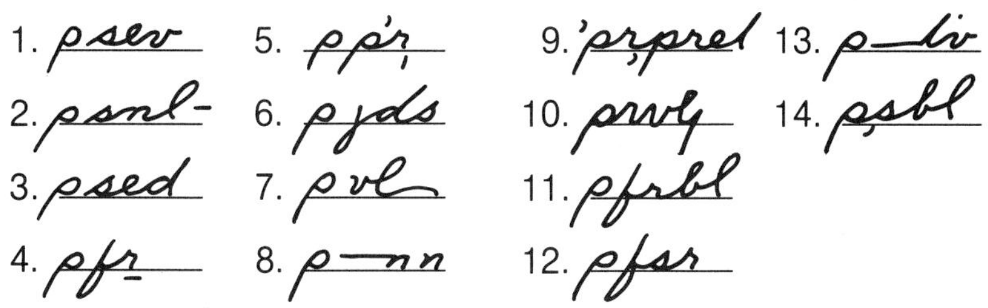

Word usage

Study the following groups of words. Notice that within the groups, the words sound similar or alike, but have different meanings. Learn the meanings of each.

Word	Definition
residents	persons living in a place
residence	place where one lives
attendance	act of attending
attendants	those who perform a service
billed	furnished with a bill
build	to construct something

assistants	helpers
assistance	help, aid
presence	being present
presents	gifts; gives
confidant	one trusted with secrets
confident	self-assured
patience	calmness
patients	people who are ill
some	part or portion
sum	whole amount; total
stair	a step
stare	to gaze

Application — **Word usage**. In your notebook number from 1 — 10. Complete each of the following sentences by writing the correct word opposite the appropriate sentence number. Check your work with the key located in Appendix G at the back of this text.

1. The (residents, residence) of the building were angry.
2. There were many (patience, patients) at the clinic.
3. Your (attendance, attendants) is required at all meetings.
4. The team was (confidant, confident) it would win.
5. You will be (build, billed) for a delivery charge.
6. The (assistants, assistance) in the lab were very helpful.
7. (Some, Sum) people are allergic to dust.
8. Their summer (residents, residence) is in South America.

9. The (presence, presents) of all staff members is requested.
10. Do not (stare, stair) at the bright sun.

APPLYING NEW PRINCIPLES

Follow these procedures in learning to read and write the sentences below.

1. Read the shorthand outlines for each of the sentences until you can read all the sentences without hesitation.
2. Using the Transcript of Shorthand Sentences, write the shorthand outlines for each sentence in your notebook.
3. Check your outlines.
4. Write correctly three times each outline that you may have written incorrectly.
5. Rewrite the shorthand outlines as you read the sentences once again from the Transcript of Shorthand Sentences.
6. Transcribe the sentences from your own notes. Compare your transcript with the text transcript and circle any errors you may have made, including spelling and punctuation errors.

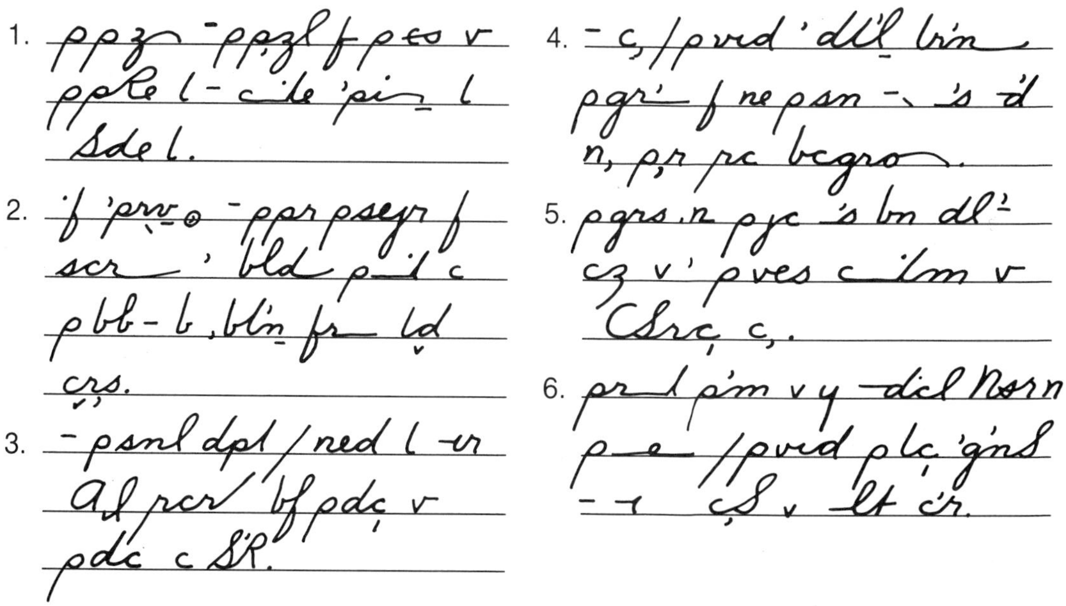

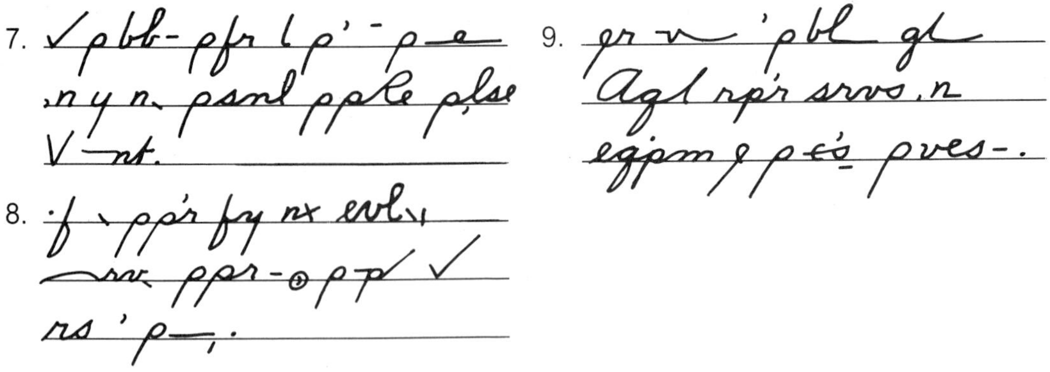

TRANSCRIPT OF SHORTHAND SENTENCES

1. Please present the proposal for the purchase of the property to the committee appointed to study it. (20)
2. If approved, the proper procedure for securing a building permit can probably be obtained from Ted Cross. (40)
3. The personnel department will need to hire additional workers before production of the product can start. (60)
4. The company will provide a detailed training program for any person who has had no prior work background. (80)
5. Progress on the project has been delayed because of a previous commitment of the construction company. (100)
6. Prompt payment of your medical insurance premium will provide protection against the high cost of health care. (120)
7. You will probably prefer to pay the premium on your new personal property policy every month. (140)
8. If you prepare for your next evaluation interview properly, perhaps you will receive a promotion. (160)
9. We are having a problem getting adequate repair service on the equipment we purchased previously. (180)

DICTATION AND TRANSCRIPTION

Write from dictation the Transcript of Shorthand Sentences. Your instructor will dictate each group of 20 words to you at various speeds. Select one set of notes, and transcribe it quickly and accurately.

SKILL-BUILDING ASSIGNMENTS

1. Complete Unit 26 in *Forkner Shorthand Skill Builder for Colleges*.

2. Select Cassette 10 Side B of the *Theory and Speed-Building Tapes for Colleges*, and follow the directions on the tape.

3. If instructed to do so, read, write and transcribe the supplementary letter for this chapter found in Appendix A, Supplementary Dictation and Transcription.

4. Take additional live dictation as provided by your instructor.

Spelling review key

1. perceive 2. personally 3. proceed, precede
4. preferred, proffered 5. preparation 6. prejudice
7. prevalent 8. permanence, preeminence* 9. appropriate
10. privilege 11. preferable 12. professor
13. primitive 14. possible

Learning tip:

*Variant spelling preeminence/pre-eminence. Your instructor will indicate the spelling preferred in your community.

BUILDING WRITING AND TRANSCRIPTION SPEEDS

New vocabulary

Read and write each word until you can do so easily.

significantly	indications	vacant	ensure	investin
analyzed	sources	caused	period	Portlan

Letter 1

Read Letter 1 under timed conditions. Calculate your reading rat Then scribble-write the letter for speed building. Write the letter i shorthand as you read it from the transcript. Transcribe the letter ar calculate your transcription rate. Use a fictitious inside addres

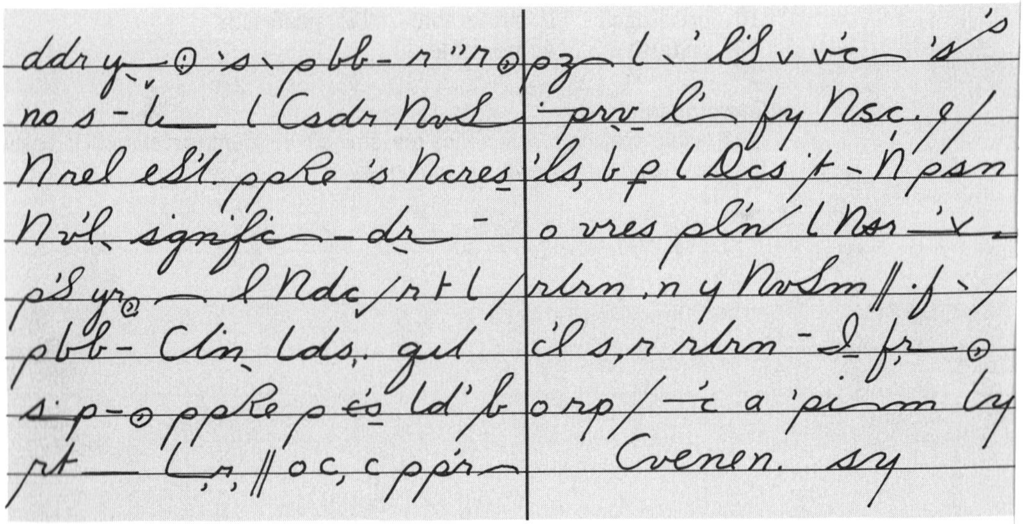

Letter 1 transcript

Dear Dr. Young: As you probably are aware, now is the time to consider investing in real estate. (20) Property has increased in value significantly during the past year, and all indications are that it (40) will probably continue to do so. Quite simply, property purchased today will be worth more tomorrow.

Our (60) company can prepare and present to you a list of vacant as well improved land for your inspection. We will also be pleased to discuss with you person our various plans to ensure ma mum return on (100) your investment.

If you will call us or return enclosed form, our representative make an appointment (120) at your con nience. Sincerely yours, (127)

Chapter 27

WRITING AX-EX-OX AND NGE

WRITING PRINCIPLES

Prefixes *ax-ex-ox*

Write a long, straight slanted, downward stroke \ to express *ax-ex-ox*. Be sure to slant the stroke so it looks like half an *x* and to prevent confusion with the *t*.

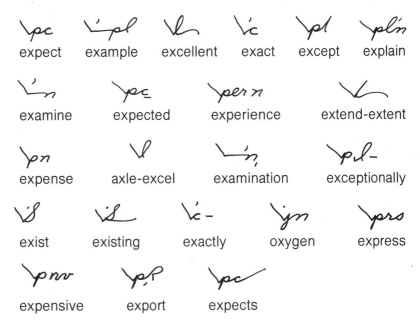

expect example excellent exact except explain

examine expected experience extend-extent

expense axle-excel examination exceptionally

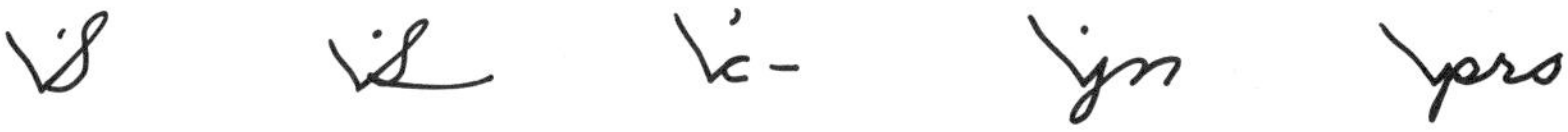

exist existing exactly oxygen express

expensive export expects

Cover the print of each line of words and read the outlines until you can read them as fast as you can read the print. Write the outlines for each word once. Read your notes. Then, increase your writing rate by scribble-writing each outline several times.

Combination *nge*

Write a dotted *j* to express the combination *nge*.

change range arrange changes changed

arrangement passengers

As you read each outline, write it three times. Do this for all the words. When you can read all the words fluently, cover the shorthand and write each outline once from the print. Read your notes.

New vocabulary

Read and write the following words until you can do so fluently.

extra — extreme — executive — substitute

television — meter-meters* — extremely

***Learning tip:**
Variant spelling meter/metre. When *meter* refers to metric measure, your instructor will indicate the spelling preferred in your community.

BUILDING TRANSCRIPTION SKILLS

Spelling review

Column A contains a list of commonly misspelled words that will really challenge your ability to spell. In your notebook number from 1–20. Complete each word and write it correctly opposite the appropriate number. Then, select the correct shorthand outline from Column B and write it in your notebook beside the appropriate transcribed word. Compare your answers with the key located at the end of the chapter. Write each outline three times in your notebook.

Column A

1. exa__er_te
2. ex_el__nt
3. _x_ept
4. ex_rci_e
5. ex_st_nce
6. exp_n_e
7. exp_r__nce
8. exp_r_m_nt
9. expl_n_t__n

Column B

10. extr_m_ly
11. arr_n__m_nts
12. a_x_l__ry
13. p_rs__de
14. pert__n
15. pr__ed_ng
16. extr__rd_n_ry
17. b_n_f_c__l
18. inc_nv_n__n_e
19. c_n_ede
20. a__o__ed

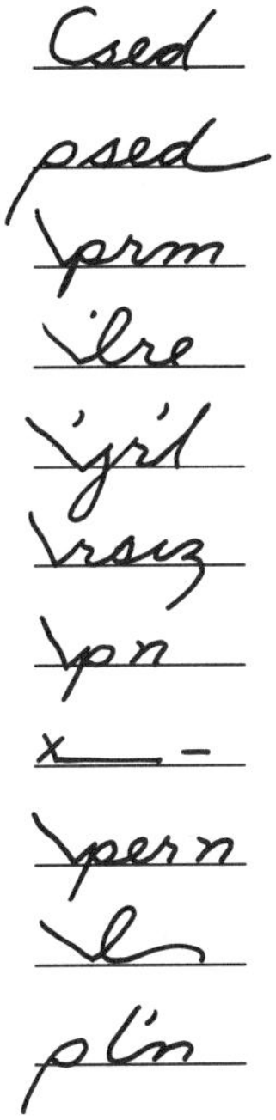

Application — **Word usage**. In your notebook number from 1–20. Select the word that properly completes each sentence, and write it opposite the appropriate number in your notebook. If necessary, use a dictionary to verify the meanings of the words. Check your work with the key located in Appendix G at the back of this text.

1. The family (least, leased) the house for the summer.
2. Jack did the (least, leased) amount of work of anyone.
3. The book has (fine, fined) print.
4. The judge (fine, fined) the driver for going through a red light.
5. A (grate, great) crowd gathered to welcome the astronauts.
6. The fireplace (grate, great) is broken.
7. The company will (higher, hire) 50 new workers.
8. He hit the ball (higher, hire) than anyone else.
9. My lunch (hour, our) starts at noon.
10. (Hour, Our) house is on Oak Street.

11. You must (wait, weight) your turn to use the computer terminal.
12. Her advice carries much (wait, weight) with her friends.
13. The light is too (weak, week) to read by.
14. We don't watch television much during the (weak, week).
15. The bride and groom walked down the (aisle, I'll, isle).
16. The small (aisle, I'll, isle) is surrounded by a sandy beach.
17. (Aisle, I'll, Isle) win the contest no matter what it takes.
18. The weather (vain, vane, vein) is on top of the fence.
19. There was a humorous (vain, vane, vein) in everything the speaker said.
20. The man at the garage made a (vain, vane, vein) effort to fix the truck.

APPLYING NEW PRINCIPLES

Follow these procedures in learning to read and write the sentences on page 193.

1. Read the shorthand outlines for each of the sentences until you can read all the sentences without hesitation.
2. Using the Transcript of Shorthand Sentences, write the shorthand outlines for each sentence in your notebook.
3. Check your outlines.
4. Write correctly three times each outline that you may have written incorrectly.
5. Rewrite the shorthand outlines as you read the sentences once again from the Transcript of Shorthand Sentences.
6. Transcribe the sentences from your own notes. Compare your transcript with the text transcript and circle any errors you may have made, including spelling and punctuation errors.

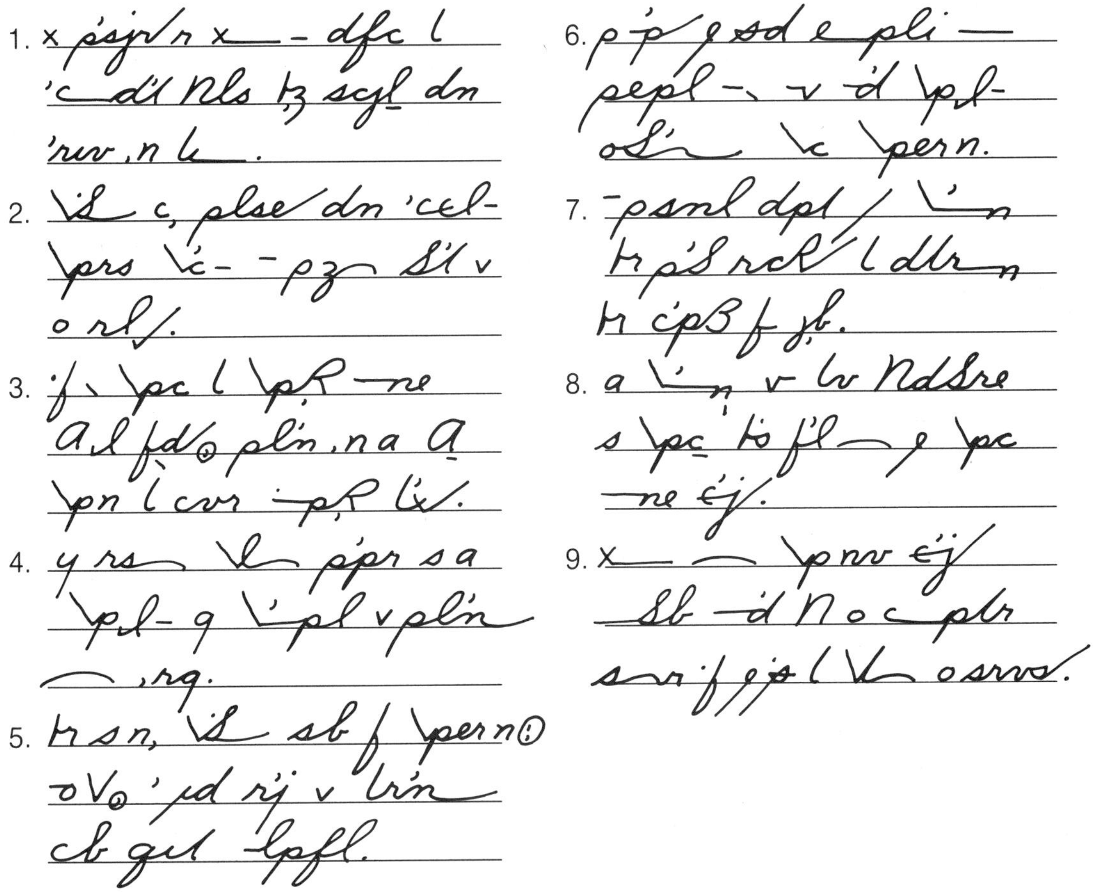

TRANSCRIPT OF SHORTHAND SENTENCES

1. Extra passengers are extremely difficult to accommodate unless those scheduled do not arrive on time. (20)
2. Existing company policies do not actually express exactly the present state of our relations. (40)
3. If you expect to export many additional foods, plan on an added expense to cover import taxes. (60)
4. Your recent excellent paper is an exceptionally good example of planning and organization. (80)
5. There is no existing substitute for experience; however, a wide range of training can be quite helpful. (100)

6. Perhaps we should employ more people who have had exceptionally outstanding executive experience. (120)
7. The personnel department will examine their past records to determine their capability for the job. (140)
8. An examination of the television industry is expected this fall, and we expect many changes. (160)
9. Extreme and expensive changes must be made in our computer center if we wish to extend our services. (180)

DICTATION AND TRANSCRIPTION

Write from dictation the Transcript of Shorthand Sentences. Your instructor will dictate each group of 20 words to you at various speeds. Select one set of notes, and transcribe it quickly and accurately.

BUILDING WRITING AND TRANSCRIPTION SPEEDS

New vocabulary

Read and write the following words until you can do so easily.

region accountants experienced unexpected excuse

extravagances unreasonable guidelines stay limits

lodging entertainment exceptions examined

examples examining forwarded

Memorandum 1

The following dictation is presented in the form of an interoffice memorandum. As you read the memorandum from the transcript, write the shorthand outlines in your notebook. Check your outlines with the text, and rewrite any outlines you may have written incorrectly. Read your notes under timed conditions, and calculate your reading rate. Keep your notes for use in Self-check 2 in *Forkner Shorthand Skill Builder for Colleges*.

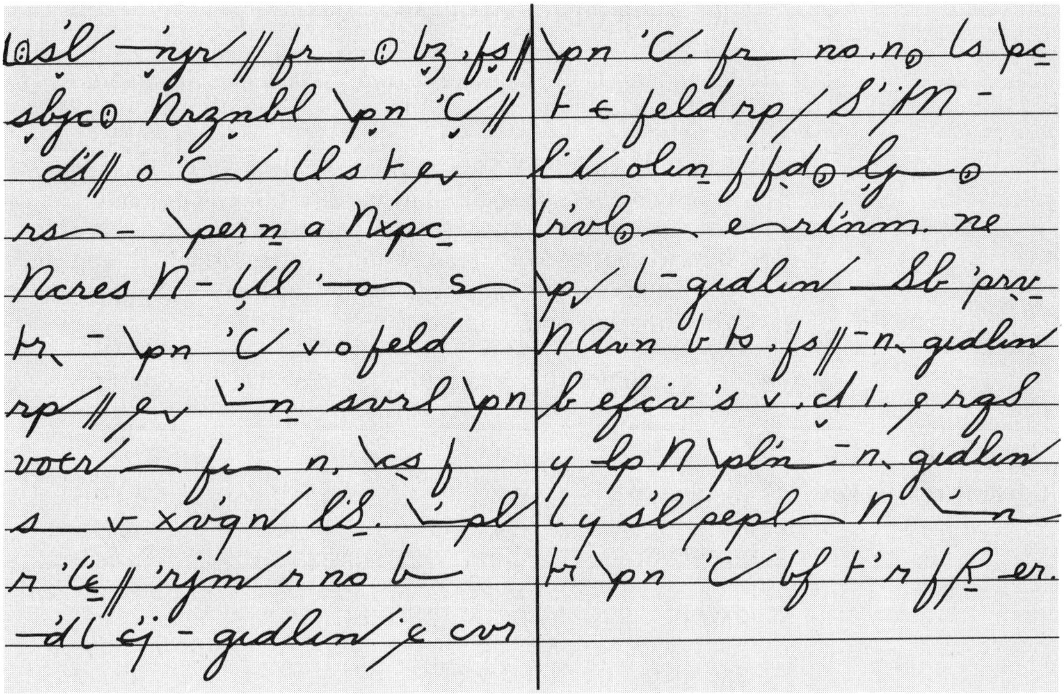

Memorandum 1 transcript

TO:	Sales Managers
FROM	Business Office
SUBJECT:	Unreasonable Expense Accounts
DATE:	Use current date

Our accountants tell us that we have recently experienced an unexpected increase in the total (20) amount spent through the expense accounts of our field representatives.

We have examined several expense vouchers (40) and find no excuse for some of the extravagances listed. Examples are attached.

Arrangements are now (60) being made to change the guidelines which cover expense accounts. From now on, it is expected that each field representative (80) will stay within the limits outlined for food, lodging, travel, and entertainment. Any exceptions to the (100) guidelines must be approved in advance by this office.

The new guidelines will be effective as of October 1. (120) We request your help in explaining the new guidelines to your sales people and in examining their expense (140) accounts before they are forwarded here. (146)

SKILL-BUILDING ASSIGNMENTS

1. Complete Unit 27 in *Forkner Shorthand Skill Builder for Colleges*.
2. Select Cassette 11 Side B of the *Theory and Speed-Building Tapes for Colleges* and follow the directions on the tape.
3. If instructed to do so, read, write, and transcribe the supplementary letters for this chapter found in Appendix A, Supplementary Dictation and Transcription.
4. Take additional live dictation as provided by your instructor.

Spelling review key

1. exaggerate
2. excellent
3. except
4. exercise
5. existence
6. expense
7. experience
8. experiment
9. explanation
10. extremely

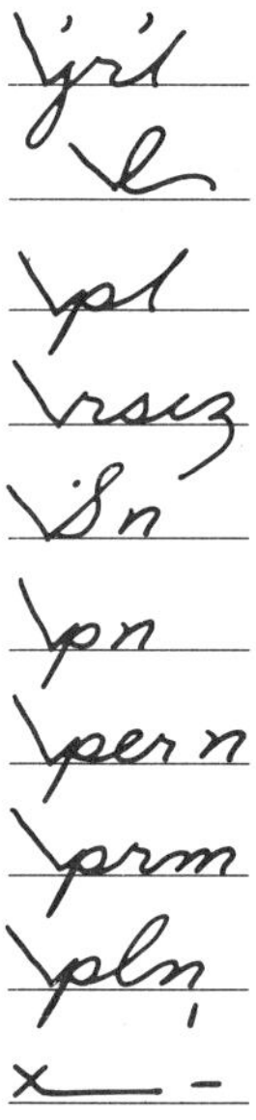

11. arrangements
12. auxiliary
13. persuade
14. pertain
15. preceding
16. extraordinary
17. beneficial
18. inconvenience
19. concede
20. allotted

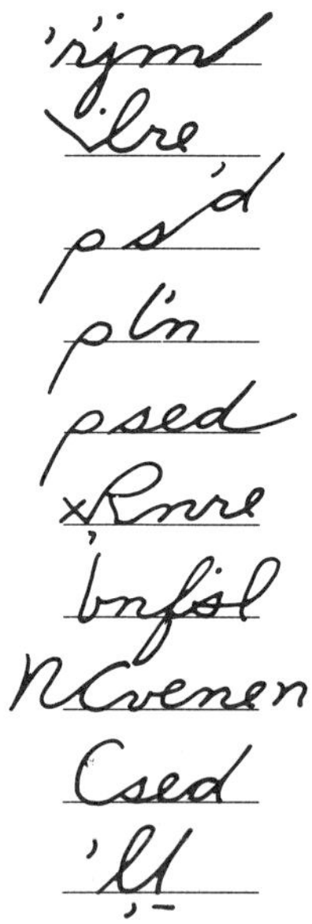

Chapter 28

BUSINESS DICTATION AND TRANSCRIPTION

BUILDING TRANSCRIPTION SKILLS

Punctuating a question

A question mark is used at the end of a sentence, phrase, or word that asks a direct question. When transcribing, space bar twice after each question mark.

1. Where is the main office?
2. Where are the files? in a central location? in each office?
3. Whom shall we nominate? Sharon? Roger?
4. She is a talented singer, isn't she?

Learning tip:

Note that a statement that comes before a question is set off by a comma.

Punctuating a courteous request

Although it may seem appropriate to use a question mark, a courteous request or suggestion is punctuated with a period.

1. Would you please send this order by September 1.
2. May I urge you to call for an appointment immediately.

Application— **Punctuating questions**. In your notebook number from 1-10. If the sentences below require one or more question marks, place the preceding word(s) and the question mark(s) opposite the appropriate number. If the sentence is correct, write OK in the space opposite the number. Check your work with the key located in Appendix G at the back of this text.

1. Where can I buy an inexpensive copier
2. Would you please call my office for an interview.
3. What would be a good return on my investment? 10 percent 15 percent
4. What does it take to get to the top of a large corporation? singleness of purpose setting objectives making decisions
5. Are local emergency and evacuation plans adequate?
6. Please refer to this letter when you return the claim form

7. Would you please refer to this letter when you return the claim form
8. Are you going to the game tonight
9. What was the basis for the criticism
10. That was a fine speech, wasn't it

Application— **Word usage**. In your notebook number from 1 – 10. Complete each of the following sentences by selecting the correct word and writing it opposite the appropriate number in your notebook. If necessary, use a dictionary to verify the meanings of the words. Check your work with the key located in Appendix G at the back of this text.

1. He doesn't believe there is (any way, anyway) to repair the automobile.
2. The (strait, straight) line indicates the route we will follow.
3. Can the tree (adopt, adapt) itself to the new location?
4. The current rate of interest has (affected, effected) our style of living.
5. The after- (diner, dinner) speaker gave an entertaining talk.
6. We have the first (addition, edition) of Shakespeare's Complete Works in our library.
7. Be sure to include the (right, write) prices on the invoice.
8. We (passed, past) by the old museum on the way to the airport.
9. The contractors had an (access, excess) of materials when they completed the building.
10. The new (device, devise) was used to shield the plane from radar.

Spelling review

The outlines which follow are for words commonly misspelled. Transcribe the outlines in your notebook. Check your spelling with a dictionary, a standard word reference list, or the *Forkner Shorthand Dictionary for Beginners*. If the shorthand outline represents more than one word, give all the spellings. Compare your answers with the key located at the end of the chapter. Write correctly any words you may have misspelled. Then, write the shorthand outlines for all the words until you can write them without hesitation.

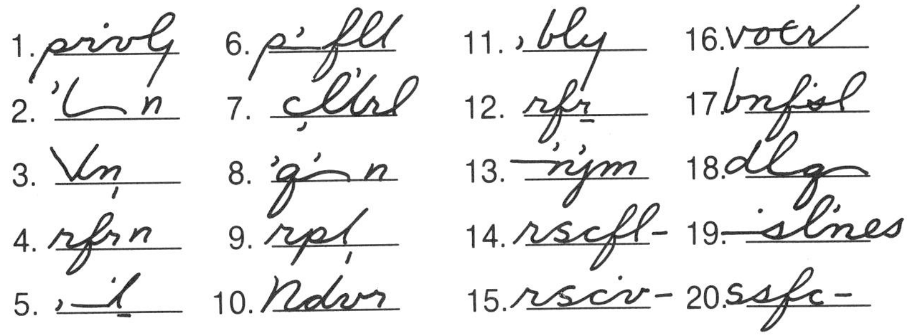

Application—**Spelling**. In your notebook number from 1–10. Complete each sentence below by selecting the missing words from the list provided in the *spelling review* and writing them opposite the appropriate number in your notebook. Each word is used only *once*. Check your work with the key located in Appendix G at the back of this text.

1. The m________ will e________ to please all tenants.
2. This letter is in r________ to your d________ account.
3. The v________ stated s________ payment was due in 30 days.
4. We do not want to see a r________ of your poor a________ record.
5. It is a p________ to make your a________.
6. A paragraph was o________ in the p________ on parking regulations.
7. The e________ of your loan will depend on what c________ you have available.
8. She r________ to her children, Bob, Dick, and Tom, who are 6, 8, and 10 years old, r________.
9. It would be b________ to price the m________ items separately.
10. You would o________ me by addressing the group r________ even though you do not share their views.

BUILDING WRITING AND TRANSCRIPTION SPEEDS

New vocabulary

Read and write the following words until you can do so without hesitation.

July ourselves unsatisfactory Brooks fastest lost

quick ten

Letter 1

Read Letter 1 following this procedure. Read sentence one. Then, go back and read sentences one and two. Then, go back to the beginning and read sentences one, two, and three. Follow this plan for reading the entire letter. By the time you have completed reading the letter, you should be able to transcribe the outlines easily.

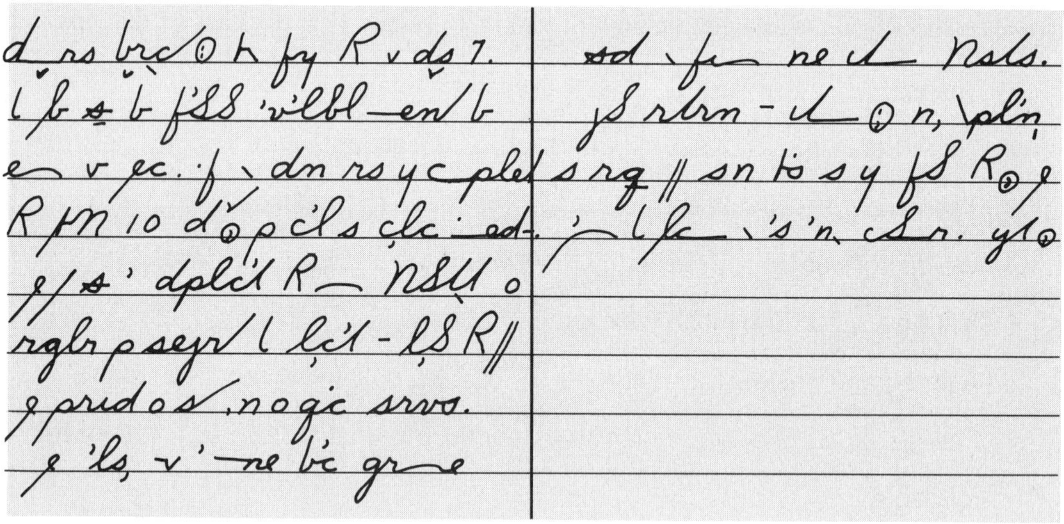

Letter 1 transcript

Dear Mrs. Brooks: Thank you for your order of December 7. It will be shipped by the fastest available (20) means by the end of the week. If you do not receive your complete order within ten days, please call us collect (40) immediately. We will ship a duplicate order and institute our regular procedures to locate the (60) lost order.

We pride ourselves on our quick service. We also have a money-back guarantee should you find any (80) item unsatisfactory. Just return the item; no explanation is required.

Since this is your first (100) order, we want to welcome you as a new customer. Yours truly, (111)

New vocabulary

As you read each of the words, write the corresponding outline three times in your shorthand notebook.

vendors supplies seeking

Letter 2

Read Letter 2 until you can read it without hesitation. Then, using the transcript, write the shorthand outlines for the letter in your notebook from self-dictation. Check the accuracy of your outlines and write the letter again. Write the sentences faster this time. Read your notes. Can you read them quickly?

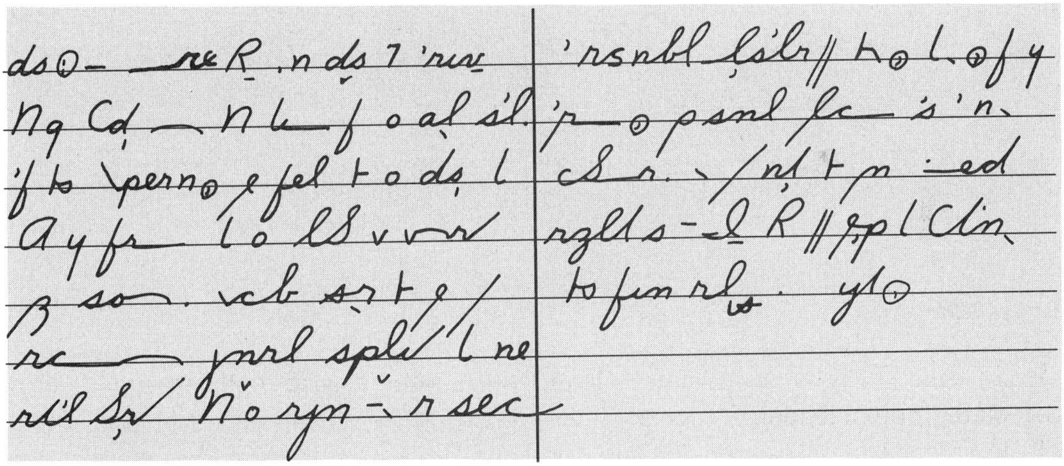

Letter 2 transcript

Dear Sir: The merchandise ordered on December 7 arrived in good condition and in time for our annual (20) sale. After this experience, we feel that our decision to add your firm to our list of vendors was sound. (40) You can be sure that we will recommend General Supplies to any retail stores in our region who are (60) seeking a responsible wholesaler.

Thank you, too, for your warm, personal welcome as a new customer. You will (80) note that one immediate result is the enclosed order.

We hope to continue this fine relationship. Yours (100) truly, (101)

New vocabulary

As you read each outline, scribble-write it for speed development.

musical comedies community

Letter 3

As you read the shorthand outlines for Letter 3, scribble-write it in your notebook until you can both read and write the letter easily.

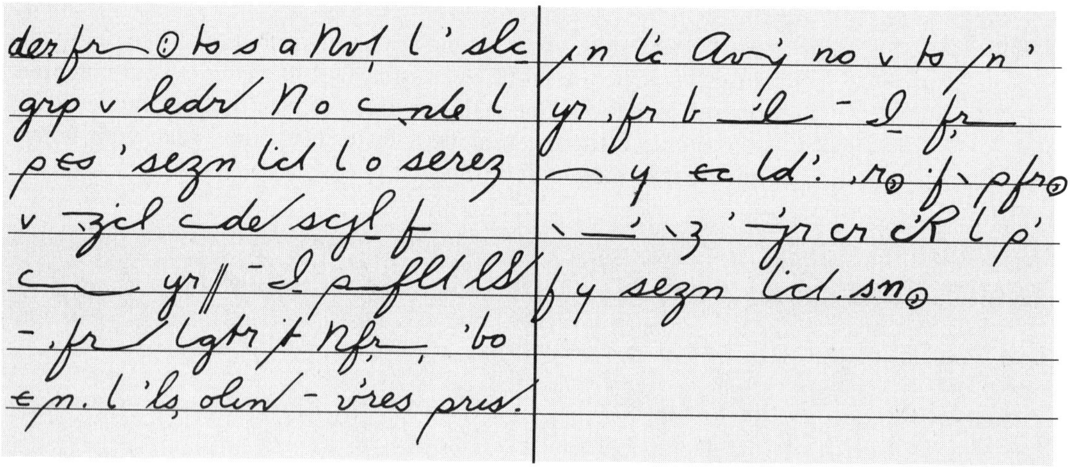

Letter 3 transcript

Dear Friend: This is an invitation to a selected group of leaders in our community to purchase a (20) season ticket to our series of musical comedies scheduled for the coming year.

The enclosed pamphlet lists (40) the offerings together with information about each one. It also outlines the various prices. Why (60) not take advantage now of this once-a-year offer by mailing the enclosed form and your check today. Or, if you (80) prefer, you may use a major credit card to pay for your season ticket. Sincerely, (96)

New vocabulary

Read and write the following outlines until you can do so easily.

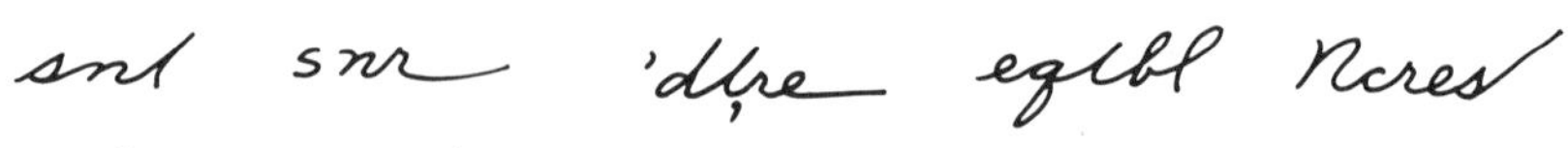

senate sponsoring auditorium equitable increases

introduce merit factor announced Hill

Memorandum 4

Read Memorandum 4 until you can read it without hesitation. Then, write the shorthand outlines for the memorandum in your notebook, making certain your outlines are correct and readable. Read them back to be sure. Transcribe the memorandum from your own notes. Correct your transcript by referring to the text transcript.

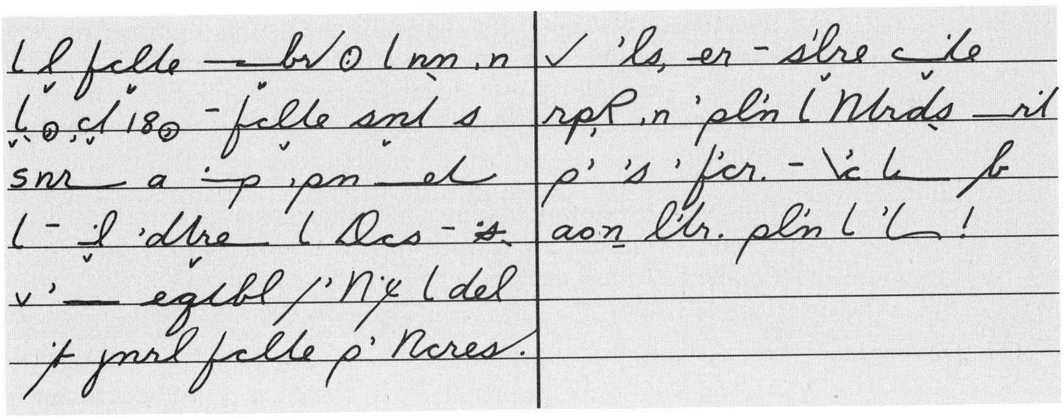

Memorandum 4 transcript

To All Faculty Members: At noon on Tuesday, October 18, the Faculty Senate is sponsoring an (20) important open meeting at the Hill Auditorium to discuss the issue of a more equitable (40) way in which to deal with general faculty pay increases. You will also hear the Salary Committee (60) report on a plan to introduce merit pay as a factor. The exact time will be announced later. Plan to (80) attend! (81)

DICTATION AND TRANSCRIPTION

Write from dictation Letters 1–3 and Memorandum 4. Your instructor will dictate each of these to you at various speeds.

Using your own notes, transcribe the letters and memorandum using an appropriate business correspondence format.

SKILL-BUILDING ASSIGNMENTS

1. Complete Unit 28 in *Forkner Shorthand Skill Builder for Colleges*.

2. Select Cassette 12 Side B of the *Theory and Speed-Building Tapes for Colleges* and follow the directions on the tape.

3. If instructed to do so, read, write, and transcribe the supplementary letter for this chapter found in Appendix A, Supplementary Dictation and Transcription.

4. Take additional live dictation as provided by your instructor.

PREVIEW EXAMINATION 7

Remove Preview Examination 7 from your *Forkner Shorthand Skill Builder for Colleges*. It follows Unit 32. This informal preview examination will help you in assessing your understanding of the Forkner principles presented in Chapters 25–28. It is similar to Examination 7 which may be administered at a later date by your instructor.

Complete Preview Examination 7 and then check your answers carefully with the key in your *Forkner Shorthand Skill Builder for Colleges*. Correct any errors you may have made.

Spelling review key

1. privilege 2. attendance 3. extension 4. reference
5. omitted 6. pamphlet 7. collateral 8. acquaintance
9. repetition 10. endeavor 11. oblige 12. referred
13. management 14. respectfully 15. respectively
16. vouchers 17. beneficial 18. delinquent
19. miscellaneous 20. specifically

Chapter 29

WRITING SYS-SESS-SUS-SIS-CESS-CIS, SCRIBE-SCRIPT, AND ULATE

WRITING PRINCIPLES

Combination *sys-sess-sus-sis-cess-cis*

Write a capital *Z* for the combinations *sys-sess-sus-sis-cess-cis*.

assist basis success successful system process

consist possess assistant assistance insist

necessity emphasis access accessories

As you read each outline, write it several times. Then cover the outlines and write each word once from the print. Verify the accuracy of your outlines.

Combinations *scribe-script*

Write a printed capital *S* S for the combinations *scribe-script*. The *S* may be joined or disjoined.

describe subscribe described subscription

transcription describes

Read the outlines until you can read them as fast as you can read from the print. Then, write the outlines from the print and read them back. If any of your outlines are difficult to read, rewrite them and read them again.

Combination *ulate*

Write a small longhand *u* to express the combination *ulate*.

congratulate regulate stimulate stipulate insulate

formulate regulation

As you read each word, write the corresponding shorthand outline three times or until you can write it accurately without hesitating. Then, write each outline once. Transcribe your notes three times.

New vocabulary

Read and write the following words until you can do so without hesitation.

necessary debit junior necessarily unnecessary

railroad

BUILDING TRANSCRIPTION SKILLS

Application —**Word usage**. In your notebook number from 1-10. Complete each of the following sentences by writing the correct word opposite the appropriate sentence number. If necessary, use a dictionary to verify the meanings of the words. Check your work with the key located in Appendix G at the back of this text.

1. Do not (lean, lien) on the railing.
2. A ship was docked at the (pier, peer) for three days.
3. Did the witness deliberately (lie, lye)?
4. Will she be (allowed, aloud) to drive the new car?
5. They set (forth, fourth) at dawn to find their ship.
6. Are you still in the planning (faze, phase)?
7. Will the construction company (raze, raise, rays) the old building?
8. We climbed the (stairs, stares) very slowly.

9. The group will (canvas, canvass) the neighborhood to raise money for the orchestra.
10. Scuba divers use (led, lead) weights to help them descend.

Spelling review

The outlines which follow are for words commonly misspelled Transcribe the outlines in your notebook. Check your spelling with a dictionary, a standard word reference list, or the *Forkner Shorthand Dictionary for Beginners*. Compare your answers with the key located at the end of the chapter. Write correctly any words you may have misspelled. Then, write the shorthand outlines for all the words until you can write them without hesitation.

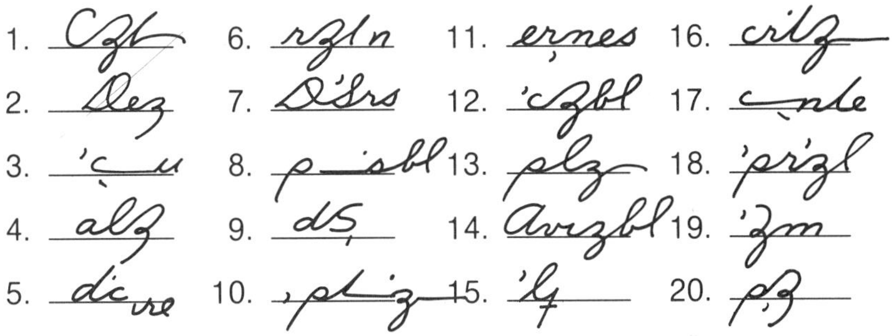

APPLYING NEW PRINCIPLES

Follow these procedures in learning to read and write the sentences on page 208.

1. Read the shorthand outlines for each of the sentences until you can read all the sentences without hesitation.

2. Using the Transcript of Shorthand Sentences, write the shorthand outlines for each sentence in your notebook.

3. Check your outlines.

4. Write correctly three times each outline that you may have written incorrectly.

5. Rewrite the shorthand outlines as you read the sentences once again from the Transcript of Shorthand Sentences.

6. Transcribe the sentences from your own notes. Compare your transcript with the text transcript and circle any errors you may have made, including spelling and punctuation errors.

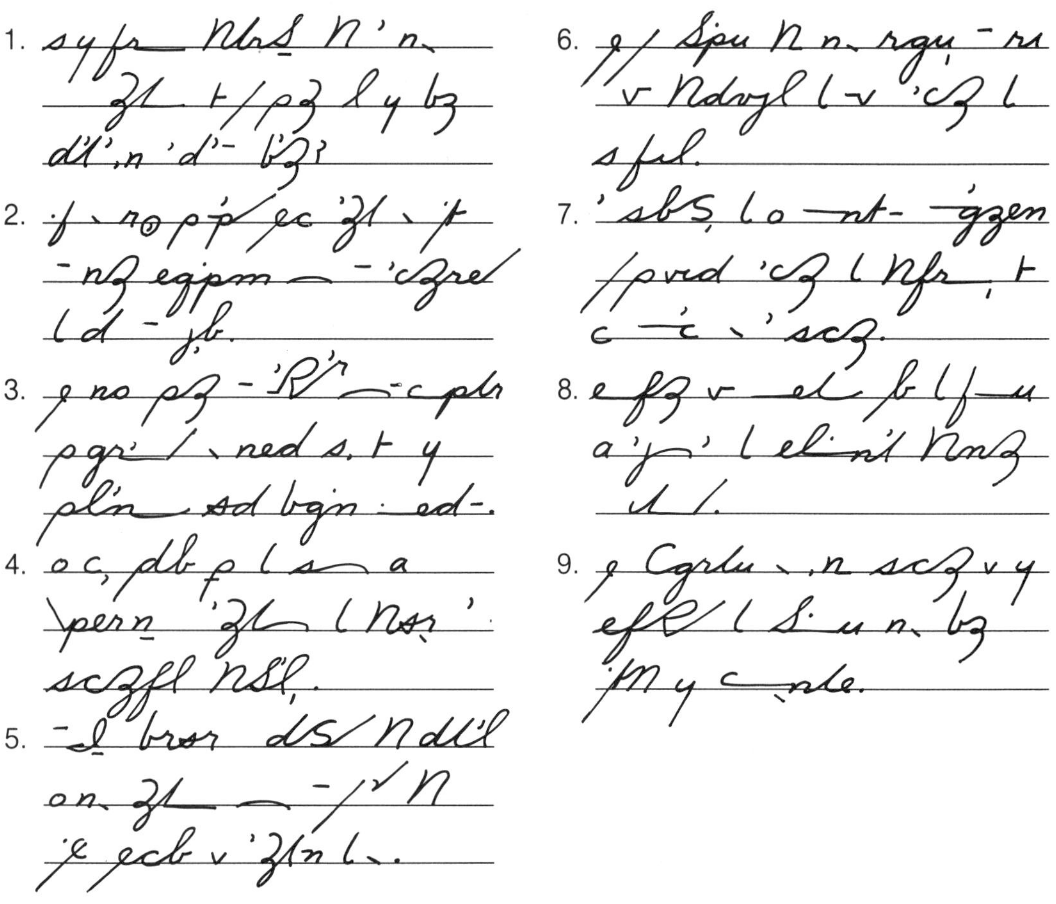

TRANSCRIPT OF SHORTHAND SENTENCES

1. Is your firm interested in a new system that will process all your business data on a daily basis? (20)
2. If you are, perhaps we can assist you with the necessary equipment and the accessories to do the job. (40)
3. We now possess the hardware and the computer programs you need so that your planning should begin immediately. (60)
4. Our company would be pleased to send an experienced assistant to ensure a successful installation. (80)
5. The enclosed brochure describes in detail our new system and the ways in which we can be of assistance to you. (100)
6. We will stipulate in the new regulation the right of the individual to have access to his file. (120)

7. A subscription to our monthly magazine will provide access to information that can make you a success. (140)
8. Emphasis of the meeting will be to formulate an agenda to eliminate unnecessary items. (160)
9. We congratulate you on the success of your efforts to stimulate new business within your community. (180)

DICTATION AND TRANSCRIPTION

Write from dictation the Transcript of Shorthand Sentences. Your instructor will dictate each group of 20 words to you at various speeds. Select one set of notes, and transcribe it quickly and accurately.

BUILDING WRITING AND TRANSCRIPTION SPEEDS

New vocabulary

Read and write the following words until you can do so easily.

afternoon congratulations draft critical expert

consultant concerns implementing calling Charles

Grace Cooper Ravel treasurer's

revision recognized

Memorandum 1

The following dictation is presented in the form of an interoffice memorandum. As you read the memorandum from the print, write the shorthand outlines in your notebook. Check your outlines with the text transcript, and rewrite correctly any outlines which you may have written incorrectly. Reread your notes under timed conditions, and calculate your reading rate. Keep your notes for use in Self-check 2 in *Forkner Shorthand Skill Builder for Colleges*.

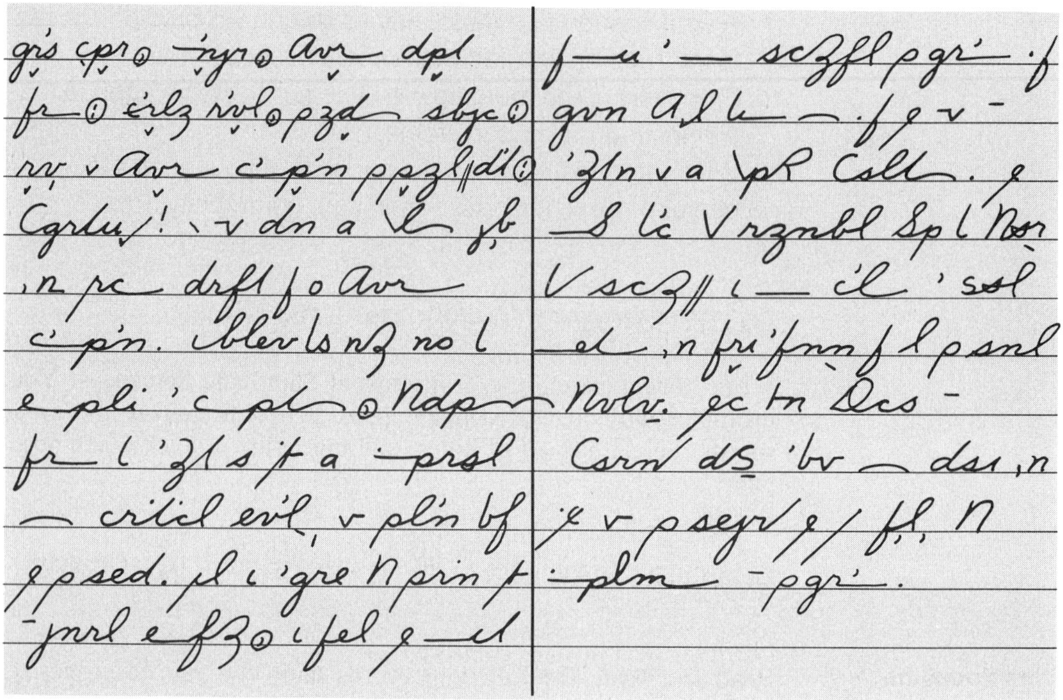

Memorandum 1
transcript

TO: Grace Cooper, Manager, Advertising Department
FROM: Charles Ravel, President
SUBJECT: Revision of Advertising Campaign Proposal
DATE: Use current date

Congratulations! You have done an excellent job on the working draft for our advertising campaign. I believe (20) it is necessary now to employ a competent, independent firm to assist us with an impartial (40) and critical evaluation of the plan before we proceed. While I agree in principle with the (60) general emphasis, I feel we might formulate a more successful program if given additional time and (80) if we have the assistance of an expert consultant. We must take every reasonable step to ensure its (100) success.

I am calling a special meeting on Friday afternoon for all personnel involved. We can then (120) discuss the concerns described above and decide on which of the procedures we will follow in implementing (140) the program. (143)

SKILL-BUILDING ASSIGNMENTS

1. Complete Unit 29 in *Forkner Shorthand Skill Builder for Colleges*.

2. Select Cassette 13 Side B of the *Theory and Speed-Building Tapes for Colleges* and follow the directions on the tape.

3. If instructed to do so, read, write, and transcribe the supplementary memorandum for this chapter found in Appendix A, Supplementary Dictation and Transcription.

4. Take additional live dictation as provided by your instructor.

Spelling review key

1. consistent 2. disease 3. accumulate 4. analysis
5. dictionary 6. resistance 7. disastrous 8. permissible
9. description 10. optimism 11. erroneous 12. accessible
13. pleasant 14. advisable 15. alleged 16. criticism
17. community 18. appraisal 19. assessment 20. possess

Chapter 30

WRITING CONTR, OVER-OTHER, AND UNDER

WRITING PRINCIPLES

Combination *contr*

Write a small longhand *k* k to express the combination *contr* and the following vowel.

contract control contrast contribute contrary

contradict contribution

As you read each outline, write it several times. Then, cover the outlines; write the outline for each word once, and read your outlines.

Over-other

Write a joined or disjoined capital *O* O to express *over* and *other*.

over-other another otherwise overcharge others

oversight overload overdue overtime overcome

overcast overnight

Read the outlines in the first line. When you can read the first line fluently, cover the shorthand and write each outline as you read from the print. Do this until you can write each word rapidly and accurately. Check your outlines. Follow the same procedure for all lines.

Combination *under*

Write a small longhand *u* u to express the combination *under*.

under understand understanding understood

undertake misunderstanding

As you read each outline, write it three times. After you have written all the words, you should be able to read and write them rapidly and accurately.

New vocabulary

Read and write the following words until you can do so without hesitation.

practical dollar dollars superintendent overall

practically moreover Dallas corporations stimulating

BUILDING TRANSCRIPTION SKILLS

Word usage

Some words, when combined to form one word, have a different meaning. Study the following words and learn their definitions or how they are correctly used.

Word	Definition/Usage
nobody	no person
no body	no group
almost	nearly
all most	all very much
anyway	in any case
any way	by any method
someone	some person
some one	some particular thing or person

everyday	usual, ordinary
every day	every single day
into	going from without to within
in to	in is an adverb; to a preposition

Application — **Word usage**. In your notebook number from 1-12. Complete each of the following sentences by writing the correct word opposite the appropriate sentence number. Check your work with the key located in Appendix G at the back of this text.

1. Mail your deposit (into, in to) the bank today.
2. The jockey walked (into, in to) the winner's circle.
3. The train was (almost, all most) three hours late.
4. We are (almost, all most) pleased with the new schedule of classes.
5. You will master the (everyday, every day) routine quickly.
6. You have been doing your job well (everyday, every day).
7. (Nobody, No body) of students is more cooperative than ours.
8. There was (nobody, no body) at the reception desk when I arrived.
9. If we can be of help in (anyway, any way), please telephone us.
10. (Anyway, Any way), it is time for the meeting to adjourn.
11. (Someone, Some one) telephoned and left a message for you.
12. Maybe (someone, some one) person on your staff would be able to deliver the package.

Spelling review

The outlines which follow are for words commonly misspelled. Transcribe the outlines in your notebook. Check your spelling in a dictionary, a standard word reference list, or in the *Forkner Shorthand Dictionary for Beginners*. Compare your answers with those located in the key at the end of the chapter. Write correctly any words you may have misspelled. Then, write the shorthand outlines for all the words until you can write them easily.

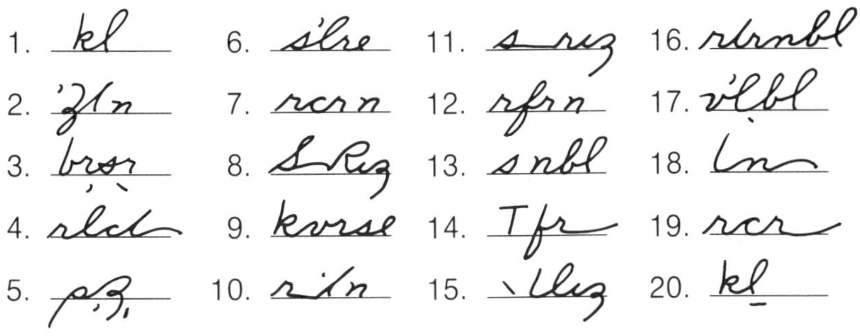

APPLYING NEW PRINCIPLES

Follow these procedures in learning to read and write the sentences below.

1. Read the shorthand outlines for each of the sentences until you can read all the sentences without hesitation.
2. Using the Transcript of Shorthand Sentences, write the shorthand outlines for each sentence in your notebook.
3. Check your outlines.
4. Write correctly three times each outline that you may have written incorrectly.
5. Rewrite the shorthand outlines as you read the sentences once again from the transcript of Shorthand Sentences.
6. Transcribe the sentences from your own notes. Compare your transcript with the text transcript and circle any errors you may have made, including spelling and punctuation errors.

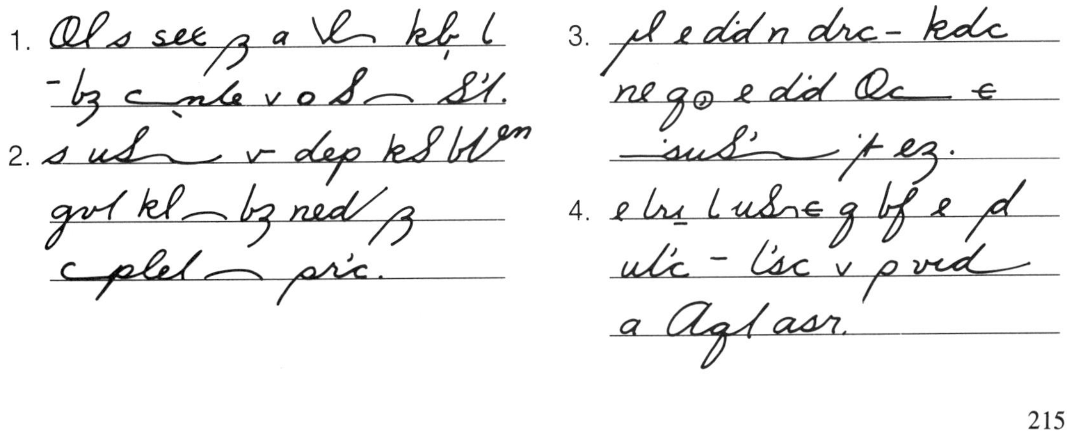

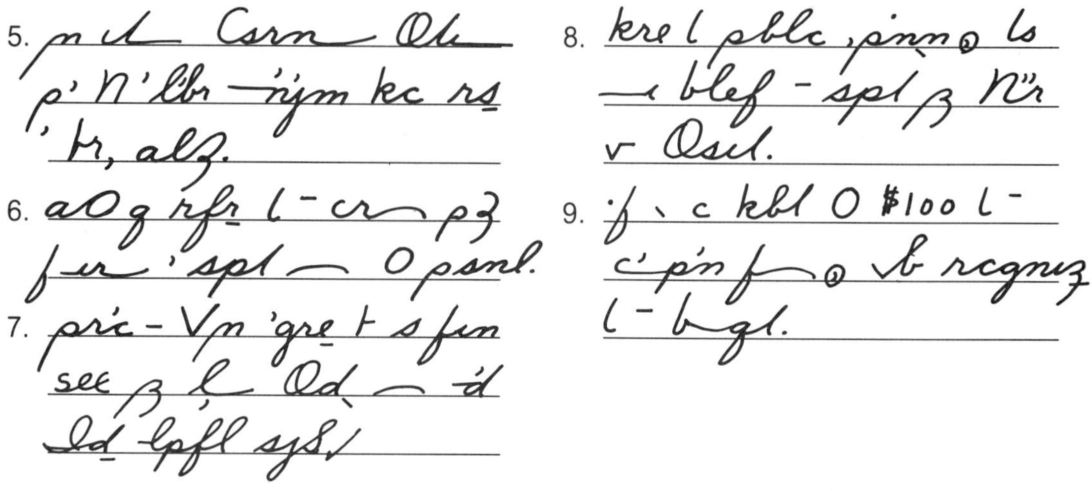

TRANSCRIPT OF SHORTHAND SENTENCES

1. Overall, his speech was an excellent contribution to the business community of our city and state. (20)
2. His understanding of the deep contrast between government control and business needs was complete and practical. (40)
3. While he did not directly contradict any question, he did overcome each misunderstanding with ease. (60)
4. He tried to understand each question before he would undertake the task of providing an adequate answer. (80)
5. One item concerning overtime pay in a labor-management contract received a thorough analysis. (100)
6. Another question referred to the current process for hiring a superintendent and other personnel. (120)
7. Practically everyone agreed that his fine speech was long overdue and had included helpful suggestions. (140)
8. Contrary to public opinion, it is my belief the superintendent was unaware of the oversight. (160)
9. If you can contribute over $100 to the campaign fund, you will be recognized at the banquet. (180)

DICTATION AND TRANSCRIPTION

Write from dictation the Transcript of Shorthand Sentences. Your instructor will dictate each group of 20 words to you at various speeds. Select one set of notes, and transcribe it quickly and accurately.

BUILDING WRITING AND TRANSCRIPTION SPEEDS

The following letter is divided into two parts. Follow this procedure for studying each part: Read through the transcript of each part, and as you read, try to write the underscored words in shorthand in your notebook. Each is a *new* word. When you have written all the new words in each part, check your outlines with the new vocabulary keys. Then, write the entire part from self-dictation until you can write it easily. After you have studied both parts, make a complete set of good notes and transcribe it in letter form.

Letter 1, Part 1
transcript

Mr. and Mrs. R. J. Harper, 2244 College Avenue, Boston, MA 02113-3111
Dear Mr. and Mrs. Harper: Thank you for your recent request for information about our investment program. (20) It is a pleasure for me to send you the enclosed folder which explains why our program appeals to many (40) individuals.

First, it is possible for you to invest as much or as little as you want. Secondly, (60) you can receive your dividends yearly, semiannually, or quarterly. These features are somewhat different (80) from the plans offered by other firms. Finally, with our investment program, it will be possible for you (100) to own interests in a cross section of businesses.

New vocabulary key

Letter 1, Part 1

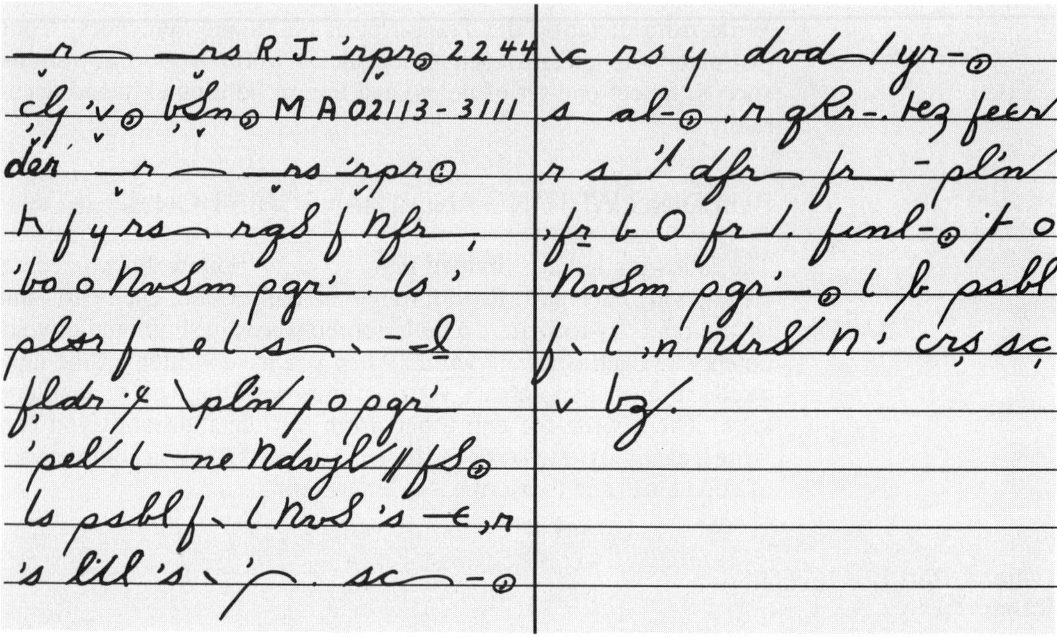

Letter 1, Part 2
transcript

If you would please indicate how much you wish to invest, (120) I would be able to make some definite recommendations to you. I would also like to know more about (140) you and your family so I could better match your goals with a plan that would be right for you.

As I'm sure you realize, (160) any information you give me will be held in strict confidence.

May I hear from you soon? Sincerely (180) yours, (181)

New vocabulary key

match

goals

confidence

Letter 1, Part 2

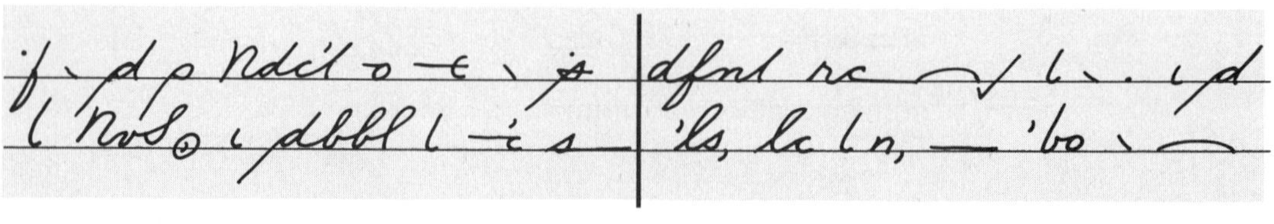

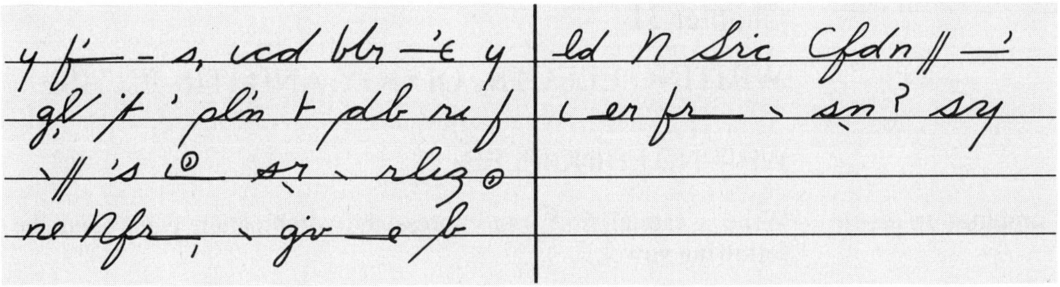

SKILL-BUILDING ASSIGNMENTS

1. Complete Unit 30 in *Forkner Shorthand Skill Builder for Colleges*.

2. Select Cassette 14 Side B of the *Theory and Speed-Building Tapes for Colleges* and follow the directions on the tape.

3. If instructed to do so, read, write, and transcribe the supplementary letter for this chapter found in Appendix A, Supplementary Dictation and Transcription.

4. Take additional live dictation as provided by your instructor.

Spelling review key

1. control 2. assistance 3. brochure 4. reluctant
5. possession 6. salary 7. recurrence 8. standardize
9. controversy 10. remittance 11. summarize
12. reference 13. sensible 14. transferring 15. utilize
16. returnable 17. valuable 18. tenant 19. recurring
20. controlled

Chapter 31

WRITING ELECTR, OLOGY, AND ITIS-ICITIS

WRITING PRINCIPLES

Combination *electr*

Write a capital *E* to express the combination *electr* and the following vowel.

electric electricity electrical electronic

electrician electrification

Read the outlines until you can read them without hestitating. Then scribble-write them for speed development.

Combination *ology*

Write a small disjoined *l* to express the combination *ology*.

biology technology psychology sociology

theology psychological

Read the first word and then write its shorthand outline in your notebook. Then read and write the outlines for the first and second words. Read and write all of the words in the same manner.

Combinations *itis-icitis*

Write a disjoined capital *I* to express the combinations *itis-icitis*. Write it close to the word to which it belongs.

arthritis bronchitis appendicitis tonsillitis

bursitis meningitis

Cover the printed words and read the shorthand outlines until you can read them without hesitating. Build your writing speed by scribble-writing the words in your notebook. Then write each word once. Read your notes.

New vocabulary

Read and write the following words until you can do so easily.

signature	degree	degrees	degrees Celsius
....	....	....	....

BUILDING TRANSCRIPTION SKILLS

Word usage

Some terms, when combined to form one word, have a different meaning. Study the following words and learn the definitions of each.

Word	Definition
always	at all times
all ways	by all means
anyone	any person
any one	any individual in a group
everyone	everybody
every one	each one
already	previously
all ready	completely ready, prepared
maybe	perhaps
may be	be able to be
sometime	some indefinite time
some time	part of a specified period

Application – **Word usage**. In your notebook number from 1 — 12. Complete each of the following sentences by writing the correct word opposite the appropriate sentence number. Check your work with the key located in Appendix G at the back of this text.

1. She left home for work (sometime, some time) ago.
2. The report will be completed (sometime, some time) tomorrow.
3. (Maybe, May be) we should telephone Mr. Booth about the late delivery.
4. The directory (maybe, may be) of some assistance in preparing our mailing list.
5. The invoices are (already, all ready) to be mailed.
6. The order had (already, all ready) been shipped.
7. (Everyone, Every one) of the fish was contaminated.
8. (Everyone, Every one) needs to be counted for the census.
9. The company tried in (always, all ways) to keep the employees satisfied.
10. The class had (always, all ways) been cooperative.
11. (Anyone, Any one) of the secretaries could have answered that particular request.
12. The group will help (anyone, any one) who needs assistance.

Spelling review

The shorthand outlines in each sentence are for words that are commonly misspelled. Transcribe each outline in your notebook. Check your spelling in a dictionary, a standard word reference list, or in the *Forkner Shorthand Dictionary for Beginners*. Compare your answers with the key located at the end of the chapter. Review any word you may have misspelled. Write the outlines until you can write them easily.

1. The  used by the  committee left much to be desired.
2. The   in the lab are a  to good classroom instruction.

3. A detailed *unrre* is *nnz* for this short trip.
4. A record of your *ixbl* income should be *rde-* available.
5. *kl* accounts *s'bl* is an *ndp nbl* business practice.
6. The engineer was *rfr* to *lcnicl* data not *rlv* to the project.
7. The package was marked *frjl*.
8. She is an extremely *lcbl* person.
9. The *vrsiz* was difficult, but *njbl*.
10. Severe flood damage has *rcr* after heavy rainfall.

APPLYING NEW PRINCIPLES

Follow these procedures in learning to read and write the sentences on page 224.

1. Read the shorthand outlines for each of the sentences until you can read all the sentences without hesitation.
2. Using the Transcript of Shorthand Sentences, write the shorthand outlines for each sentence in your notebook.
3. Check your outlines.
4. Write correctly three times each outline that you may have written incorrectly.
5. Rewrite the shorthand outlines as you read the sentences once again from the Transcript of Shorthand Sentences.
6. Transcribe the sentences from your own notes. Compare your transcript with the text transcript and circle any errors you may have made, including spelling and punctuation errors.

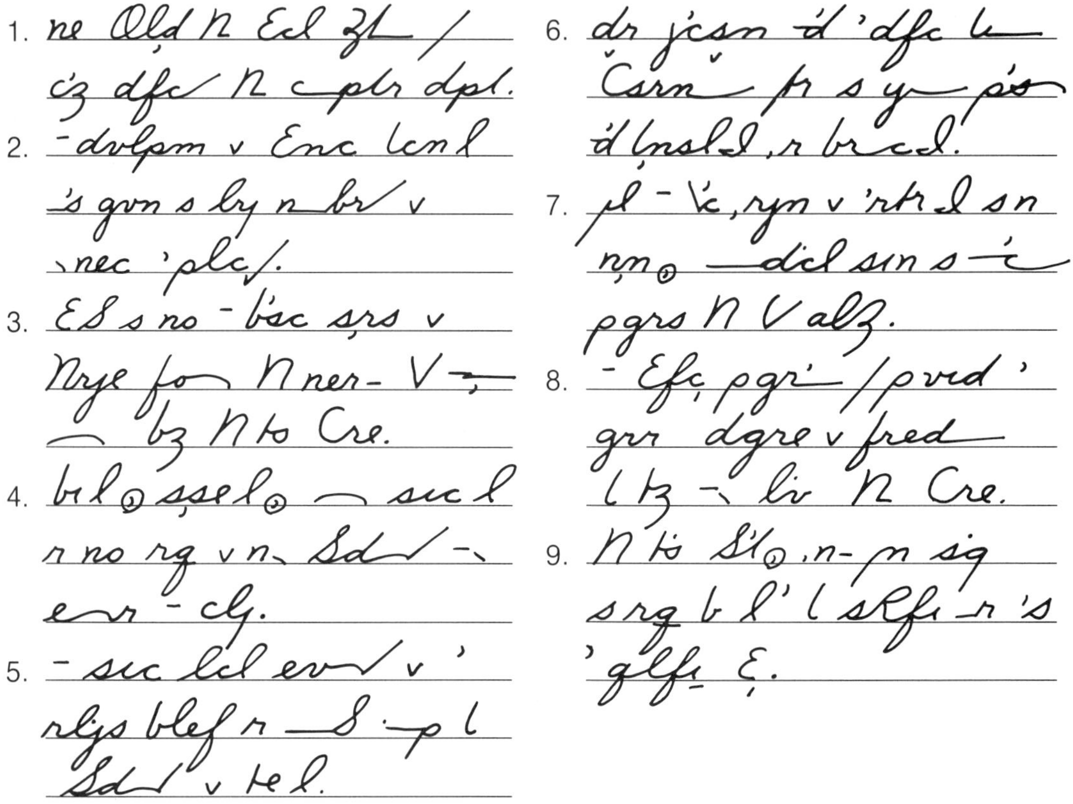

TRANSCRIPT OF SHORTHAND SENTENCES

1. Any overload in the electrical system will cause difficulties in the computer department. (20)
2. The development of electronic technology has given us large numbers of unique applications. (40)
3. Electricity is now the basic source of energy found in nearly every home and business in this country. (60)
4. Biology, sociology, and psychology are now required of new students who enter the college. (80)
5. The psychological events of a religious belief are most important to students of theology. (100)
6. Dr. Jackson had a difficult time concerning whether his young patient had tonsillitis or bronchitis. (120)
7. While the exact origin of arthritis is not known, medical science is making progress in its analysis. (140)

8. The electrification program will provide a greater degree of freedom to those who live in the country. (160)
9. In this state, only one signature is required by law to certify her as a qualified electrician. (180)

DICTATION AND TRANSCRIPTION

Write from dictation the Transcript of Shorthand Sentences. Your instructor will dictate each group of 20 words to you at various speeds. Select one set of notes, and transcribe it quickly and accurately.

BUILDING WRITING AND TRANSCRIPTION SPEEDS

New vocabulary

Read and write the following words until you can do so easily.

crowds doors apologize bargains enlarged

Los Angeles Paula comprehensive participant

Letter 1

Read the following letter until you can read it fluently. Scribble-write the letter once for speed development. Then, as you read the letter from the transcript, make one good set of notes. Transcribe your notes.

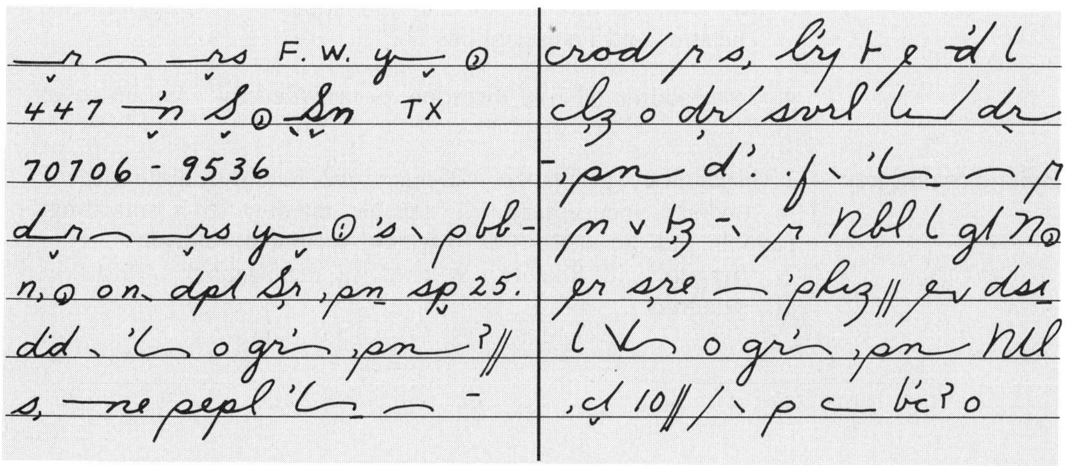

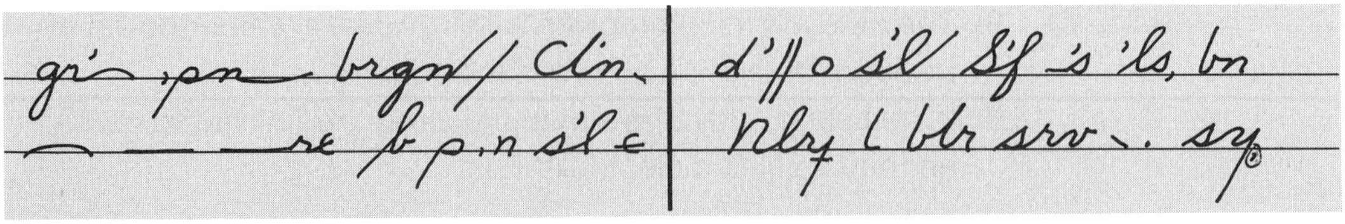

Letter 1

Mr. and Mrs. F. W. Young, 447 Main Street, Houston, TX 70706-9536

Dear Mr. and Mrs. Young: As you probably know, our new department store opened September 25. Did (20) you attend our grand opening?

So many people attended and the crowds were so large that we had to close our (40) doors several times during the opening day. If you attended and were one of those who were unable to (60) get in, we are sorry and apologize.

We have decided to extend our grand opening until October (80) 10.

Will you please come back? Our grand opening bargains will continue, and more merchandise will be put on sale each day. (100)

Our sales staff has also been enlarged to better serve you. Sincerely yours, (113)

SKILL-BUILDING ASSIGNMENTS

1. Complete Unit 31 in *Forkner Shorthand Skill Builder for Colleges*.
2. Select Cassette 15 Side B of the *Theory and Speed-Building Tapes for Colleges* and follow the directions on the tape.
3. If instructed to do so, read, write, and transcribe the supplementary letter for this chapter found in Appendix A, Supplementary Dictation and Transcription.
4. Take additional live dictation as provided by your instructor.

Spelling review key

1. psychology, grievance 2. electrical, facilities, hindrance 3. itinerary, unnecessary 4. taxable, readily 5. Controlling, payable, indispensable 6. referring, technical, relevant 7. "fragile" 8. likable 9. exercise, manageable 10. recurred

Chapter 32

BUSINESS DICTATION AND TRANSCRIPTION

BUILDING TRANSCRIPTION SKILLS

Spelling review

The following words have been selected from words you have learned in this text. In each group of four words, one has been misspelled. Write the correct spelling of that word in your notebook. Compare your work with the key located at the end of the chapter.

1.	amateur	absense	apparent	attendance
2.	appraisel	achievement	arrangement	accessible
3.	beginning	brilliant	bookeeper	business
4.	concede	consistent	concievable	ceiling
5.	calendar	column	tradgedy	chief
6.	desirable	disappear	deductable	deferred
7.	definite	decision	dissatisfied	disipline
8.	enforceable	exagerate	experience	essential
9.	foresee	friend	fascinate	Febuary
10.	goverment	guarantee	guidance	generally
11.	hopeful	heretofor	humorous	hardware
12.	invoicing	identical	temperment	indebtedness
13.	jealous	lodging	legable	library
14.	mortgage	transfered	misspell	mediocre
15.	negotiate	neccesary	noticeable	itinerary
16.	occurence	omitted	offering	occurred
17.	pleasant	proffessor	privilege	precede
18.	questionaire	quantity	referred	recommend
19.	serviceable	seperate	submitted	studying

20. usually	undoubtly	usable	uniform
21. vegetable	villain	visable	voucher
22. whose	written	weather	writting
23. yield	knowlege	interfere	foreign

Application—**Word usage**. How well have you mastered the word-usage exercises in the Business Transcription Skills sections throughout this text? In your notebook number from 1—25. Select from the words in parentheses the word that best fits the definition and write it opposite the appropriate number. Check your work with the key located in Appendix G at the back of this text.

1. writing materials (stationary, stationery)
2. also (to, too, two)
3. smallest in size or degree (leased, least)
4. not strong (weak, week)
5. completely ready (already, all ready)
6. payable (do, dew, due)
7. belonging to them (there, their, they're)
8. the act of being present (attendance, attendants)
9. a city that is a government seat (capital, capitol)
10. to perform addition (ad, add)
11. aid, help (assistance, assistants)
12. basic law (principal, principle)
13. large (grate, great)
14. permitted (allowed, aloud)
15. futile, conceited (vain, vane, vein)
16. to counsel (advice, advise)
17. an erasing (eraser, erasure)

18. to praise (complement, compliment)
19. to be aware of (know, no)
20. a portion (peace, piece)
21. a view (scene, seen)
22. communication by letter (correspondence, correspondents)
23. join, come together (meet, meat, mete)
24. change (vary, very)
25. climate (weather, whether)

Correcting errors in dictation

A very important transcription skill is the ability of the secretary to detect obvious errors and to correct them during transcription. In the following letter to Mr. Brown there are obvious mistakes. An alert secretary would assume the responsibility for correcting such errors *without first consulting the dictator*. Read through the letter and then transcribe it making all of the necessary corrections. Mr. Brown is four months (March, April, May, and June) delinquent in the amount of $400.

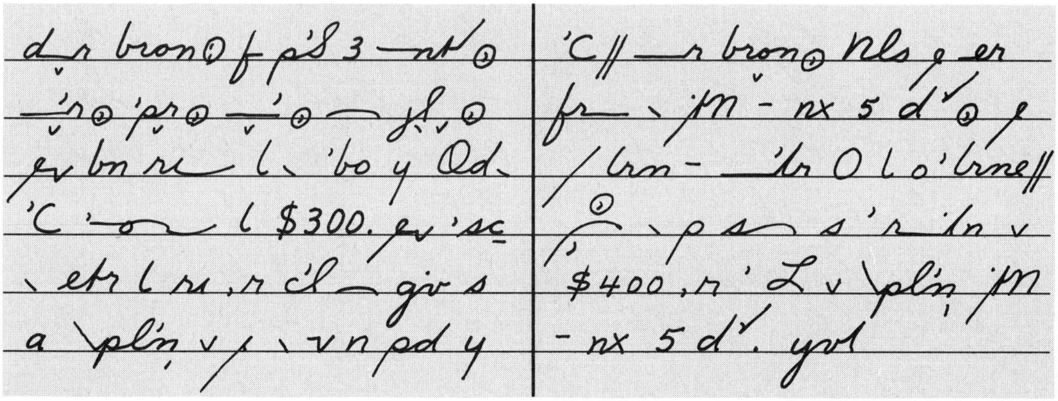

Transcript

Dear Mr. Brown: For the past four months, March, April, May, and June, we have been writing to you about your overdue account amounting to $400. We have asked you either to write or call and give us an explanation of why you have not paid your account.

Mr. Brown, unless we hear from you within the next five days, we will turn the matter over to our attorney.

Won't you please send us a remittance of $400 or a letter of explanation within the next five days. Yours very truly,

BUILDING WRITING AND TRANSCRIPTION SKILLS

Passage 1

The following passage contains 226 standard words, some of which may be new to you. Read the passage twice, and calculate your reading rate each time. The second reading should be faster than the first. When finished reading and calculating, scribble-write the passage twice for speed development.

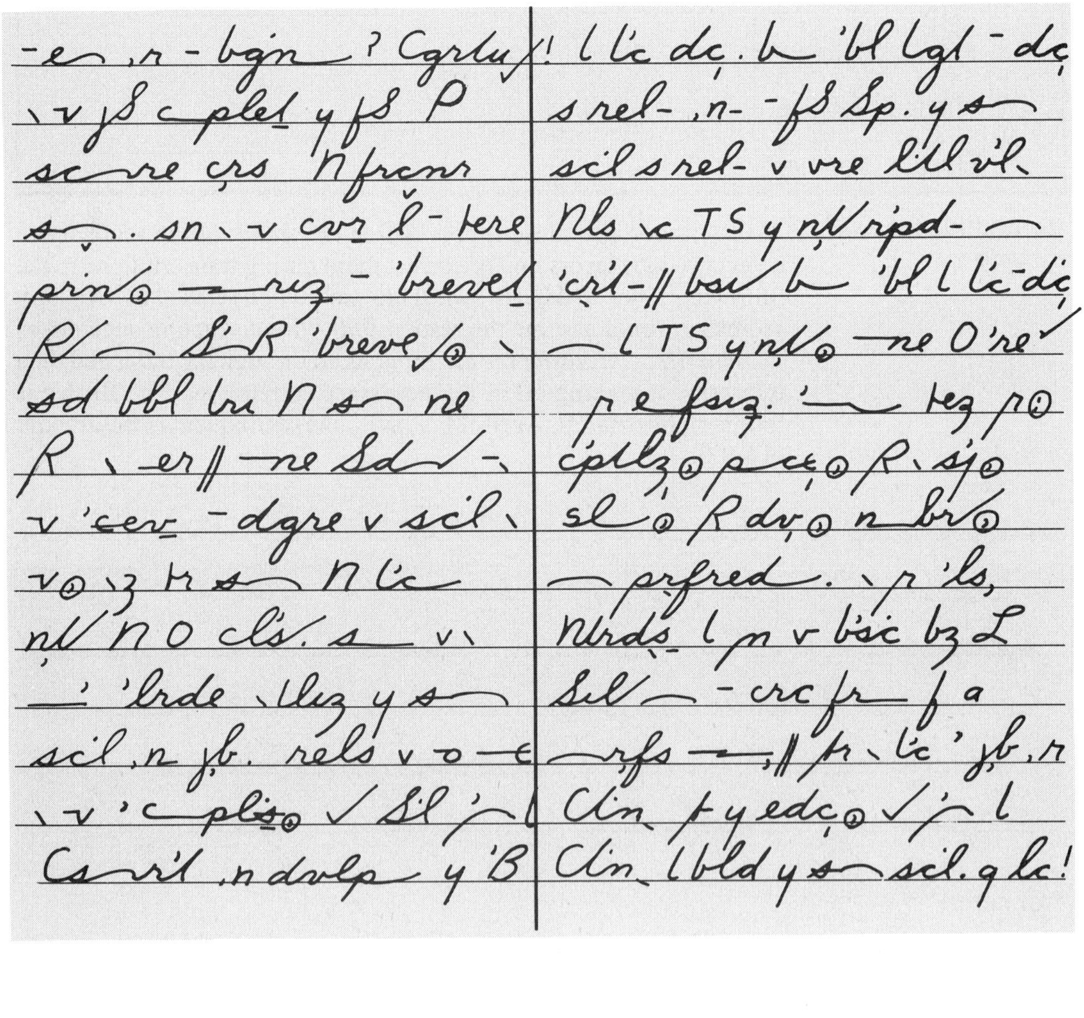

Passage 1 transcript

THE END OR THE BEGINNING?
Congratulations! You have just completed your first post-secondary course in Forkner Shorthand. Since you have covered (20) all the theory principles, memorized the abbreviated words and standard

abbreviations, you should be (40) able to write in shorthand any word you hear.

Many students who have achieved the degree of skill you have, use (60) their shorthand in taking notes in other classes. Some of you may already utilize your shorthand skill on the (80) job. Regardless of how much you have accomplished, you will still want to concentrate on developing your ability (100) to take dictation. Being able to get the dictation is really only the first step. Your shorthand (120) skill is really of very little value unless you can transcribe your notes rapidly and accurately.

Besides (140) being able to take the dictation and to transcribe your notes, many other areas were emphasized. (160) Among these were: capitalization, punctuation, word usage, spelling, word division, numbers, and proofreading. (180) You were also introduced to one of the basic business letter styles and the correct form for an interoffice (200) memorandum.

Whether you take a job or continue with your education, you will want to continue (220) to build your shorthand skill. Good luck! (226)

DICTATION AND TRANSCRIPTION

Write from dictation Passage 1. Your instructor will dictate it to you at various speeds.

Using your own notes, transcribe the passage using an appropriate format for an unbound manuscript.

SKILL-BUILDING ASSIGNMENTS

1. Complete Unit 32 in *Forkner Shorthand Skill Builder for Colleges*.
2. Select Cassette 16 Side B of the *Theory and Speed-Building Tapes for Colleges* and follow the directions on the tape.
3. If instructed to do so, read, write, and transcribe the supplementary letter for this chapter found in Appendix A, Supplementary Dictation and Transcription.
4. Take additional live dictation as provided by your instructor.

REVIEWING THE WRITING PRINCIPLES

All the writing rules, abbreviated words, and standard abbreviations you have learned in Chapters 25 through 32 are reviewed on Cassette 18 Side B of the *Theory and Speed-Building Tapes for Colleges*. Take dictation from this tape before completing Preview Examination 8.

PREVIEW EXAMINATION 8

Remove Preview Examination 8 from your *Forkner Shorthand Skill Builder for Colleges*. It follows Unit 32. This informal preview examination will help you in assessing your understanding of the Forkner principles presented in Chapters 29—32. It is similar to Examination 8 which may be administered at a later date by your instructor.

Complete Preview Examination 8 and then check your answers carefully with the key in your *Forkner Shorthand Skill Builder for Colleges*. Correct any errors you may have made.

FINAL EXAMINATION

Remove and complete the Final Examination at the back of your *Forkner Shorthand Skill Builder for Colleges*.

Spelling review key

1. absence 2. appraisal 3. bookkeeper 4. conceivable
5. tragedy 6. deductible 7. discipline 8. exaggerate
9. February 10. government 11. heretofore
12. temperament 13. legible 14. transferred
15. necessary 16. occurrence 17. professor
18. questionnaire 19. separate 20. undoubtedly
21. visible 22. writing 23. knowledge

APPENDIXES

Appendix A Supplementary Dictation and Transcription 237

There are 34 supplementary passages for dictation and transcription practice—a minimum of one passage for each text chapter. Each passage contains words that illustrate the writing principles introduced up to and including that chapter. For example, the supplementary letter headed Chapter 10, Letter 2 in this appendix would be used only after study of Chapter 10 is completed. Vocabulary used in the passages is drawn from the text and from the *Skill Builder*.

Appendix B Abbreviated Words 266

Numbers in parentheses refer to the chapter in which the abbreviated word is introduced.

Appendix C Standard Abbreviations, Standard Symbols 268

Appendix D Abbreviations for Days; Months; States, Districts, and Territories; Provinces and Territories 269

Appendix E Summary of Writing Principles 271

This appendix contains a summary of all the principles of Forkner Shorthand cross-referenced to the chapter in which the principle was introduced. Following the list of principles are eight sentences each of which illustrates the principles introduced in each four-chapter text sequence. For example, the sentence headed Chapters 1–4 illustrates all of the writing principles introduced in Chapters 1–4.

Appendix F Summary of English Principles 278

Numbers in parentheses refer to the chapter in which the principle was introduced.

Appendix G Keys to Application Exercises 281

APPENDIX A

SUPPLEMENTARY DICTATION AND TRANSCRIPTION

Chapter 1, Passage 2

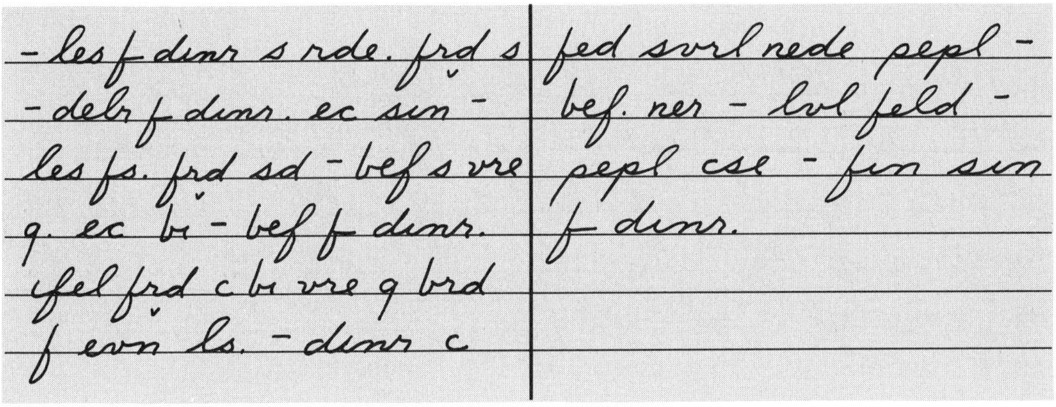

Chapter 1, Passage 2 Transcript

The lease for the diner is ready. Fred is the dealer for the diner. He can sign the lease for us. Fred said the (20) beef is very good. He can buy the beef for the diner. I feel Fred can buy very good bread for even less. (40) The diner can feed several needy people the beef. Near the level field the people can see the fine sign for (60) the diner. (62)

Chapter 2, Letter 2

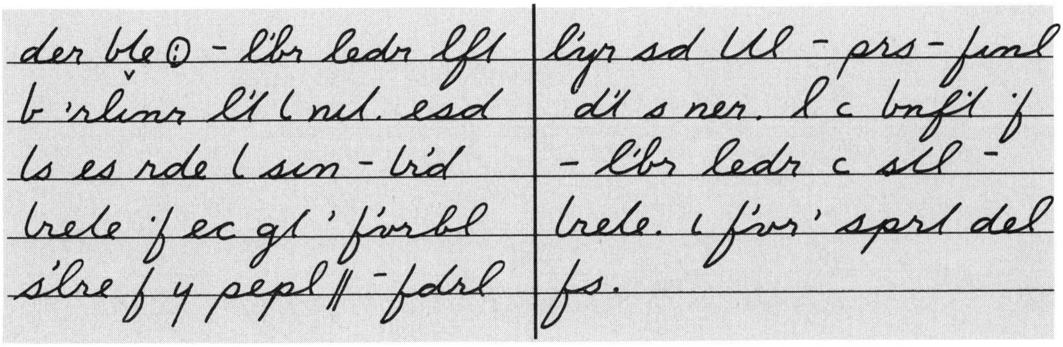

Chapter 2, Letter 2 Transcript

Dear Betty: The labor leader left by airliner late at night. He said to us he is ready to sign the trade (20) treaty if he can get a favorable salary for your people.

The federal lawyer said to tell the (40) press the final date is near. All can benefit if the labor leader can settle the treaty. I favor a (60) separate deal for us. (64)

Chapter 3, Letter 2

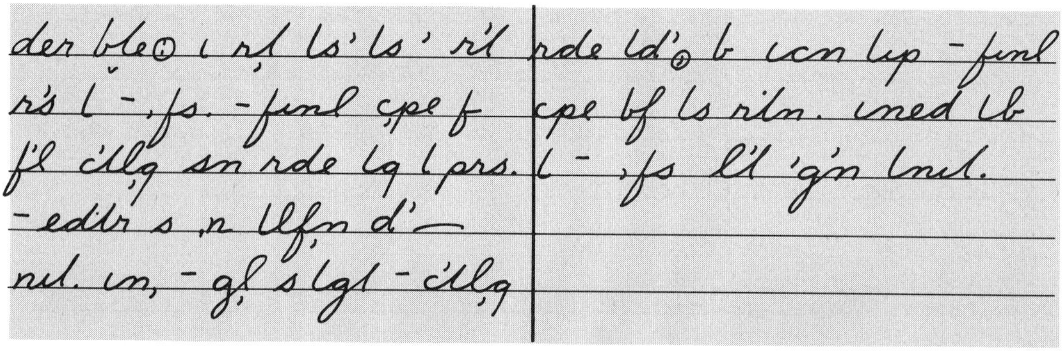

Chapter 3, Letter 2 Transcript

Dear Betty: I wrote to say it is a rat race at the office. The final copy for the fall catalog is (20) not ready to go to press. The editor is on the telephone day and night. I know the goal is to get the (40) catalog ready today, but I cannot type the final copy before it is written. I need to be at (60) the office late again tonight. (66)

Chapter 4, Letter 3

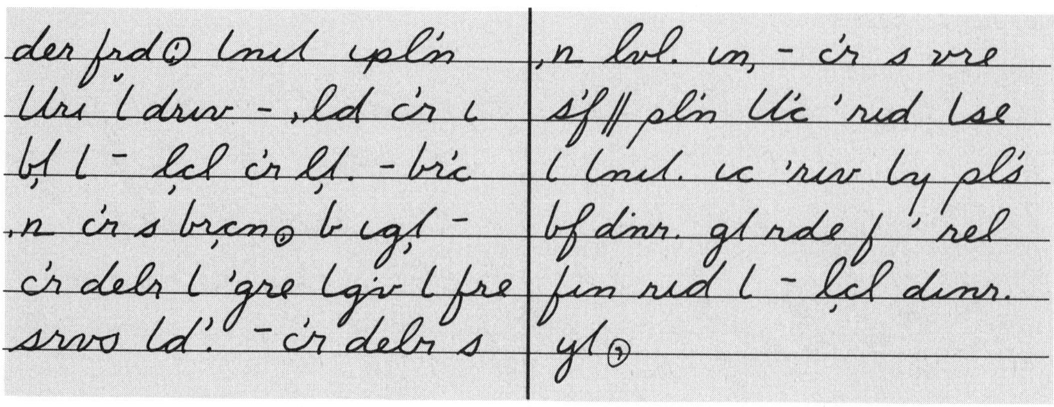

Chapter 4, Letter 3 Transcript

Dear Fred: Tonight I plan to try to drive the old car I bought at the local car lot. The brake on the car is (20) broken, but I got the car dealer to agree to give it free service today. The car dealer is on the level. (40) I know the car is very safe.

Plan to take a ride to see it tonight. I can arrive at your place before (60) dinner. Get ready for a real fine ride to the local diner. Yours truly. (73)

Chapter 5, Letter 2

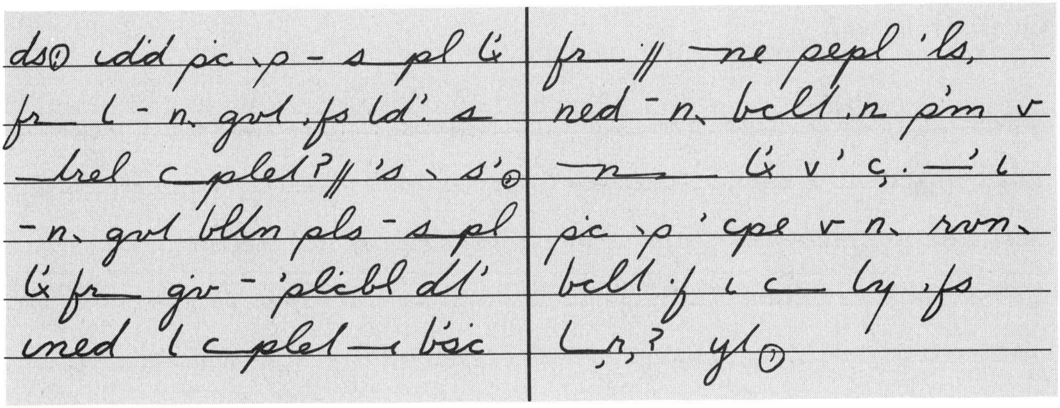

Chapter 5, Letter 2 Transcript

Dear Sir: I did pick up the sample tax form at the new government office today. Is the material (20) complete?

As you say, the new government bulletin plus the sample tax form give the applicable data I need (40) to complete my basic form.

Many people also need the new booklet on the payment of the minimum tax (60) of a company. May I pick up a copy of the new revenue booklet if I come to your office (80) tomorrow? Yours truly, (83)

Chapter 6, Letter 2

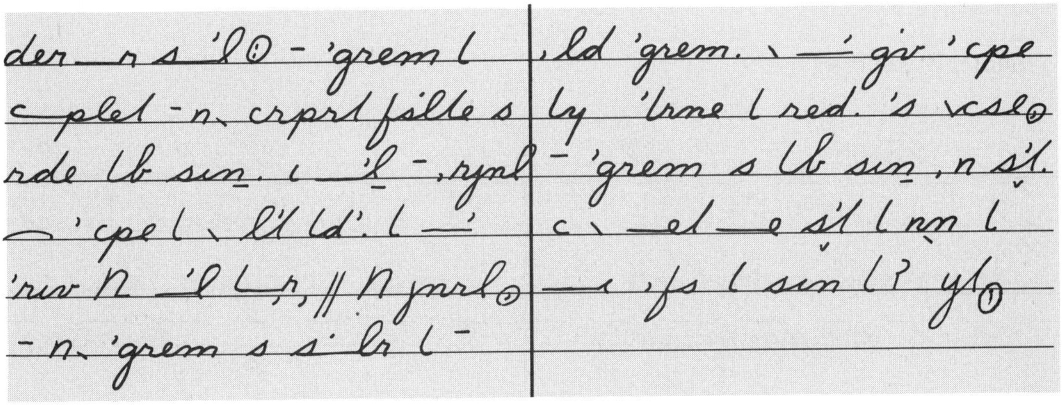

Chapter 6, Letter 2 Transcript

Dear Mr. Small: The agreement to complete the new corporate facility is ready to be signed. I mailed (20) the original and a copy to you late today. It may arrive in the mail tomorrow.

In general, (40) the new agreement is similar to the old agreement. You may give a copy to your attorney to read. (60) As you can see, the agreement is to be signed on Saturday. Can you meet me Saturday at noon at my (80) office to sign it? Yours truly, (85)

Chapter 7, Letter 2

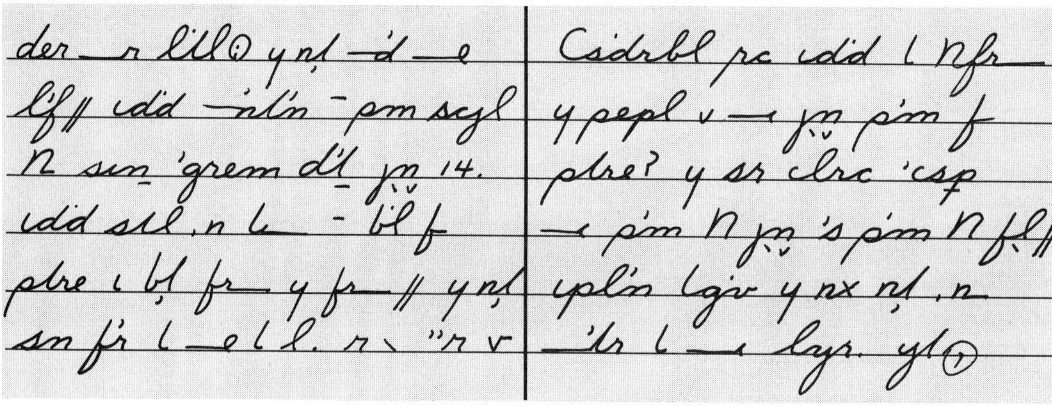

Chapter 7, Letter 2 Transcript

Dear Mr. Little: Your note made me laugh.

I did maintain the payment schedule in the signed agreement dated June 14. (20) I did settle on time the bill for the pottery I bought from your firm.

Your note is not fair to me at all. (40) Are you aware of the considerable work I did to inform your people of my June payment for the pottery? (60) Your senior clerk accepted my payment in June as payment in full.

I plan to give your next note on the matter (80) to my lawyer. Yours truly, (86)

Chapter 8, Letter 4

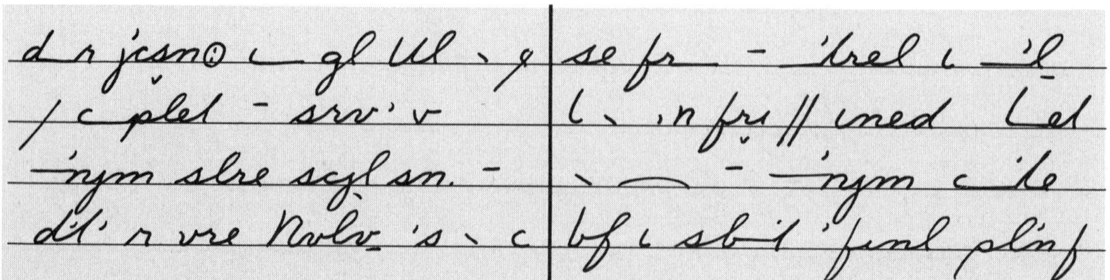

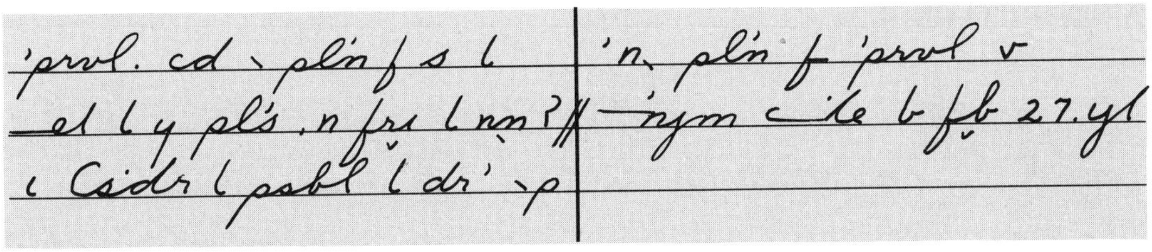

Chapter 8, Letter 4 Transcript

Dear Mr. Jackson: I am glad to tell you we will complete the survey of the management salary schedule soon. (20) The data are very involved as you can see from the material I mailed to you on Friday.

I need to (40) meet you and the management committee before I submit a final plan for approval. Could you plan for us (60) to meet at your place on Friday at noon?

I consider it possible to draw up a new plan for the approval (80) of the management committee by February 27. Yours truly, (95)

Chapter 9, Letter 2

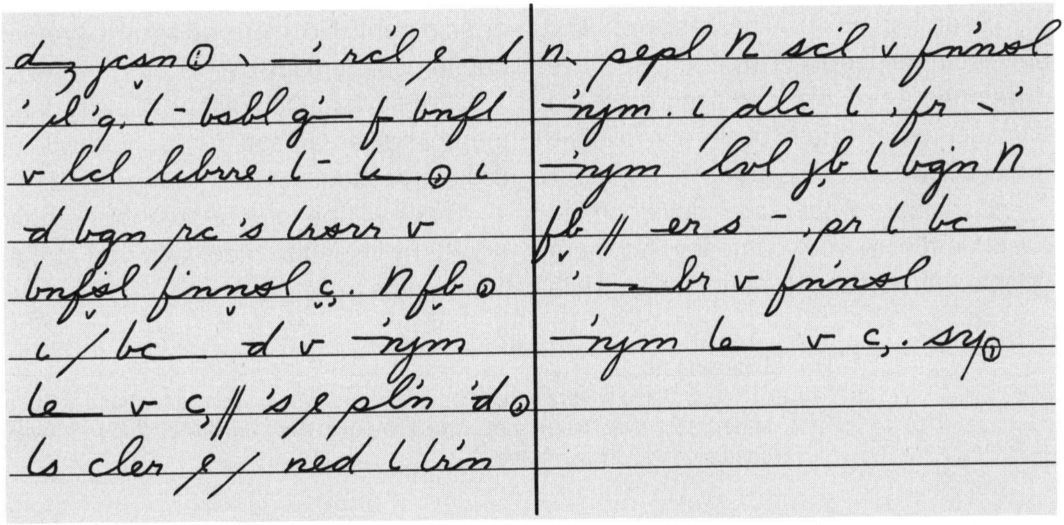

Chapter 9, Letter 2 Transcript

Dear Ms. Jackson: You may recall we met a while ago at the baseball game for the benefit of the local (20) library. At the time, I had begun work as treasurer of the Beneficial Financial Company. In (40) February, I will become head of the management team of the company.

As we plan ahead, it is clear (60) we will need to train new people in the skill of financial management. I would like to offer you a management (80)-level job to begin in February.

Here is the opportunity to become a member of the (100) financial management team of the company. Sincerely yours, (111)

Chapter 10, Letter 2

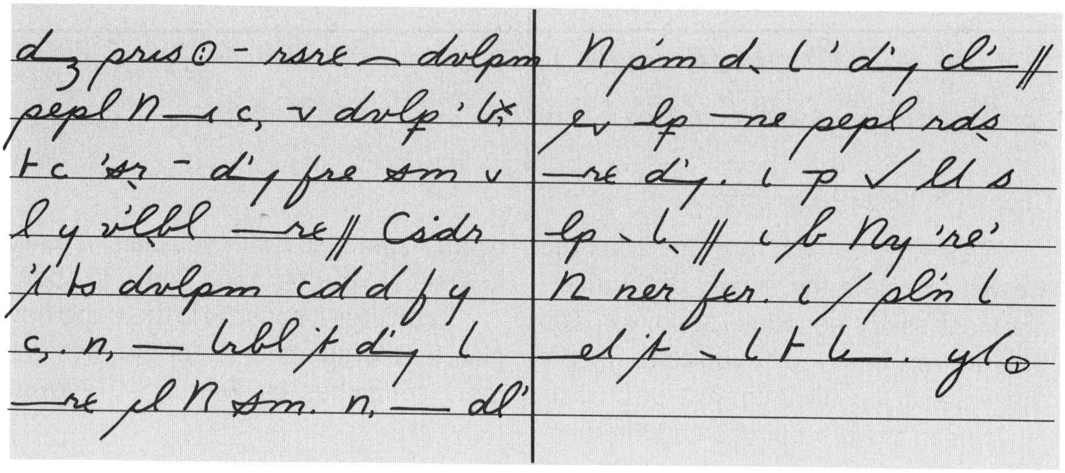

Chapter 10, Letter 2 Transcript

Dear Ms. Price: The research and development people in my company have developed a box that can assure (20) the damage-free shipment of all your valuable merchandise.

Consider what this development could do for (40) your company. No more trouble with damage to merchandise while in shipment. No more delay in payment due to (60) a damage claim.

We have helped many people reduce merchandise damage. I hope you will let us help you too.

I (80) will be in your area in the near future. I will plan to meet with you at that time. Yours truly. (98)

Learning tip:

Shorthand writers usually omit hyphens when writing shorthand notes at speed. However, when a hyphen is written, it is normally circled to prevent confusion with the word *the*.

Chapter 11, Letter 2

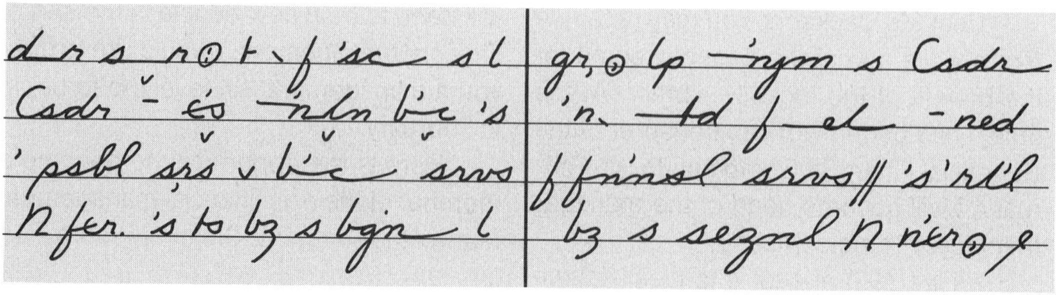

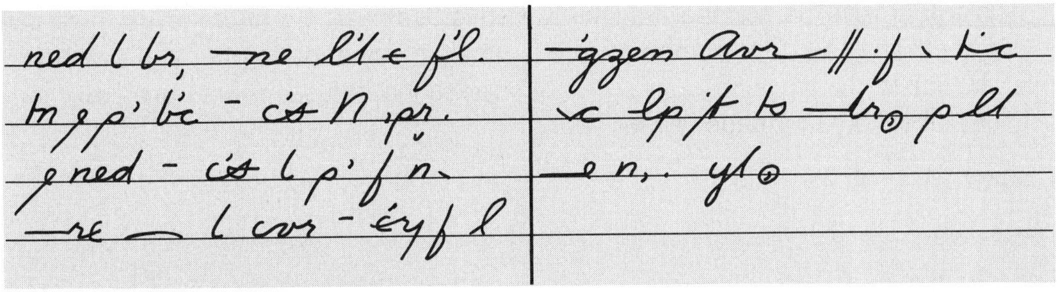

Chapter 11, Letter 2 Transcript

Dear Mr. Summer: Thank you for asking us to consider the Chase Manhattan Bank as a possible source of (20) banking service in the future. As this business is beginning to grow, top management is considering a (40) new method for meeting the need for financial service.

As a retail business is seasonal in nature, we (60) need to borrow money late each fall. Then we pay back the cash in April. We need the cash to pay for new merchandise (80) and to cover the charge for all magazine advertising.

If you think you can help with this matter, please let (100) me know. Yours truly, (104)

Chapter 12, Letter 3

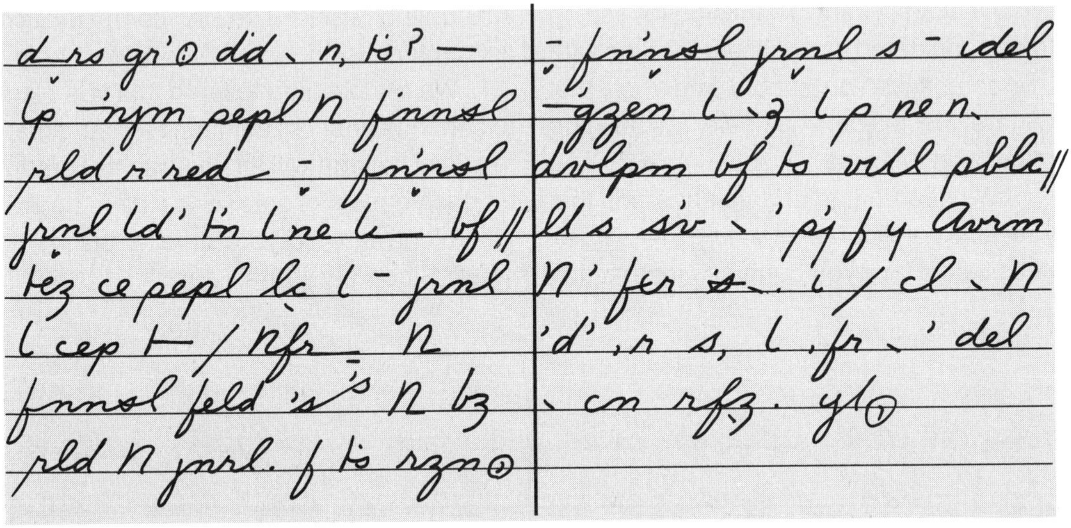

Chapter 12, Letter 3 Transcript

Dear Mrs. Gray: Did you know this? More top management people in the financial world are reading <u>The Financial</u> (20) <u>Journal</u> today than at any time before.

These key people look to <u>The Journal</u> to keep them well informed in the (40) financial field as well as in the business world in general. For this reason, <u>The</u>

Financial Journal is the (60) ideal magazine to use to put any new development before this vital public.

Let us save you a page (80) for your advertisement in a future issue. I will call you in a day or so to offer you a deal you (100) cannot refuse. Yours truly, (105)

Chapter 13, Letter 2

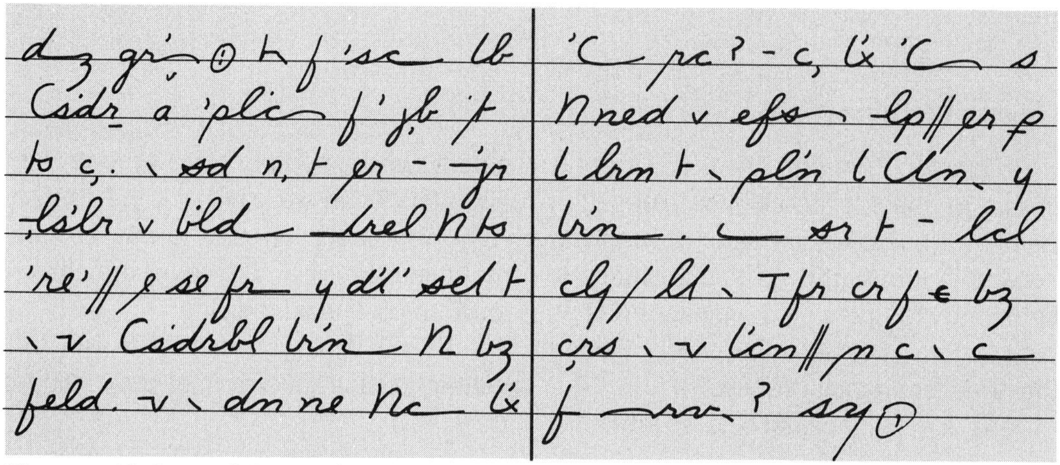

Chapter 13, Letter 2 Transcript

Dear Ms. Grant: Thank you for asking to be considered an applicant for a job with this company. You should know (20) that we are the major wholesaler of building material in this area.

We see from your data sheet (40) that you have considerable training in the business field. Have you done any income tax accounting work? The (60) company tax accountant is in need of efficient help.

We are pleased to learn that you plan to continue your (80) training. I am sure that the local college will let you transfer credit for each business course you have taken.

When can (100) you come for the interview? Sincerely yours, (108)

Chapter 14, Letter 2

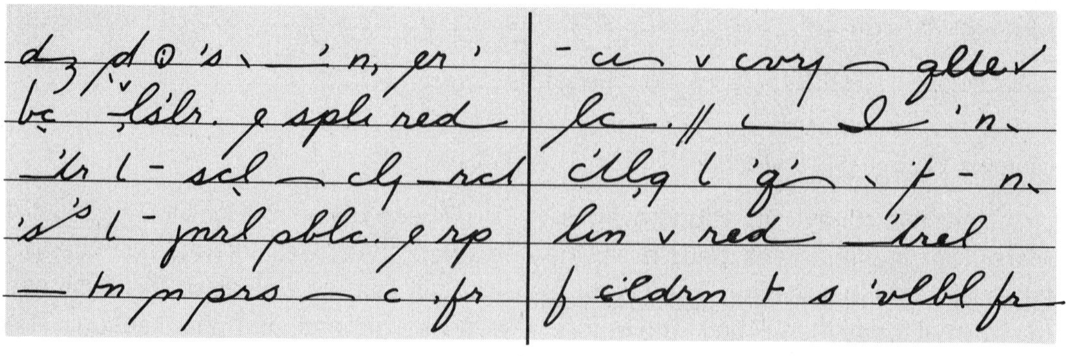

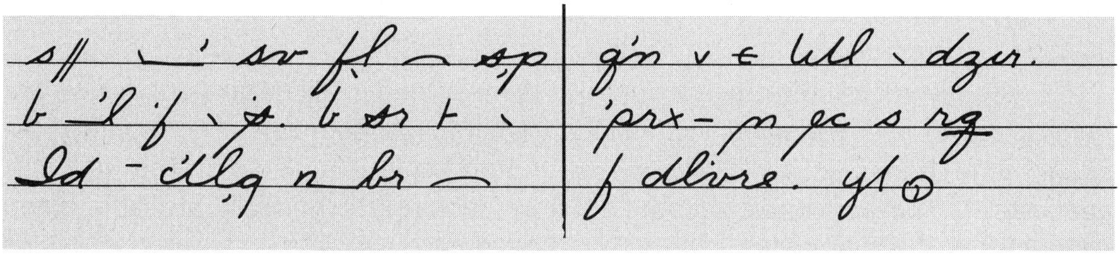

Chapter 14, Letter 2 Transcript

Dear Ms. Wood: As you may know, we are a book wholesaler. We supply reading matter to the school and college (20) market as well as to the general public. We represent more than one press and can offer the kind of coverage (40) and quality you will welcome.

I am enclosing a new catalog to acquaint you with the new line of (60) reading material for children that is available from us.

You may save fuel and shop by mail if you wish. (80) Be sure that you include the catalog number and quantity of each title you desire. Approximately (100) one week is required for delivery. Yours truly, (110)

Chapter 15, Memorandum 2

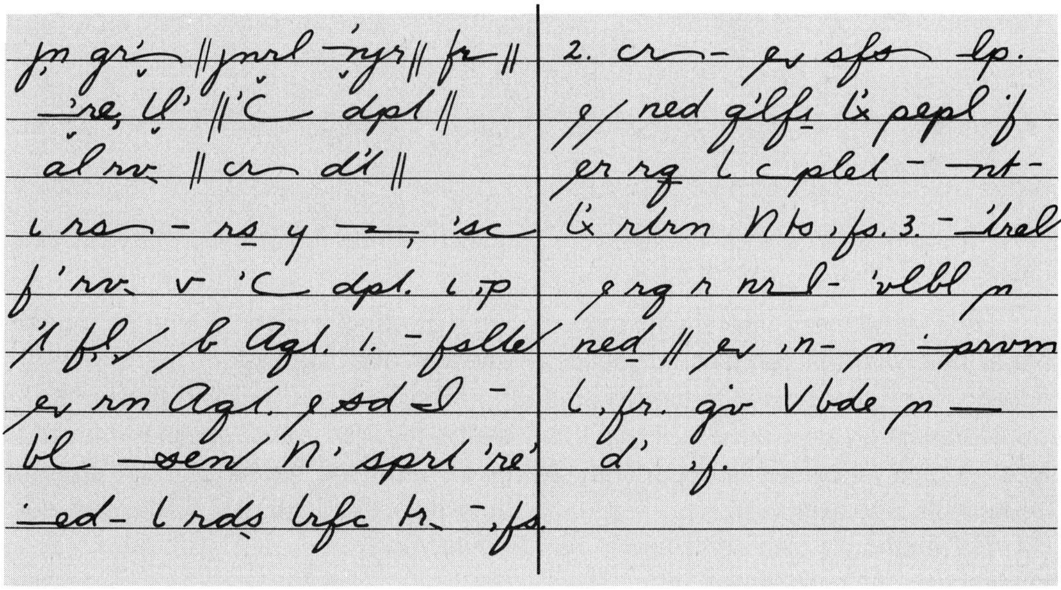

Chapter 15, Memorandum 2 Transcript

TO: John Grant, General Manager

FROM: Mario Tella, Accounting Department

CONTENT: Annual Review
DATE: Current date

I recently received your memorandum asking for a review of the accounting department. I hope what (20) follows will be adequate. 1. The facilities we have are not adequate. We should enclose the billing (40) machines in a separate area immediately to reduce traffic through the office. 2. Currently we (60) have sufficient help. We will need qualified tax people if we are required to complete the monthly tax return (80) in this office. 3. The materials we require are normally available when needed.

We have only (100) one improvement to offer. Give everybody one more day off. (112)

Chapter 16, Letter 3

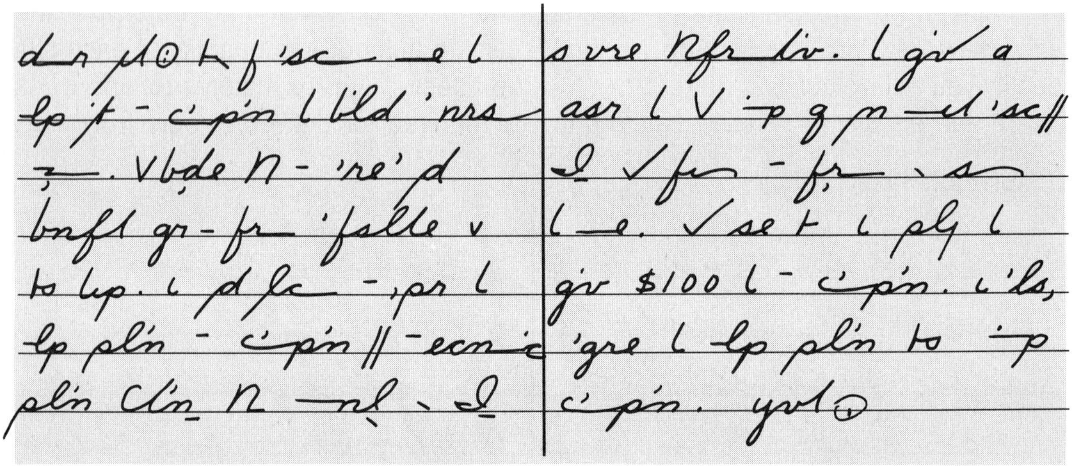

Chapter 16, Letter 3 Transcript

Dear Mr. White: Thank you for asking me to help with the campaign to build a nursing home. Everybody in the (20) area would benefit greatly from a facility of this type. I would welcome the opportunity to (40) help plan the campaign.

The economic plan contained in the manual you enclosed is very informative. (60) It gives an answer to every important question one might ask.

Enclosed you will find the form you sent to me. You (80) will see that I pledge to give $100 to the campaign. I also agree to help plan this important (100) campaign. Yours very truly, (105)

Chapter 17, Memorandum 2

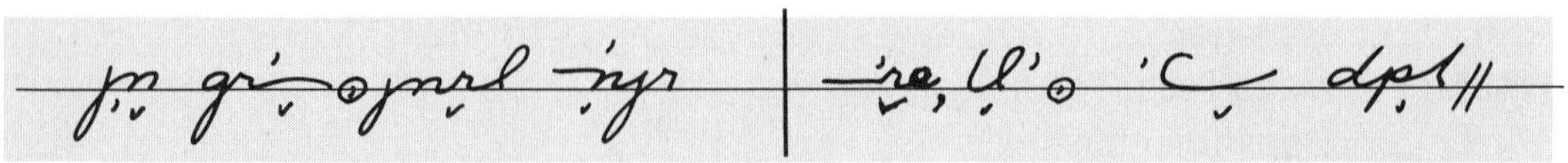

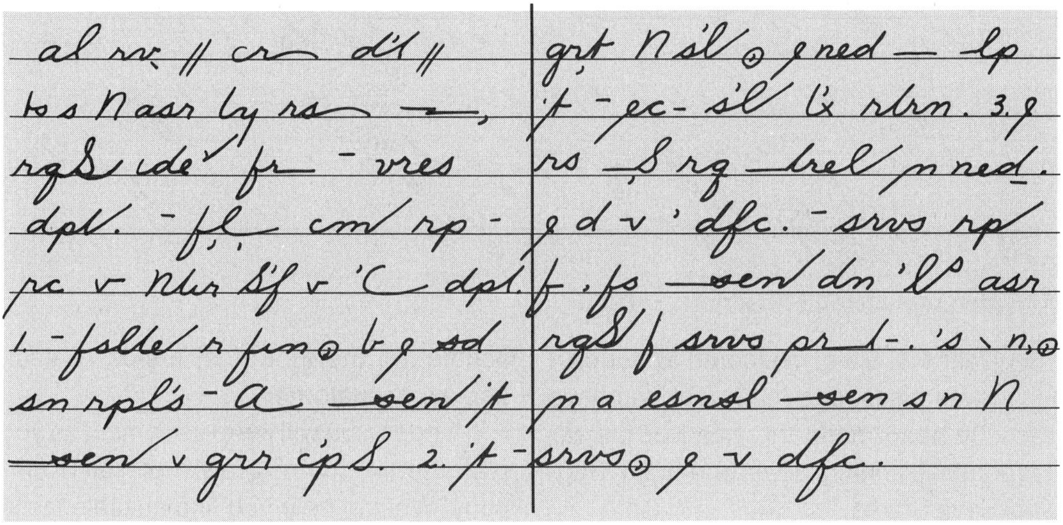

Chapter 17, Memorandum 2 Transcript

TO: John Grant, General Manager
FROM: Mario Tella, Accounting Department
SUBJECT: Annual Review
DATE: Current date

This is in answer to your recent memorandum requesting ideas from the various departments. The (20) following comments represent the work of the entire staff of the accounting department. 1. The facilities (40) are fine, but we should soon replace the adding machines with machines of greater capacity. 2. With the growth in sales, (60) we need more help with the weekly sales tax return. 3. We receive most required materials when needed. We do have a (80) difficulty. The service representatives for the office machines do not always answer requests for (100) service promptly. As you know, when an essential machine is not in service, we have difficulty. (117)

Chapter 18, Letter 2

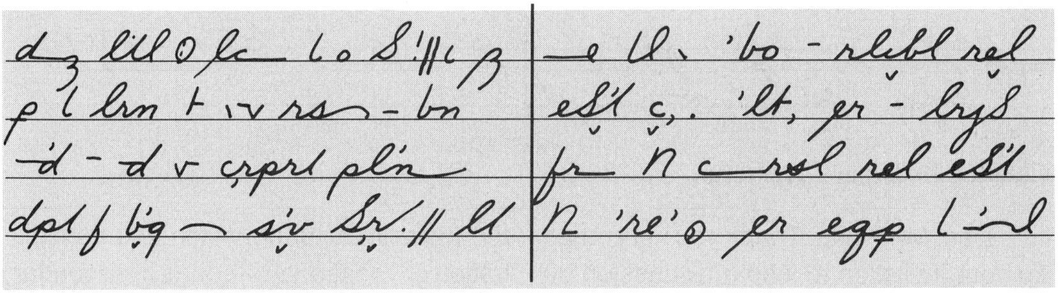

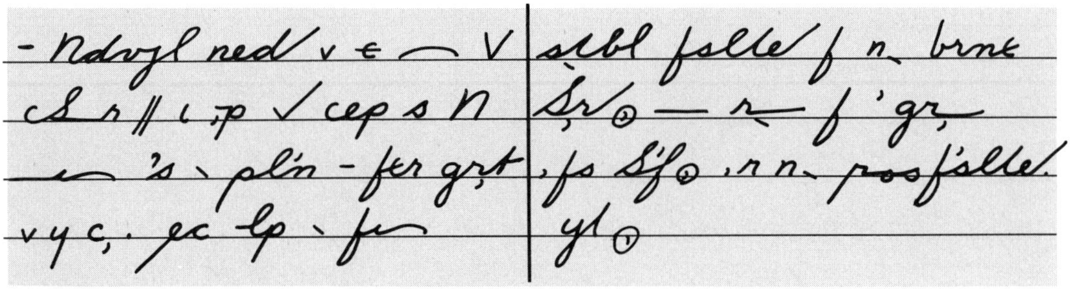

Chapter 18, Letter 2 Transcript

Dear Ms. Little: Welcome to our city!

I was pleased to learn that you have recently been made the head of the (20) corporate planning department for Bag-and-Save Stores.

Let me tell you about the Reliable Real Estate Company. (40) Although we are the largest firm in commercial real estate in the area, we are equipped to handle (60) the individual needs of each and every customer.

I hope you will keep us in mind as you plan the (80) future growth of your company. We can help you find suitable facilities for new branch stores, more room for a (100) growing office staff, or new warehouse facilities. Yours truly, (111)

Chapter 19, Letter 2

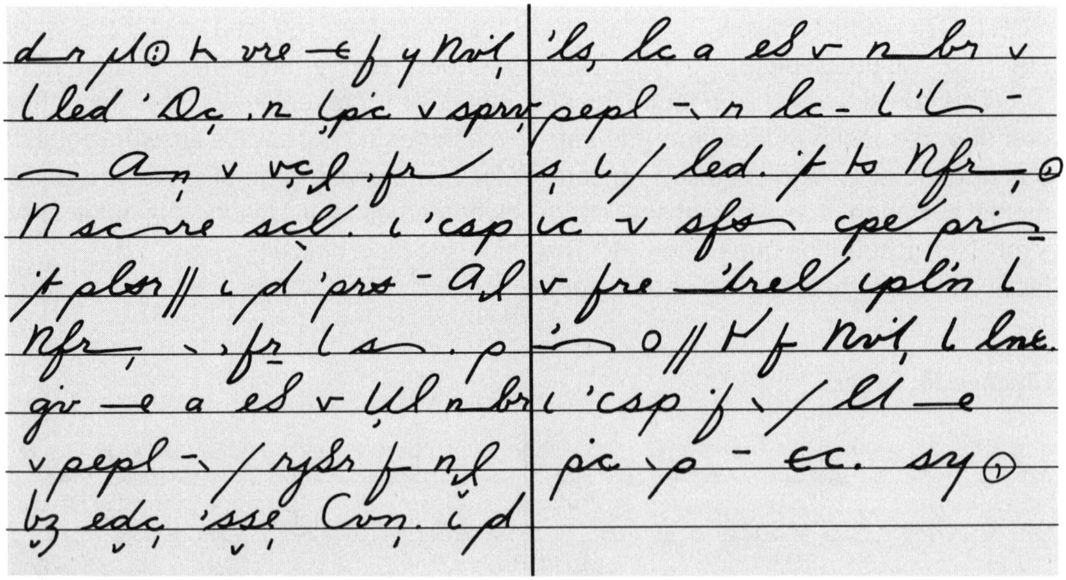

Chapter 19, Letter 2 Transcript

Dear Mr. White: Thank you very much for your invitation to lead a discussion on the topic of (20) supervision and administration of vocational offerings in secondary schools. I accept with pleasure. (40)

I would appreciate the additional information you offered to send. Please give me an estimate of (60) the total number of people who will register for the National Business Education Association (80) Convention. I would also like an estimate of the number of people who are likely to attend the (100) session I will lead. With this information, I can have sufficient copies printed of the free materials I plan (120) to hand out.

Thanks for the invitation to lunch. I accept if you will let me pick up the check! Sincerely (140) yours, (141)

Chapter 20, Letter 5

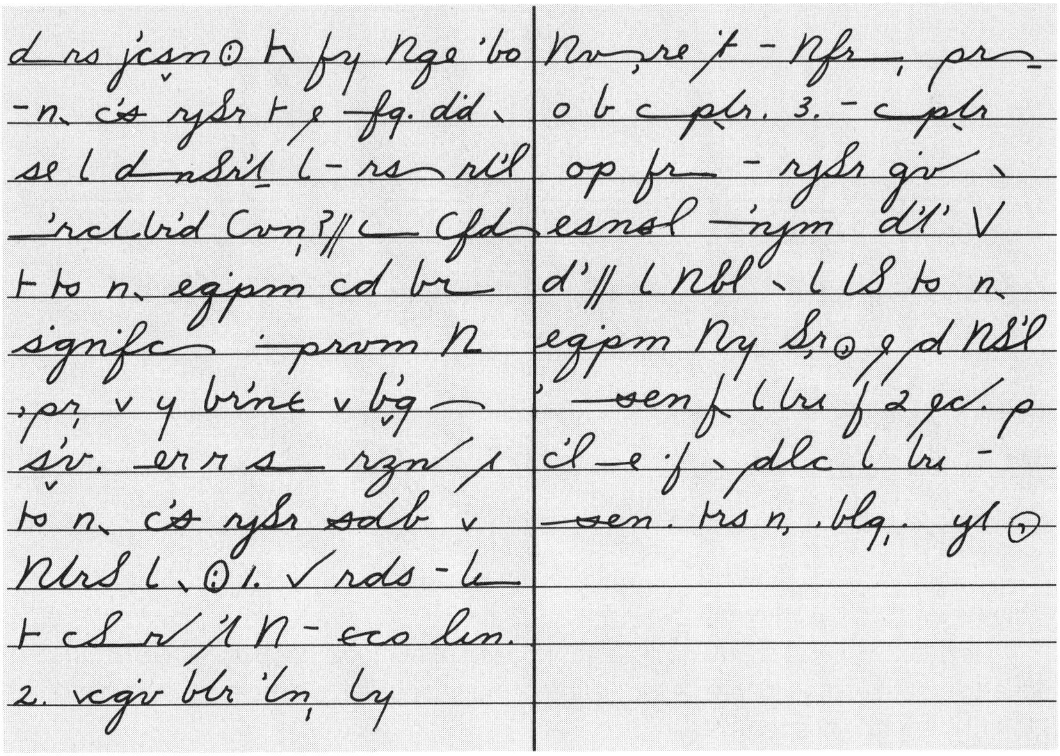

Chapter 20, Letter 5 Transcript

Dear Mrs. Jackson: Thank you for your inquiry about the new cash register that we manufacture. Did you (20) see it demonstrated at the recent retail marketing trade convention?

I am confident that this new (40) equipment could bring significant improvement in the operation of your branch of Bag-and-Save. Here are some (60) reasons why this new cash register should be of interest to you: 1. You will reduce the time that customers wait (80) in the check-out line. 2. You can give better attention to your inventory with the information printed out (100) by computer. 3. The computer output from the register gives you essential management data every (120) day.

To enable you to test this new equipment in your store, we would install a machine for you to try for (140) two weeks. Please call me if you would like to try the machine. There is no obligation. Yours truly, (157)

Chapter 21, Letter 2

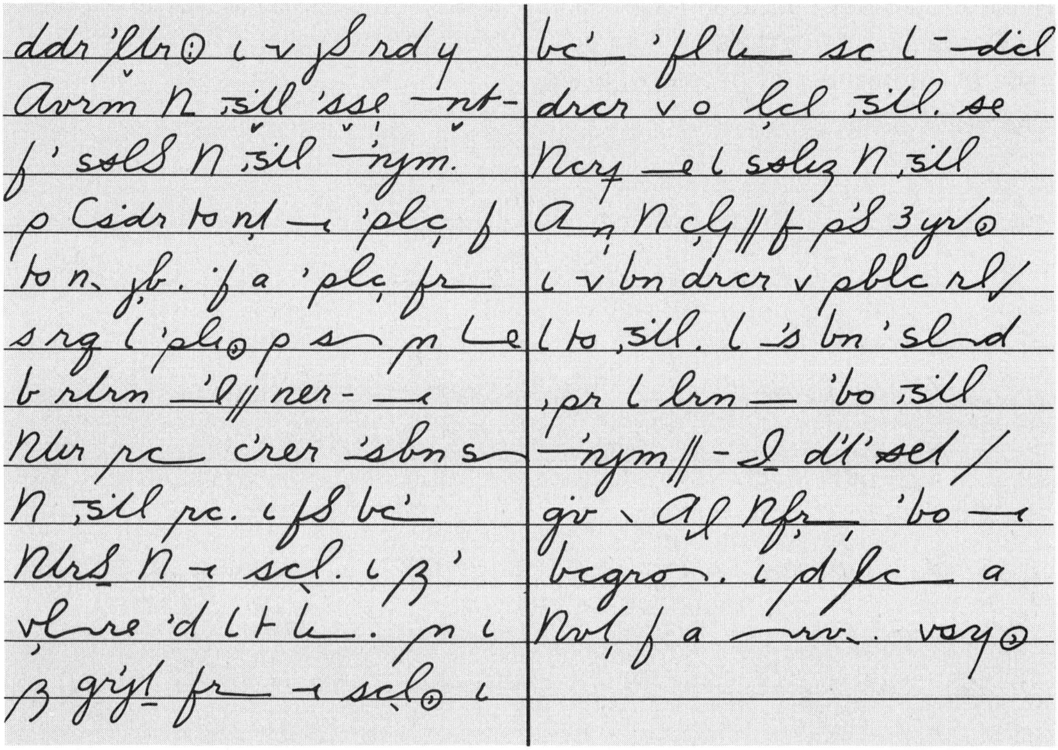

Chapter 21, Letter 2 Transcript

Dear Dr. Walter: I have just read your advertisement in the Hospital Association Monthly for a (20) specialist in hospital management. Please consider this note my application for this new job. If an (40) application form is required to apply, please send one to me by return mail.

Nearly my entire working career (60) has been spent in hospital work. I first became interested in high school. I was a voluntary aide at (80) that time. When I was graduated from high school, I became a full-time secretary to the medical director (100) of our local hospital. She encouraged me to specialize in hospital administration in college. (120)

For the past three years, I have been director of public relations at this hospital. It has been a splendid (140) opportunity to learn more about hospital management.

The enclosed data sheet will give you additional (160) information about my background. I would welcome an invitation for an interview. Very sincerely (180) yours, (182)

Chapter 21, Letter 3

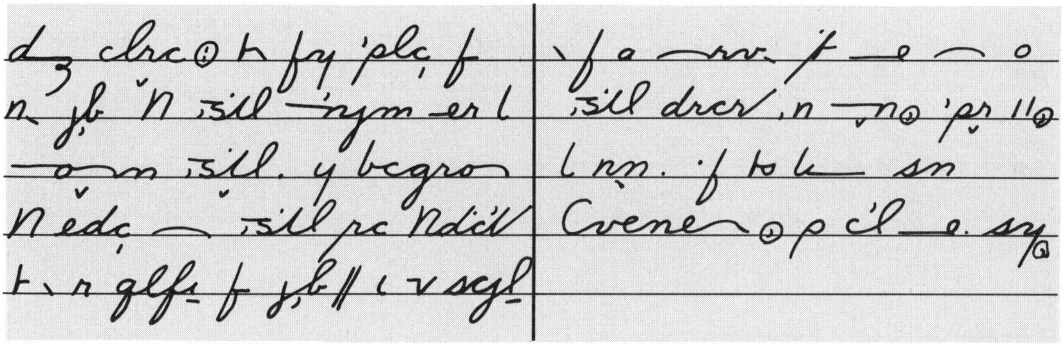

Chapter 21, Letter 3 Transcript

Dear Ms. Clark: Thank you for your application for the new job in hospital management here at Mountain Hospital. (20) Your background in education and hospital work indicates that you are qualified for the job.

I have (40) scheduled you for an interview with me and our hospital directors on Monday, April 11, at noon. If (60) this time is not convenient, please call me. Sincerely yours, (70)

Chapter 22, Letter 2

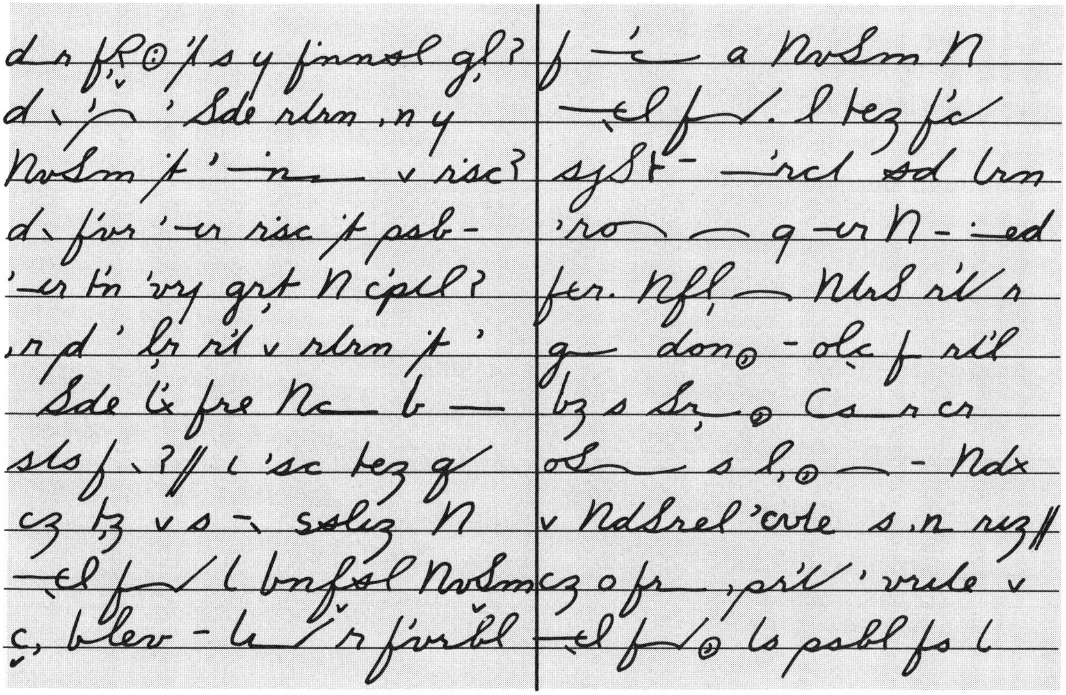

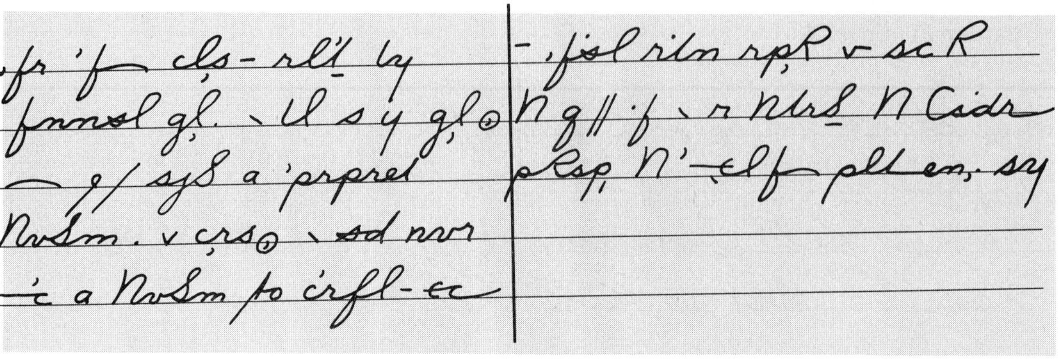

Chapter 22, Letter 2 Transcript

Dear Mr. Ford: What is your financial goal? Do you want a steady return on your investment with a minimum (20) of risk? Do you favor a higher risk with possibly a higher-than-average growth in capital? Or (40) would a lower rate of return with a steady tax-free income be more satisfactory for you?

I ask these (60) questions because those of us who specialize in mutual funds at Beneficial Investment Company believe (80) the times are favorable for making an investment in mutual funds. All these facts suggest that the market should turn (100) around and go higher in the immediate future. Inflation and interest rates are going down, the (120) outlook for the retail business is strong, consumer credit outstanding is low, and the index of industrial (140) activity is on the rise.

Because our firm operates a variety of mutual funds, it is (160) possible for us to offer a fund closely related to your financial goal. You tell us your goal, and we will (180) suggest an appropriate investment. Of course, you should never make an investment without carefully checking the (200) official written report of the security in question.

If you are interested in considering (220) participation in a mutual fund, please let me know. Sincerely yours, (233)

Chapter 23, Letter 2

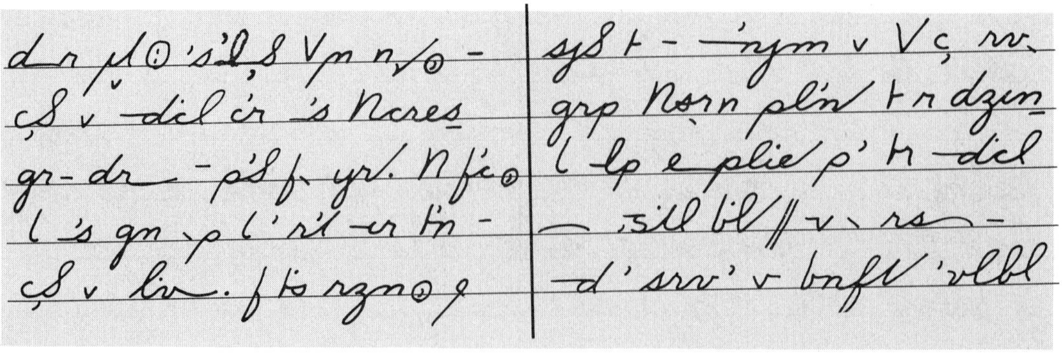

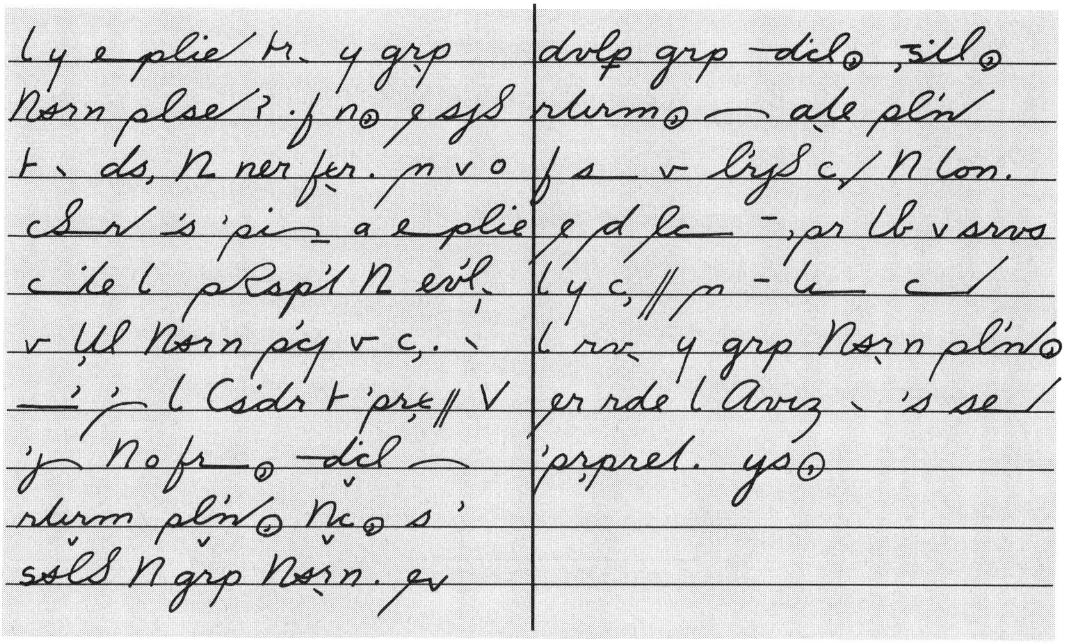

Chapter 23, Letter 2 Transcript

Dear Mr. White: As almost everyone knows, the cost of medical care has increased greatly during the past few years. In (20) fact, it has gone up at a rate higher than the cost of living. For this reason, we suggest that the management (40) of every company review group insurance plans that are designed to help employees pay their medical and (60) hospital bills.

Have you recently made a survey of the benefits available to your employees through (80) your group insurance policies? If not, we suggest that you do so in the near future. One of our customers (100) has appointed an employee committee to participate in the evaluation of the total (120) insurance package of the company. You may want to consider that approach.

Every agent in our firm, Medical (140) and Retirement Plans, Incorporated, is a specialist in group insurance. We have developed group (160) medical, hospital, retirement, and annuity plans for some of the largest companies in town. We would (180) welcome the opportunity to be of service to your company.

When the time comes to review your group insurance (200) plans, we are ready to advise you as seems appropriate. Yours sincerely, (214)

Chapter 24, Letter 3

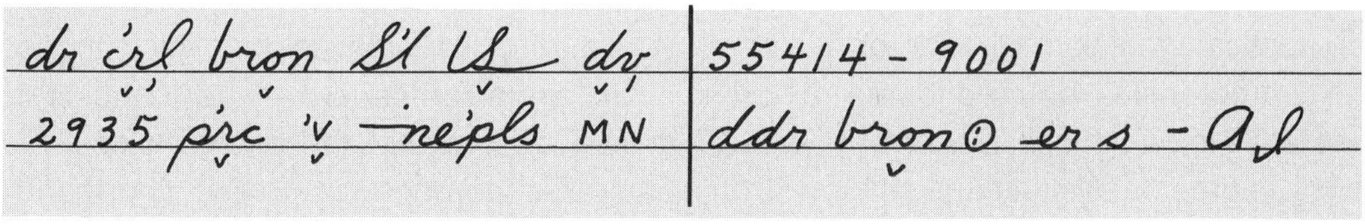

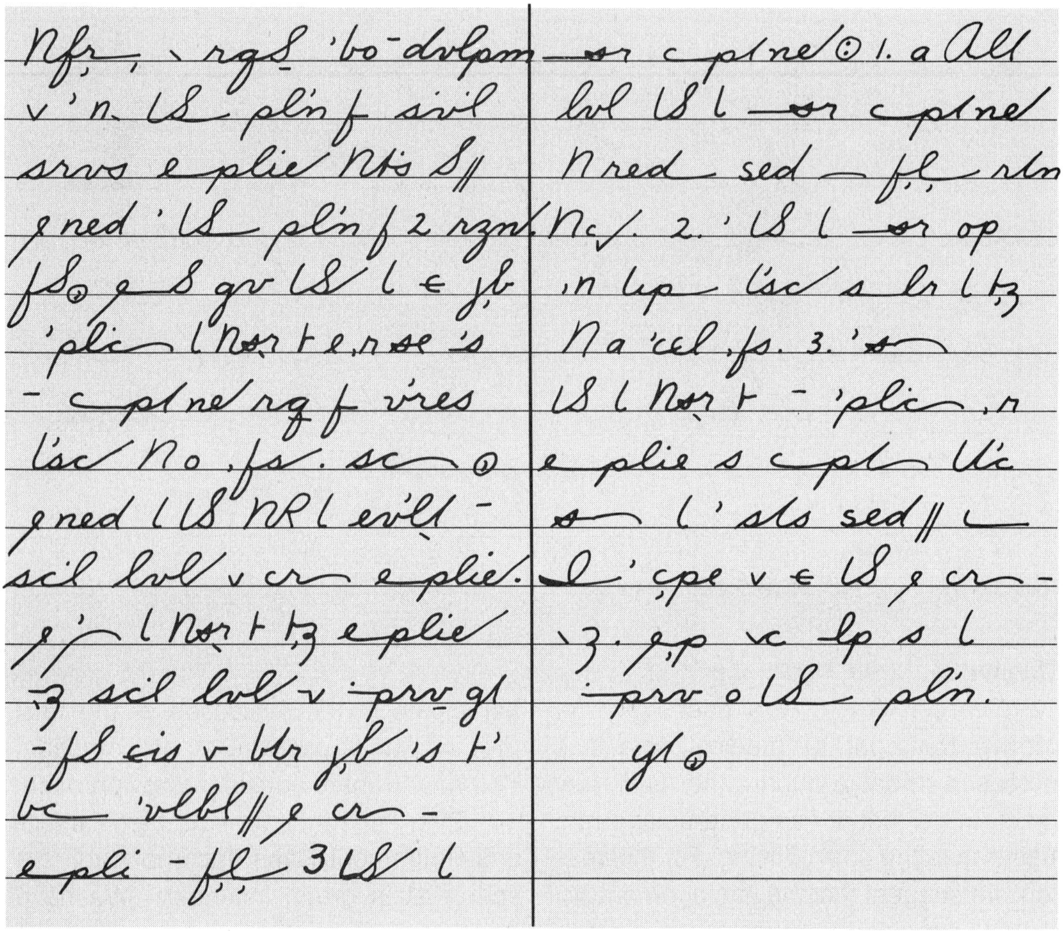

Chapter 24, Letter 3 Transcript

Dr. Carol Brown, State Testing Division, 2935 Park Avenue, Minneapolis, MN 55414-9001

Dear Dr. Brown: Here is the additional information you requested about the development of a (20) new testing plan for the civil service employees in this city.

We need a testing plan for two reasons. First, (40) we must give tests to each job applicant to ensure that he or she has the competencies required for the (60) various tasks in our offices. Second, we need to test in order to evaluate the skill levels of current (80) employees. We want to ensure that those employees whose skill levels have improved get the first choice of the better (100) jobs as they become available.

We currently employ the following three tests to measure competencies: (120) 1. An adult-level test to measure competencies in reading speed and following written instructions. 2. (140) A test to measure output on typing tasks similar to those in an actual office. 3. A shorthand test to (160) ensure that the applicant or employee is competent to take shorthand at a satisfactory speed.

I (180) am enclosing a copy of each test we currently use. We hope you can help us to improve our testing (200) plan. Yours truly, (203)

Chapter 25, Letter 2

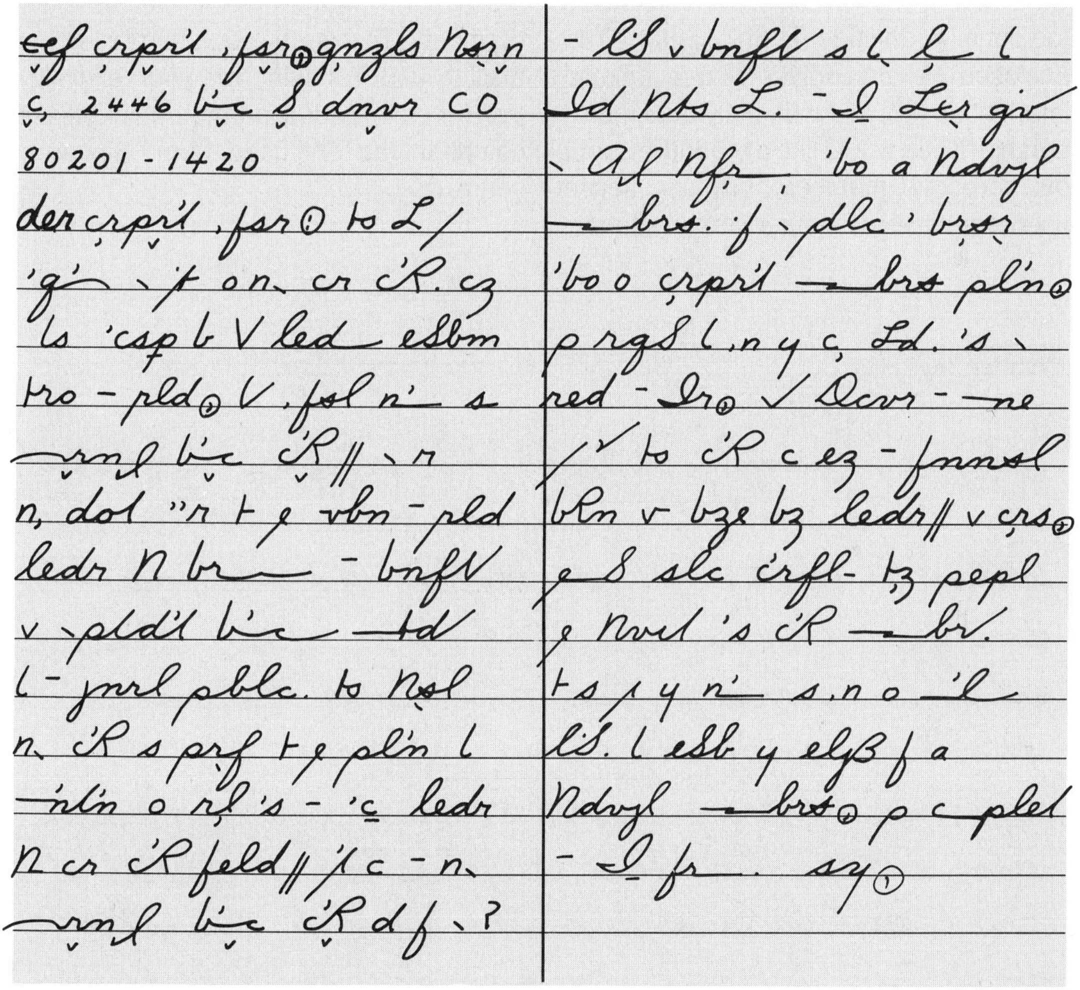

Chapter 25, Letter 2 Transcript

Chief Corporate Officer, Gonzales Insurance Company, 2446 Bank Street, Denver, CO 80201-1420

Dear Corporate Officer: This letter will acquaint you with our new credit card. Because it is accepted by (20) every leading establishment throughout the world, its official name is the International Bank Card.

You are (40) no doubt aware that we have been the world leader in bringing the benefits of up-to-date banking methods to

(60) the general public. This unusual new card is proof that we plan to maintain our role as the acknowledged (80) leader in the credit card field.

What can the new International Bank Card do for you? The list of benefits (100) is too long to include in this letter. The enclosed literature gives you additional information (120) about an individual membership. If you would like a brochure about our corporate membership plan, please (140) request it on your company letterhead. As you read the enclosure, you will discover the many ways this (160) card can ease the financial burden of the busy business leader.

Of course, we must select carefully those (180) people we invite as card members. That is why your name is on our mailing list. To establish your eligibility (200) for an individual membership, please complete the enclosed form. Sincerely yours, (216)

Chapter 26, Letter 2

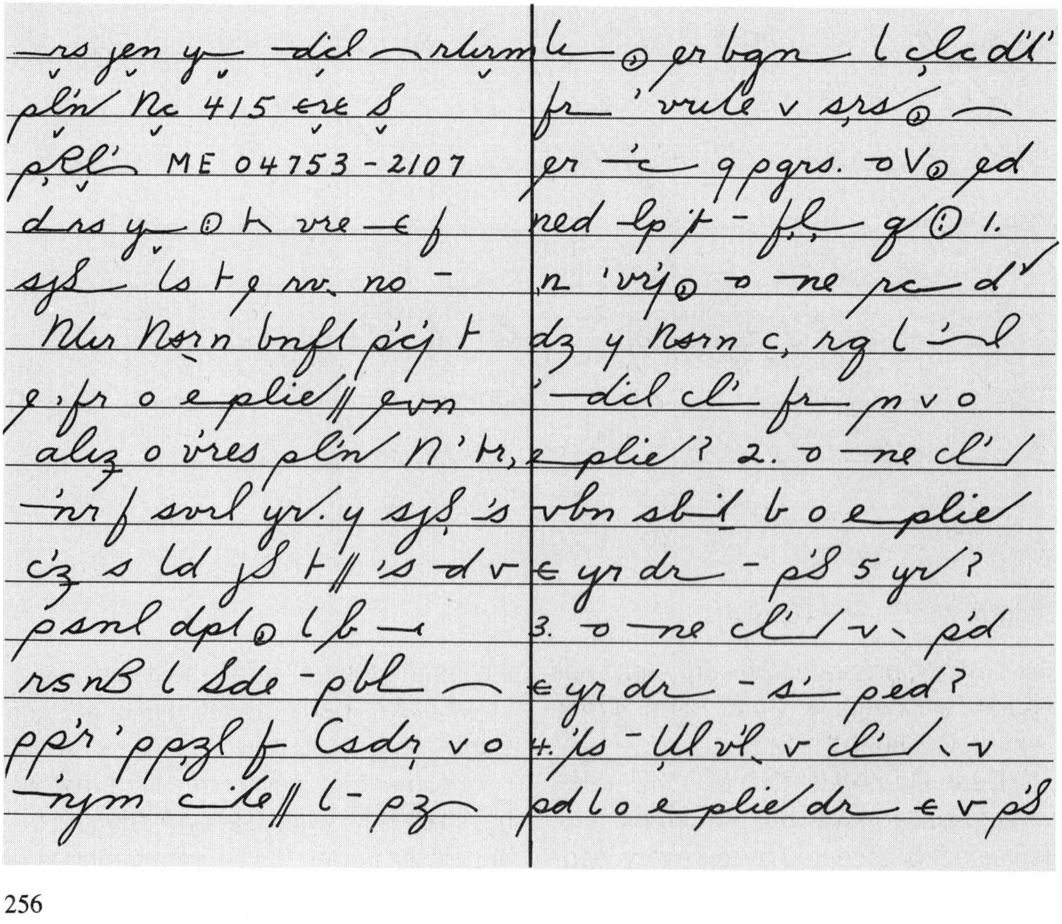

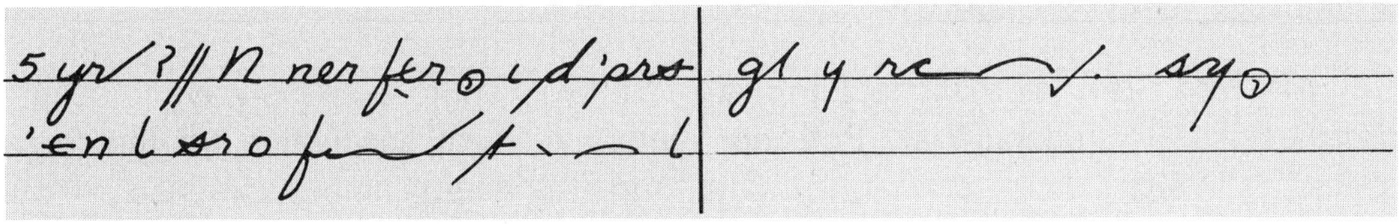

Chapter 26, Letter 2 Transcript

Mrs. Jean Young, Medical and Retirement Plans, Incorporated, 415 Church Street, Portland, ME 04753-2107

Dear Mrs. Young: Thank you very much for suggesting to us that we review now the entire insurance benefit (20) package that we offer our employees. We have not analyzed our various plans in a thorough manner (40) for several years. Your suggestion has caused us to do just that.

As head of the personnel department, it will (60) be my responsibility to study the problem and prepare a proposal for the consideration (80) of our management committee.

At the present time, we are beginning to collect data from a variety (100) of sources, and we are making good progress. However, we do need help with the following questions: 1. On the (120) average, how many working days does your insurance company require to handle a medical claim from (140) one of our employees? 2. How many claims have been submitted by our employees each year during the past five (160) years? 3. How many claims have you paid each year during the same period? 4. What is the total value of the (180) claims you have paid to our employees during each of the past five years?

In the near future, I would appreciate (200) a chance to share our findings with you and to get your recommendations. Sincerely yours, (216)

Chapter 27, Letter 2

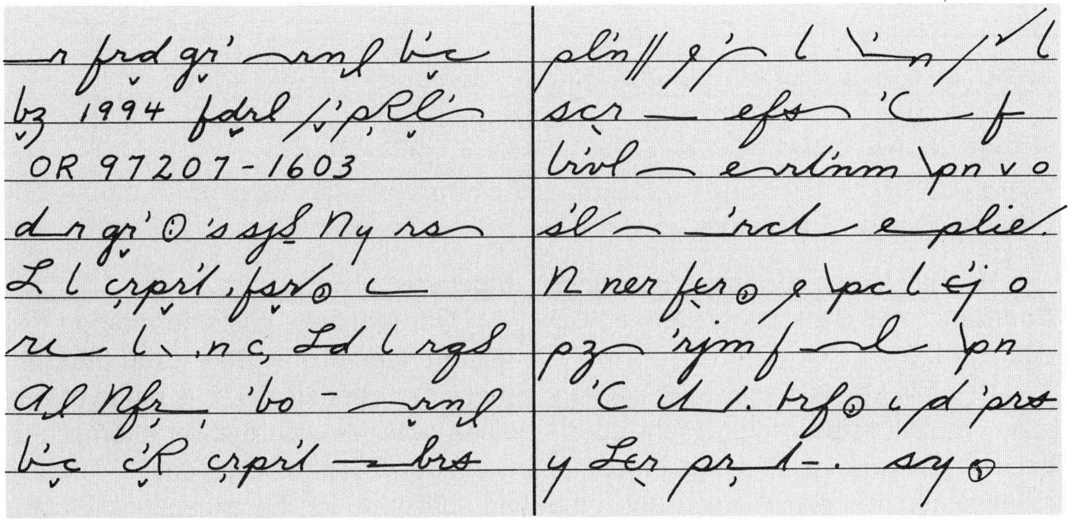

Chapter 27, Letter 2 Transcript

Mr. Fred Gray, International Banking Business, 1994 Federal Way, Portland, OR 97207-1603

Dear Mr. Gray: As suggested in your recent letter to corporate officers, I am writing to you on (20) company letterhead to request additional information about the International Bank Card (40) corporate membership plan.

We want to examine ways to secure more efficient accounting for the travel and (60) entertainment expense of our sales and marketing employees. In the near future, we expect to change our (80) present arrangement for handling expense account items. Therefore, I would appreciate your literature promptly. (100) Sincerely yours, (103)

Chapter 27, Letter 3

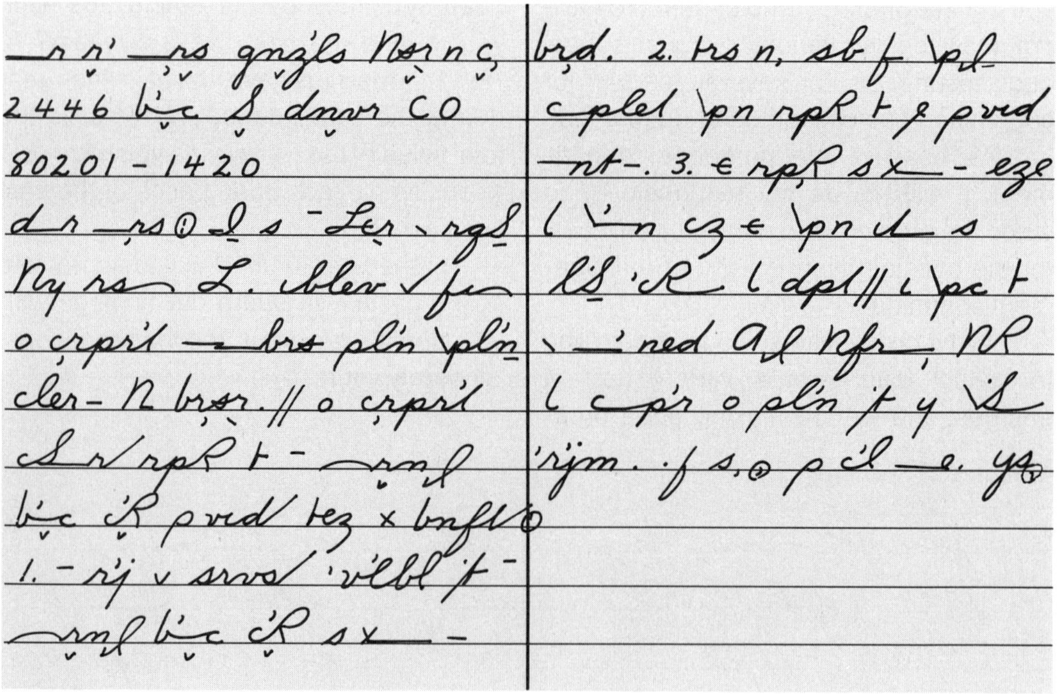

Chapter 27, Letter 3 Transcript

Mr. Ray Morris, Gonzales Insurance Company, 2446 Bank Street, Denver, CO 80201-1420

Dear Mr. Morris: Enclosed is the literature you requested in your recent letter. I believe you will (20) find our corporate membership plan explained clearly in the brochure.

Our corporate customers report that (40) the International Bank Card provides these extra benefits: 1. The range of services available with the (60) International Bank Card is extremely broad. 2. There is no substitute for the exceptionally complete (80) expense report that we provide monthly. 3. Each report is extremely easy to examine because each (100) expense item is listed according to department.

I expect that you may need additional information (120) in order to compare our plan with your existing arrangement. If so, please call me. Yours sincerely, (138)

Chapter 28, Letter 5

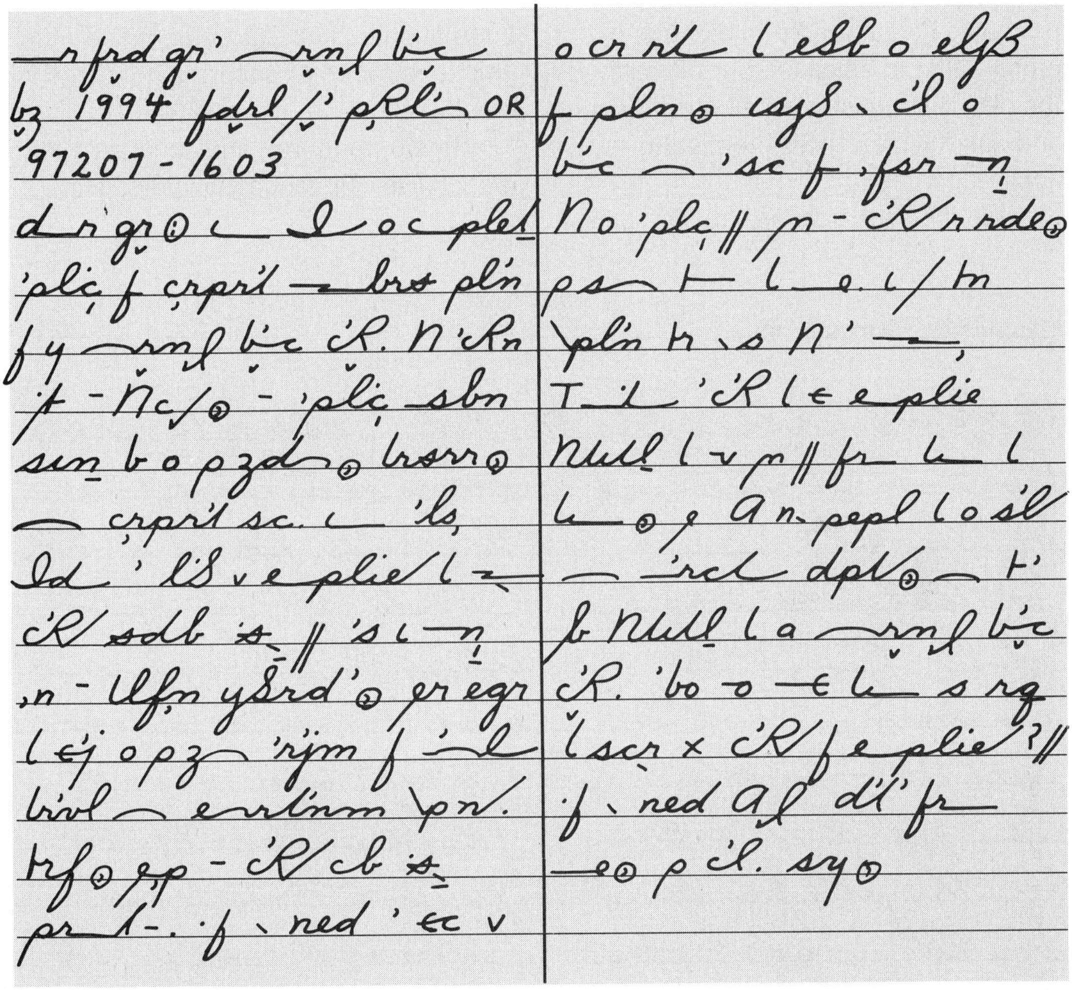

Chapter 28, Letter 5 Transcript

Mr. Fred Gray, International Banking Business, 1994 Federal Way, Portland, OR 97207-1603

Dear Mr. Gray: I am enclosing our completed application for the corporate membership plan for your (20) International Bank Card. In accordance with the instructions, the application has been signed by our president, (40) treasurer, and corporate secretary. I am also including a list of employees to whom cards (60) should be issued.

As I mentioned on the telephone yesterday, we are eager to change our present arrangement (80) for handling travel and entertainment expenses. Therefore, we hope the cards can be issued promptly. If you need (100) a check of our credit rating to establish our eligibility for the plan, I suggest you call our (120) bank and ask for the officer mentioned in our application.

When the cards are ready, please send them to me. I (140) will then explain their use in a memorandum transmitting a card to each employee entitled to have one. (160)

From time to time, we add new people to our sales and marketing departments, and they will be entitled to an (180) International Bank Card. About how much time is required to secure extra cards for employees?

If you need (200) additional data from me, please call. Sincerely yours, (210)

Chapter 29, Memorandum 2

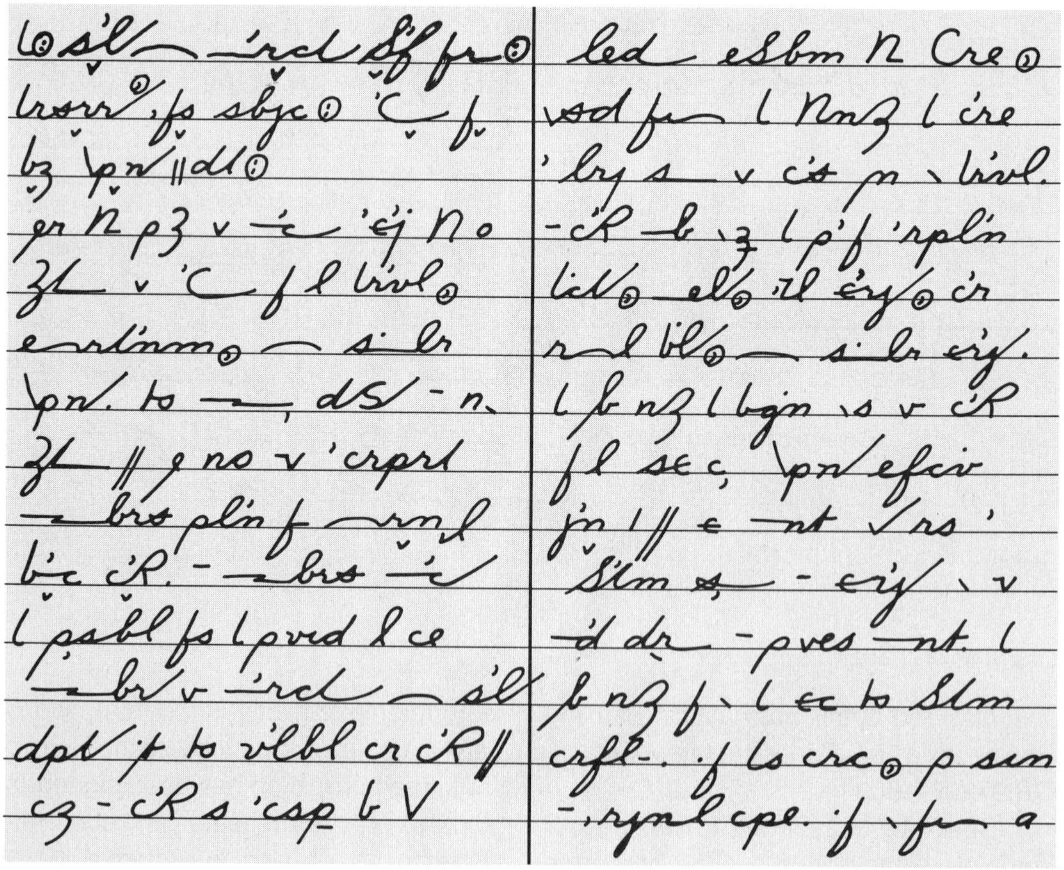

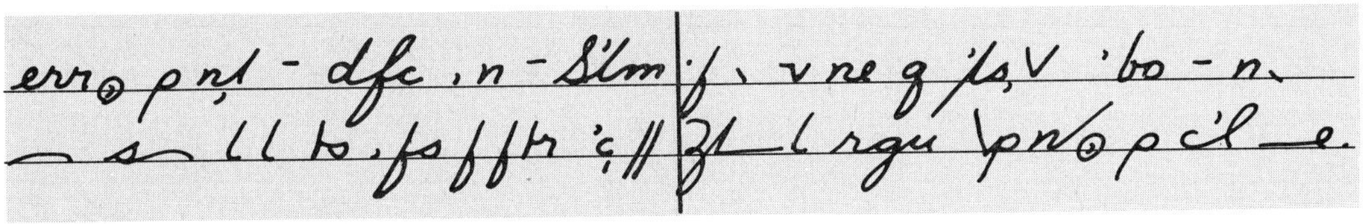

Chapter 29, Memorandum 2 Transcript

TO: Sales and Marketing Staff
FROM: Treasurer's Office
SUBJECT: Accounting for Business Expenses
DATE: Current date

We are in the process of making a change in our system of accounting for all travel, entertainment, and (20) similar expenses. This memorandum describes the new system.

We now have a corporate membership plan (40) for the International Bank Card. The membership makes it possible for us to provide all key members of (60) the marketing and sales departments with this valuable credit card.

Because the card is accepted by every (80) leading establishment in the country, you should find it unnecessary to carry a large sum of cash when (100) you travel. The card may be used to pay for airplane tickets, meals, hotel charges, car rental bills, and similar charges. (120) It will be necessary to begin use of the card for all such company expenses effective January (140) 1.

Each month you will receive a statement showing the charges you have made during the previous month. It will (160) be necessary for you to check this statement carefully. If it is correct, please sign the original copy. (180) If you find an error, please note the difficulty on the statement and send it to this office for further (200) action.

If you have any question whatsoever about the new system to regulate expenses, please call (220) me. (221)

Chapter 30, Letter 2

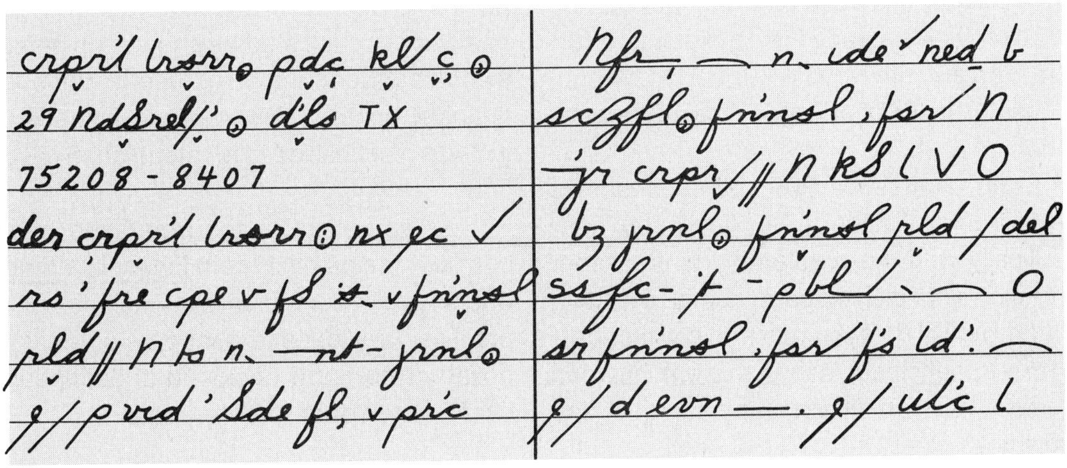

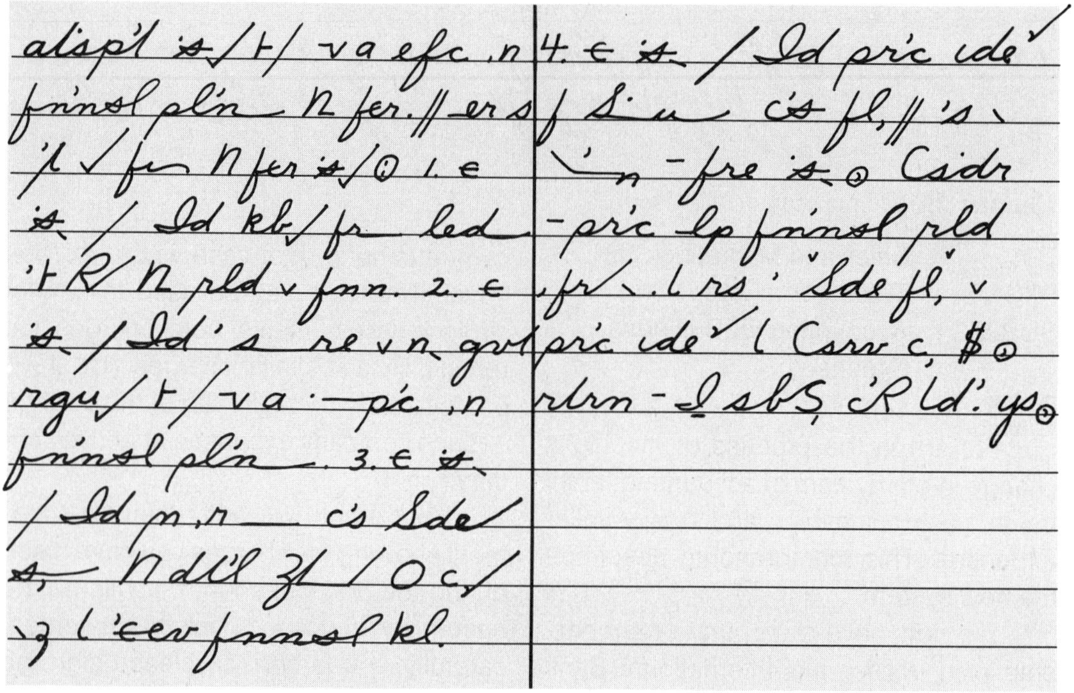

Chapter 30, Letter 2 Transcript

Corporate Treasurer, Production Controls Company, 29 Industrial Way, Dallas, TX 75208-8407

Dear Corporate Treasurer: Next week you will receive a free copy of the first issue of Financial World.

In (20) this new monthly journal, we will provide a steady flow of practical information and new ideas (40) needed by successful financial officers in major corporations.

In contrast to every other business (60) journal, Financial World will deal specifically with the problems you and other senior financial officers (80) face today. And we will do even more. We will undertake to anticipate issues that will have an effect (100) on financial planning in the future.

Here is what you will find in future issues: 1. Each issue will include (120) contributions from leading authorities in the world of finance. 2. Each issue will include a summary (140) of new government regulations that will have an impact on financial planning. 3. Each issue will include (160) one or more case studies showing in detail systems other companies use to achieve financial control. (180) 4. Each issue will include practical ideas for stimulating cash flow.

As you examine the free issue, (200) consider the practical help Financial World offers you. To receive a steady flow of practical (220) ideas to conserve company dollars, return the enclosed subscription card today. Yours sincerely, (238)

Chapter 31, Letter 2

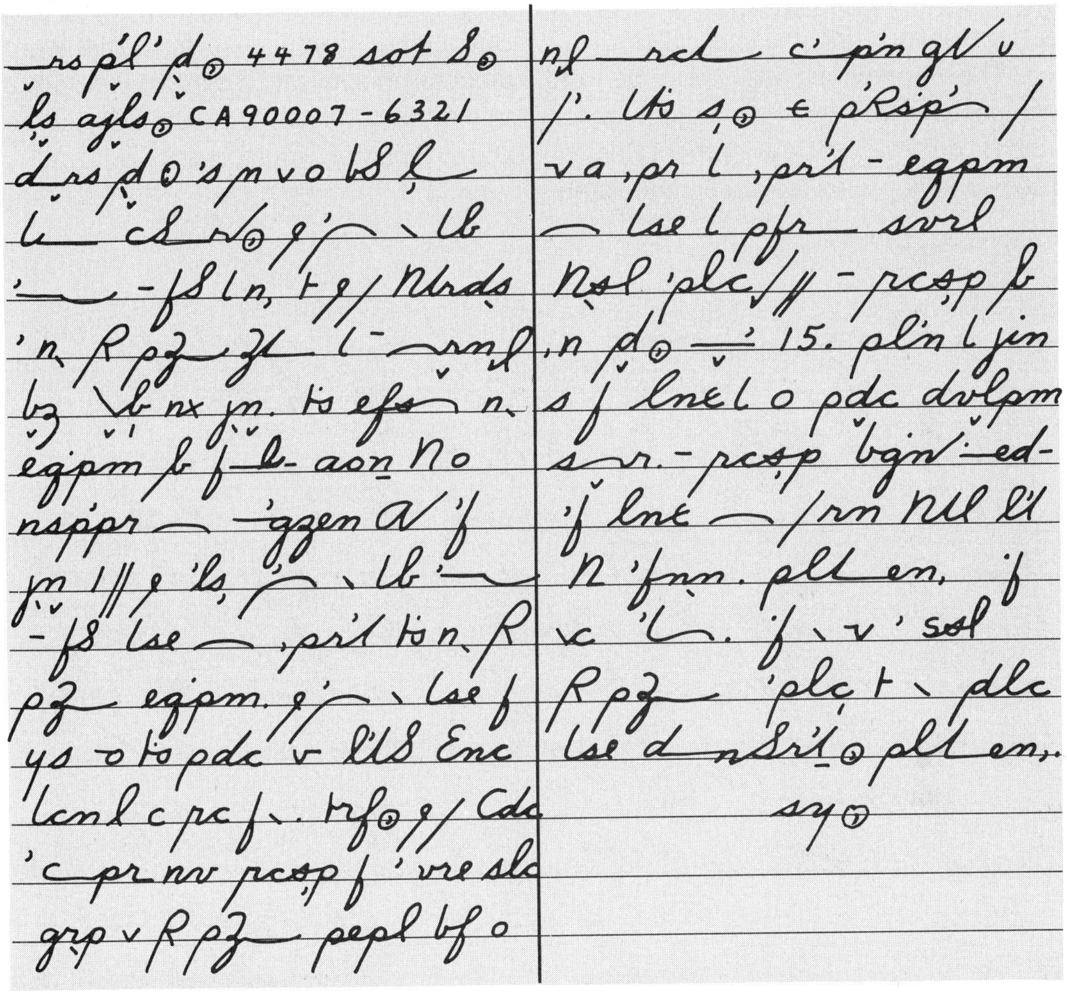

Chapter 31, Letter 2 Transcript

Mrs. Paula Wood, 4478 South Street, Los Angeles, CA 90007-6321

Dear Mrs. Wood: As one of our best long-time customers, we want you to be among the first to know that we will (20) introduce a new word processing system at the International Business Exhibition next June. This (40) efficient new equipment will be formally announced in our newspaper and magazine ads after June 1.

We (60) also want you to be among the first to see and operate this new word processing equipment. We want you to (80) see for yourself how this product of the latest electronic technology can work for you. Therefore, we will (100) conduct a comprehensive workshop for a very select group of word processing people before our national (120) marketing campaign gets under way. At this session, each participant will have an opportunity to (140) operate the equipment and to see it perform several unusual applications.

The workshop will (160) be on Wednesday, May 15. Plan to join us for lunch at our Product Development Center. The workshop (180) begins immediately after lunch and will run until late in the afternoon. Please let me know if you (200) can attend. If you have a special word processing application that you would like to see demonstrated, please (220) let me know. Sincerely yours, (205)

Chapter 32, Letter 2

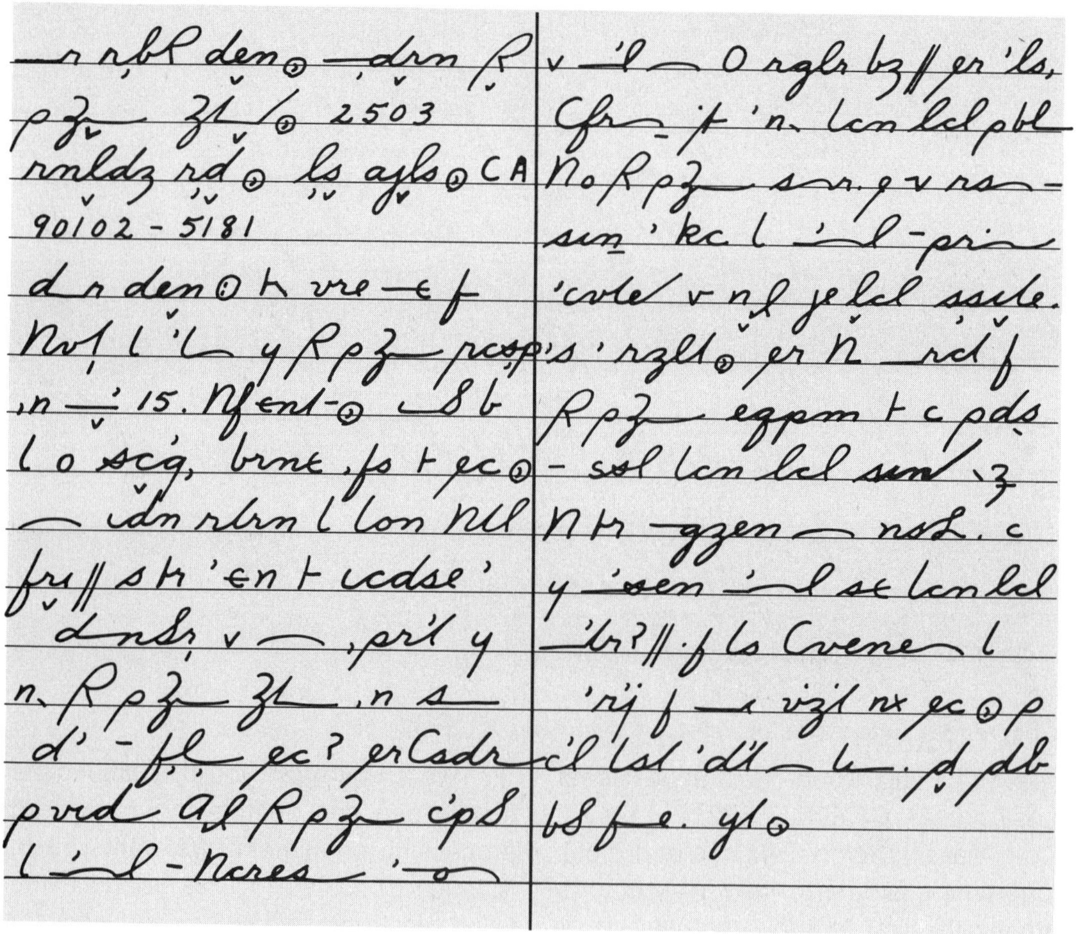

Chapter 32, Letter 2 Transcript

Mr. Robert Dean, Modern Word Processing Systems, 2503 Reynolds Road, Los Angeles, CA 90102-5181

Dear Mr. Dean: Thank you very much for the invitation to attend your word processing workshop on May 15. (20) Unfortunately, I must be at our Chicago branch office that week, and I do not return to town (40) until Friday.

Is there a chance that I could see a demonstration of and operate your new word processing system (60) on some day the following week? We are considering providing additional word processing (80) capacity to handle the increasing amount of mail and other regular business.

We are also confronted (100) with a new technological problem in our word processing center. We have recently signed a contract to (120) handle the printing activities of the National Geological Society. As a result, we (140) are in the market for word processing equipment that can produce the special technological signs used (160) in their magazine and newsletter. Can your machine handle such technological matter?

If it is convenient (180) to arrange for my visit next week, please call to set a date and time. Wednesday would be best for me. Yours truly, (200)

APPENDIX B

ABBREVIATED WORDS

about (18)*	'bo	decide (9)	dsi	important (15)	-p
accept (6)	'csp	difficult (13)	dfc	inquire (19)	Nq
acknowledge (17)	'c	difficulty (13)	dfc	is (1)	s
administer (17)	an	distribute (22)	Db	it (2)	t
advertise (11)	avr	do (3)	d	like (5)	lc
after (7)	'f	each (10)	e	merchandise (10)	—se
all (2)	l	establish (19)	esb	more (6)	—
am (6)	—	extra (27)	x	necessary (29)	nz
and (3)	⌒	extreme (27)	x—	next (3)	nx
any (7)	ne	first (18)	fs	not (3)	n
appreciate (9)	'prs	for (1)	f	of (2)	v
are (7)	r	glad (6)	gl	opportunity (6)	,pr
as (5)	's	go (1)	g	order (22)	R
at (2)	t	good (1)	g	organization (19)	,rg
be (2)	b	great (6)	gr	organize (19)	,rg
because (17)	cz	has (11)	's	our (18)	o
business (11)	bz	have (9)	-v	out (18)	o
but (2)	b	he (1)	e	particular (22)	plc
by/bye (2)	b	his (1)	s	please (9)	p
can (1)	c	hour (18)	o	practical (30)	prc
correspond (21)	crs	immediate (15)	-ed	principal (15)	prn
correspondence (21)	crs	importance (15)	-p	principle (15)	prn

*The number in parentheses which follows each item indicates the chapter in which the word appears.

put (9)		ship (9)		the (1)	
quantity (14)		short (9)		to (2)	
question (14)		side (9)		us (1)	
receive (9)		sincere (23)		well (7)	
remember (23)		sincerely (23)		will (7)	
require (14)		suggest (17)		write (5)	
right (5)		thank (10)		you (5)	
satisfactory (6)		that (10)		your (2)	
satisfy (6)					

APPENDIX C

STANDARD ABBREVIATIONS

approximate (approx.)	'prx
avenue (ave.)	'v
certificate (cert.)	sP
Company/company (Co.)	c,
credit (cr)	cr
debit (dr)	dr
department (dept.)	dpt
doctor (Dr.)	dr
estimate (est.)	eS
et cetera (etc.)	etc
executive (exec.)	\c
gentlemen (gent.)	j
government (govt.)	gvt
Incorporated (Inc.)	Nc
invoice (inv.)	Nv
junior (Jr.)	jr
laboratory (lab.)	l'b
Limited (Ltd.)	ltd
manufacture (mfg.)	—fg
memorandum (memo)	—,
Mr.	—r
Mrs.	—rs
Ms.	—z
purchase order (P.O.)	p,
regard (re)	re
represent (rep.)	rp
representative (rep.)	rp
secretary (sec.)	sc
senior (Sr.)	sr
signature (sig.)	sg
stenographer (steno)	Sn,
street (St.)	S
substitute (sub.)	sb
superintendent (supt.)	spt
television (TV)	tv
year (yr.)	yr

STANDARD SYMBOLS*

Celsius	C
centimeter/centimetre	cm
degree	°
dollar	$
dollars	$$
gram	g
kilogram	kg
kilometer/kilometre	km
liter/litre	L
meter/metre	m
milligram	mg
millimeter/millimetre	mm

*The metric symbols represent both the singular and plural forms of the terms.

APPENDIX D

ABBREVIATIONS FOR DAYS AND MONTHS

Sunday (Sun.)	
Monday (Mon.)	
Tuesday (Tue.)	
Wednesday (Wed.)	
Thursday (Thu.)	
Friday (Fri.)	
Saturday (Sat.)	
January (Jan.)	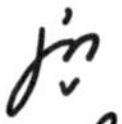
February (Feb.)	
March (Mar.)	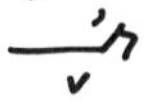
April (Apr.)	
May	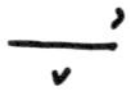
June	
July (Jul.)	
August (Aug.)	
September (Sep.)	
October (Oct.)	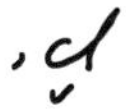
November (Nov.)	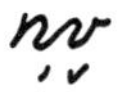
December (Dec.)	

STATES, DISTRICTS, AND TERRITORIES

Alabama	AL	Montana	MT
Alaska	AK	Nebraska	NE
Arizona	AZ	Nevada	NV
Arkansas	AR	New Hampshire	NH
California	CA	New Jersey	NJ
Colorado	CO	New Mexico	NM
Connecticut	CT	New York	NY
Delaware	DE	North Carolina	NC
District of Columbia	DC	North Dakota	ND
Florida	FL	Ohio	OH
Georgia	GA	Oklahoma	OK
Guam	GU	Oregon	OR
Hawaii	HI	Pennsylvania	PA
Idaho	ID	Puerto Rico	PR
Illinois	IL	Rhode Island	RI
Indiana	IN	South Carolina	SC
Iowa	IA	South Dakota	SD
Kansas	KS	Tennessee	TN
Kentucky	KY	Texas	TX
Louisiana	LA	Utah	UT
Maine	ME	Vermont	VT
Maryland	MD	Virginia	VA
Massachusetts	MA	Virgin Islands	VI
Michigan	MI	Washington	WA
Minnesota	MN	West Virginia	WV
Mississippi	MS	Wisconsin	WI
Missouri	MO	Wyoming	WY

CANADIAN PROVINCES AND TERRITORIES

Alberta	AB	Nova Scotia	NS
British Columbia	BC	Ontario	ON
Labrador	LB	Prince Edward Island	PE
Manitoba	MB	Quebec	PQ
New Brunswick	NB	Saskatchewan	SK
Newfoundland	NF	Yukon Territory	YT
Northwest Territories	NT		

APPENDIX E

SUMMARY OF WRITING PRINCIPLES

Sound or Sound Combinations	Expressed by		Illustrations				Text Chapter
a	'		fall-fail	f'l	fat	f'l	2
ad (p)[1]	A		address	Ars			11
an (p)	a		answer	asr			13
awa (p)	"		aware	"r			7
ax-ex-ox (p)	\		axle-excel	\l	oxide	\id	27
be	b		believe	blev			9
bility	B		ability	'B			25
c-k (hard)	c		tack-take	t'c			3
c (soft)	s		face	f's			3
cess-cis-sess-sis-sus-sys	ʒ		recess	rʒ			29
ch	€		chair	€'r			10
city-sity	S	(d)[3]	capacity	c'pS			17
con-coun-count	C		consider	Csidr	country	Cre	7
contr	k		contrary	kre			30
ct (ending)	c		fact	f'c			21
de (p)	d		delight	dlit			9
des-dis (p)	D		desperate	Dpr't	dispatch	Dp'€	13
e (long)	e		seed	sed			1

[1] (p) = prefix

[2] (s) = suffix

[3] (d) = disjoined

e (short)			said	sd			1
ed (past tense)	–	(d)	mailed	—'l–			6
electr	E		electrical	Ecl			31
en-in-un (p)	N		ensure-insure-unsure	Nsr			6
enclose-incl	I		enclosed	I–	include	Id	14
ever (p) (s)^{2}every (p)	V	(d)	evergreen	Vgren	every day	Vd'	15
for-fore-fer-fur (p)	f	(d)	forbear-forebear	fbr	furlough	fl,	25
g (soft)-j	/		page	pj			6
h	–		hold	hld			9
i (long)	ι		fight	fil			1
i (short)	·		fit	fil			2
icitis-itis	I	(d)	appendicitis	'pnI	tonsillitis	lnslI	31
ing-ng-thing	‿		trying	tri‿	nothing	n‿	11
incl-enclose	I		include	Id	enclosed	I–	14
instr	N	(d)	instruct	Nc			21
k	c		keep	cep			3
letter-liter (p)	L		letterhead	Ld	literal	Ll	25
ly (s)	–	(d)	totally	ll-			14
m	—		member	—br			5
ment	m		mental	ml			5
nce-nse	n	(d)	dance-dense	dn			23
nd-nt	⌒		renter-render	r⌒r			13
ng	‿		rang	r'‿			11
nge	j		arrange	'rj			27
o	,		boat-bought	bl			3
oi-oy	i		toy	li	toil	lil	23

ology	(d)	biology			31
oo-u		fool-full			5
other-over		otherwise	another		30
ou-ow		foul-fowl			18
out (**p**) (s)		outline			18
over-other		overseas			30
per-pre-pri-pro-pur	(d)	proceed-precede	pertain		26
		privacy	pursue		
position-post		imposition	postage		23
qu		quote			14
re (p)		reverse			9
rd-rt		card-cart			22
rity	(d)	security			22
s-z (hard)		use (v)	use (n)		10
s (added to root word)		says	items		15
scribe-script		subscribe	transcription		29
self (**p**s) (s)	(d)	self-service	herself		18
sh		she			9
sion-tion		session	edition		19
sp		speak			21
st		test			17
t		light			2
th		this			10
trans (p)		translate			11
u		duty			5
ulate		regulate			29

under	u	underline	ulin	30
w-wh	/	were-where	/r	7
y (long e)	e	needy	nede	1

Chapters 1—4

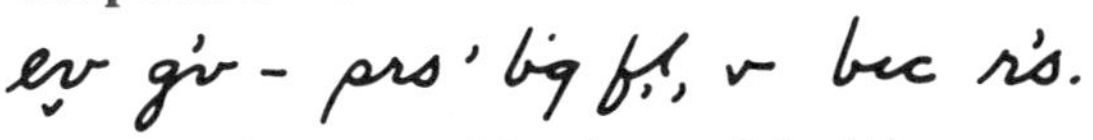

Eve gave the press a big photo of the bike race.

Sound of the long *e*	Sound of *a*	Sound of hard *c* and *k*
Sound of short *e*	Sound of *t*	Sounds of *o*
Sound of long *i*	Sound of short *i*	Sound of soft *c*

Chapters 5—8

Are you aware the general may not approve the payment when due unless

he is consulted?

Sounds of *u-oo*	Sound of soft *g* and *j*	Sounds of *w-wh*
Sound of *m*	Prefixes *in-en-un*	*awa-away*
Syllable *ment*	*d* or *ed* added to a root word	Prefixes *con-coun-count*

Chapters 9—12

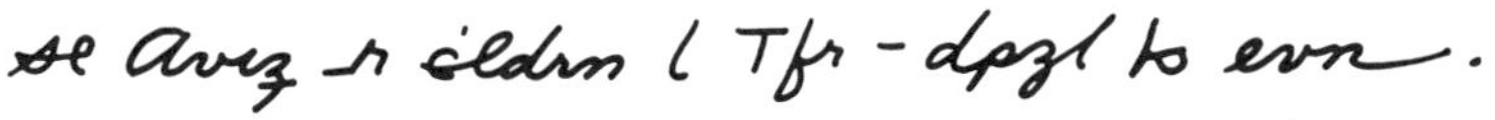

She advised her children to transfer the deposit this evening.

Sound of *h*	Sound of *ch*	Sounds of *ng-ing-thing*
Sound of *sh*	Sound of *th*	Prefix *ad-add*
Prefixes *be-de-re*	Sound of hard *s* and *z*	Prefix *trans*

Chapters 13—16

Everybody left the annual school display quickly, including my friends.

nt-nd	*qu*	Adding *s* to root words
Prefix *an*	*incl-enclose*	Prefix or suffix *ever-every*
Prefixes *dis-des*	*ly*	

Chapters 17—20

The booklet outlines information and publicity on the self-service store

downtown.

st	Sound of *ou-ow*	Prefix or suffix *self*
sity-city	Prefix or suffix *out*	Sound of *"shun"*

Chapters 21—24

The director instructed the employee to postpone the report at the special

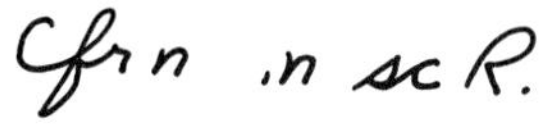

conference on security.

sp	*rt-rd*	*nce-nse*
ct	*rity*	*post-position*
instr	Sound of *oi-oy*	

Chapters 25—28

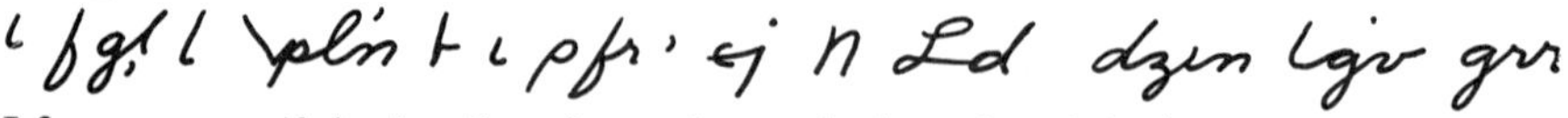

I forgot to explain that I prefer a change in letterhead design to give greater

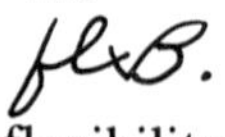

flexibility.

Prefixes *for-fore-fer-fur*	*letter-liter*	Prefixes *ax-ex-ox*
bility	Prefixes *pre-pri-pro-per-pur*	*nge*

Chapters 29—32

They undertake, with some success, to regulate, overcome, or control the

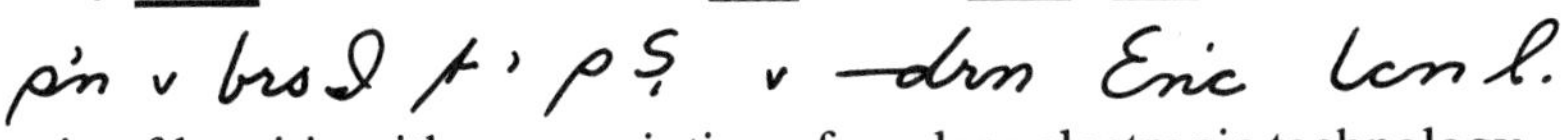

pain of bursitis with a prescription of modern electronic technology.

Syllables *sys-sess-sus-sis-cess-cis*
ulate
scribe-script
contr
over-other
under
electr
ology
itis-icitis

APPENDIX F

SUMMARY OF ENGLISH PRINCIPLES

Addresses

Use a comma to set off elements in addresses. (12)*

Apostrophe

The apostrophe is used to show the omission of a letter or letters in contractions such as isn't (is not) and can't (can not). (13)

The apostrophe is used to show the possessive case, i.e., ownership. (14)

Appositives

A comma is used to set off words or phrases that identify a preceding noun or phrase. Some authorities do not use commas to set off a one-word appositive. (12)

Capitalization

When transcribing, always capitalize names of places, days of the week, months, and names of holidays. Do not abbreviate days of the week or months. (4)

Type in all capitals the titles of books, magazines, newspapers, booklets, pamphlets, and other printed works or capitalize the first letter of the important words and underscore. (17)

Capitalize the important words in titles of parts of unpublished works (chapters, articles, editorials, column) and names of movies, songs, lectures, and television shows. Enclose such titles in quotation marks. (17)

Compound Sentences

The most common way to form a compound sentence is to join two complete sentences with a comma and one of these connecting words: *and, but, for, or either, neither*, and *nor*. (10)

Two complete sentences may be joined with a semicolon followed by a transitional word or phrase. Common transitional words or phrases include: *accordingly, however, then, so, therefore, still, finally, consequently, hence, in fact, as a matter of fact*. Most authorities agree that a transitional word must be followed by a comma. (10)

*The numbers in parentheses indicate chapters where examples may be found.

Two or more complete sentences may be joined with a semicolon without a connecting word or a transitional word or phrase. (10)

Courteous Request or Suggestion

Although it may seem appropriate to use a question mark, a courteous request or a suggestion is punctuated with a period. (28)

Dates

Use a comma to set off elements in dates. (12)

Geographic Locations

Use a comma to set off elements in geographic locations. (12)

Hyphen

Use a hyphen to join two or more words used as a single descriptive word before a noun. Use a hyphen to mark the division of a word at the end of a line of type or printing. (16)

Introductory Words, Phrases, and Clauses

Place a comma after all expressions that introduce the reader to the rest of the sentence. (4)

Numbers

In this text isolated numbers under eleven are spelled out and all numbers over ten are written in figures. When appearing at the beginning of a sentence, all numbers should be spelled out. If this results in an awkward sentence, rewrite the sentence. (20)

Figures are used to write age, dates, and time of day. (20) Dollar signs precede dollar amounts. If the amount is in even dollars, omit the decimal and zeros. (20)

Spell out ordinal numbers that are not part of an address or a date. Ordinal numbers are forms of numbers that indicate order or succession, such as first, tenth, and twenty-fifth. (20)

Parenthetical Expressions

Place a comma before and after all parenthetical words, expressions, or phrases. They can be identified because they may be omitted from a sentence without changing its meaning. (6)

Possessives

See Apostrophe.

Question Mark

A question mark is used at the end of a sentence, phrase, or word that asks a direct question. (28)

Each question within a sentence should be followed by a question mark. (24)

A courteous request or a suggestion is punctuated with a period. (28)

Series

Use a comma to separate more than two words, phrases, or clauses in a series. A comma should be used before *and*, *nor*, and *or* when they connect the last two elements in a series. (8)

Use a colon to introduce a series beginning with expressions such as *these*, *as follows*, and *the following*. (22)

Titles

Use a comma to set off elements in titles. (12)

Titles Used with Personal Names

Abbreviate the following titles when they are used with personal names: Dr., Mr., Mrs., Ms. These abbreviations should be followed by a period. Miss and Misses are not abbreviations and should not be followed with periods. (21)

In general, spell out all other titles used with personal names: Professor, President, and Prime Minister. (21)

APPENDIX G

KEYS TO APPLICATIONS EXERCISES

Chapter 1 — **Writing by sound**

f-e-l-d, l-e-v, d-r-i, f-r-e, s-t-r-a-t, m-i-t, s-l-o, d-a, e-j, t-r-e-t-e, g-o-l, s-i-n, o-n, p-a, b-r-i-t

Chapter 4 — **Punctuating introductory expressions; capitalization**

1. know, 2. Buenos Aires 3. Consequently, 4. OK 5. result, Jean/Mexico 6. OK 7. right, 8. Christmas/ Tuesday 9. Fultons/West Fourth Street, 10. Furthermore,

Chapter 6 — **Punctuating parenthetical expressions**

1. shall, course, 2. Fields, programmer, 3. computer, predecessor, 4. OK 5. try, nevertheless, 6. not, rule, 7. operating, information, 8. OK 9. difficult, unfortunately, 10. package, condition,

Chapter 7 — **Word usage**

1. It's 2. cite 3. effect 4. later 5. great 6. their 7. to 8. stationary 9. adopt 10. counsel

Chapter 8 — **Punctuating items in a series**

1. single, double, 2. house, garage, 3. homework, television, 4. OK 5. Canada, States, 6. educated, date, 7. teacher, counselors, 8. OK 9. overhead, up, 10. soccer, match,

Chapter 9 — **Spelling**

1. hoping 2. scene 3. surprise 4. arrangement 5. nickel 6. several 7. height 8. sense 9. niece 10. shining 11. loneliness 12. criticize 13. separate 14. schedule 15. referred

Chapter 10 — **Punctuating compound sentences**

1. Our financial kit has been updated and expanded, and it will help you to determine actual costs. (*comma plus connecting word*)

Our financial kit has been updated and expanded; consequently, it will help you to determine actual costs. (*semicolon plus transitional word and comma*)

Our financial kit has been updated and expanded; it will help you to determine actual costs. (*semicolon only*)

2. The fire was burning brightly, and it kept the room warm and cozy. (*comma plus connecting word*)

The fire was burning brightly; therefore, it kept the room warm and cozy. (*semicolon plus transitional word and comma*)

The fire was burning brightly; it kept the room warm and cozy. (*semicolon only*)

Chapter 10 — **Word usage** (*All sentences may be written in shorthand*)

1. *Choose* the right color for the play area.
2. The company *chose* to market the new machine.
3. I would like to ride rather *than* walk to the game.
4. If you go, *then* I can go.
5. *Their* group began before the agreed date.
6. We arrived *there* in time for the club meeting.
7. John attached the *loose* wire.
8. My class can *lose* the vote Tuesday.
9. She is able to do a *thorough* job on her paper.
10. They are *through* with the book for today.

Chapter 11 — **Word usage** (*All sentences may be written in shorthand*)

1. The Congress will meet in January at the *Capitol*.
2. Do you have enough *capital* to begin your own business?
3. He will give you some *advice* on each course available.
4. The counselor will *advise* you on which course to take.
5. Keep your *eraser* near your typewriter.
6. Did you make a clean *erasure* on your paper?
7. You will need to *pare* the apple before you eat it.
8. Jean bought a *pear* at the fruit market.
9. The class will *pair* off to visit the library.

Chapter 12 — **Punctuating appositives, dates, addresses, and titles**

1. Thursday, 30, 2. Mallory, counselor, 3. 15, 1977,
4. Avenue, Phoenix, 5. OK

Chapter 13 — **The apostrophe**

1. he's 2. weren't 3. I've 4. '70 5. they're 6. o'clock
7. there's 8. you're 9. won't 10. let's

Chapter 14 — **Possessives**

1. girls' 2. Marie's 3. OK 4. OK 5. weeks'

Chapter 15 — **Word usage** (*All sentences may be written in shorthand*)

1. We would like to place the *ad* in the paper for four days.
2. Be sure to *add* your new address to the brochure.
3. The company has its full *complement* of officers.

4. We would like to *compliment* you on your fine delivery service.
5. We bought new equipment *for* the baseball team.
6. A new group of women is coming to the *fore* in government.
7. The new library opened *four* days ago.
8. *No*, the door was not left open.
9. I *know* you will do whatever the job requires.
10. The *piece* of land near the river is not for sale.
11. The *peace* treaty was signed on February 4.
12. The *scene* of the accident is near the college.
13. I have not *seen* the new office building yet.
14. Her *principal* job is to answer the telephone.
15. On what *principle* does this engine operate?

Chapter 16 — **Hyphenation**

1. up-to-date 2. OK 3. two-thirds 4. city-wide 5. well-known 6. OK 7. above-average 8. high-grade 9. one-way 10. OK

Chapter 16 — **Word division**

1. about 2. December 25 3. straight 4. OK 5. November 30, 1972 6. Samuel Clemens 7. OK 8. OK 9. shipped 10. c.o.d.

Chapter 17 — **Words that sound alike**

1. s 2. o 3. c 4. d 5. h 6. k 7. v 8. b 9. g 10. n 11. p 12. r 13. q 14. w 15. x 16. j 17. m 18. a 19. t 20. u 21. e 22. i 23. f 24. 1

Chapter 20 — **Transcribing numbers**

1. $70 000 2. $250.55 3. One hundred, $50 4. OK 5. $1.60 6. OK 7. first

Chapter 22 — **Introducing a series**

1. prices: 2. items: 3. marks: 4. directions:

Chapter 25 — **Word usage**

1. lessen 2. know 3. fare, fair 4. ate, eight 5. you're, your

Chapter 26 — **Word usage**

1. residents 2. patients 3. attendance 4. confident 5. billed 6. assistants 7. Some 8. residence 9. presence 10. stare

Chapter 27 — **Word usage**

1. leased 2. least 3. fine 4. fined 5. great 6. grate 7. hire 8. higher 9. hour 10. Our 11. wait 12. weight 13. weak 14. week 15. aisle 16. isle 17. I'll 18. vane 19. vein 20. vain

Chapter 28 — **Punctuating questions**

1. copier? 2. OK 3. percent? percent? 4. purpose? objectives? decisions? 5. OK 6. form. 7. form. 8. tonight? 9. criticism? 10. it?

Chapter 28 — **Word usage**

1. any way 2. straight 3. adapt 4. affected 5. dinner 6. edition 7. right 8. passed 9. excess 10. device

Chapter 28 — **Spelling**

1. management, endeavor 2. reference, delinquent 3. voucher, specifically 4. repetition, attendance 5. privilege, acquaintance 6. omitted, pamphlet 7. extension, collateral 8. referred, respectively 9. beneficial, miscellaneous 10. oblige, respectfully

Chapter 29 — **Word usage**

1. lean 2. pier 3. lie 4. allowed 5. forth 6. phase 7. raze 8. stairs 9. canvass 10. lead

Chapter 30 — **Word usage**

1. in to 2. into 3. almost 4. all most 5. everyday 6. every day 7. no body 8. nobody 9. any way 10. anyway 11. someone 12. some one

Chapter 31 — **Word usage**

1. some time 2. sometime 3. maybe 4. may be 5. all ready 6. already 7. Every one 8. Everyone 9. all ways 10. always 11. any one 12. anyone

Chapter 32 — **Word usage**

1. stationery 2. too 3. least 4. weak 5. all ready 6. due 7. their 8. attendance 9. capital 10. add 11. assistance 12. principle 13. great 14. allowed 15. vain 16. advise 17. erasure 18. compliment 19. know 20. piece 21. scene 22. correspondence 23. meet 24. vary 25. weather